Bargain Hunting
in the Bay Area

# BARGAIN HUNTING
## in the Bay Area

by SALLY SOCOLICH

Wingbow Press • Berkeley

4th
Revised
Edition

ISBN: 0-914728-32-6

Wingbow Press books are published and distributed by Bookpeople, 2940 Seventh Street, Berkeley, California 94710

Designed by Bonnie Jean Smetts

Revised Edition
First Printing, April 1976
Second Printing, September 1976
Third Printing, April 1977
Fourth Printing, September 1977

Second Revised Edition
Fifth Printing, July 1978
Sixth Printing, December 1978
Seventh Printing, June 1979

Third Revised Edition
Eighth Printing, June 1980
Ninth Printing, February 1981

Fourth Revised Edition
Tenth Printing, June 1982

# Contents

# INTRODUCTION

Savvy bargain hunters realize you can save money on most of the things you buy—if you know *where* to buy. Now you need not confine your "sale buying" to just a few weeks or months a year. Armed with *Bargain Hunting in the Bay Area* you can enjoy year-round savings on the widest range of consumer products. You'll be able to stretch your dollar on everyday necessities: food, clothing, housewares, furniture, as well as on luxury items like diamonds, gold, sterling silver, and hobby and sporting goods, too. Bargain hunting is an interest that appeals to shoppers of all income levels. As the cost of living continues to rise and more demands are put on our family budgets we must look for ways to make our dollar do more. That is the purpose of this book.

The first four editions of *Bargain Hunting in the Bay Area* were so well-received it was clear readers wanted to know yet more about where to find good shopping values. I did worry that the rise in gasoline prices would greatly effect the success of bargain stores, that perhaps they might decline due to a lack of customers. While some stores have closed, new stores have opened, and old stores continue to thrive as more enlightened consumers seek them out. You will find that branches of larger stores have opened in your local neighborhood shopping centers saving you costly trips around the Bay Area.

This revision of *Bargain Hunting in the Bay Area* leads you in the same direction as previous editions...to over 400 stores offering the *best quality goods for the lowest prices.* Of these entries I have kept my basic bargain criterion of "at least 20% off the retail price," though *most* entries offer far greater reductions. Many readers of the first four editions have shared their bargain discoveries with me and I have researched and included a number of them. This book is intended as a guide, of course, and not as an endorsement of the stores listed. Those included are strictly personal selections for which I have accepted no kindnesses or gratuities to insure their inclusion. To maximize the number of entries for this book I have avoided lengthy descriptions of each store or business, just wordy enough to reveal its "personality" and spark your interest.

**A WORD OF WARNING, BEFORE YOU SHOP:** Even a seasoned bargain hunter has trouble keeping up with the outlets and discount stores that move and seem to play hopscotch around the Bay Area. Outlets have been known to quietly move across the street, or even close permanently on a few days notice. Rent increases, changes of building ownership, or management shifts can force a bargain outlet to seek new, lower priced locations. *Since store hours are subject to change, I recommend that you call those shops you intend to visit before driving across town.* Addresses and phone numbers were correct at the time of publication, but these may change. Subsequent printings will include corrections, and readers are encouraged to notify the author, in care of the publisher of any such changes.

Please glance over the *Hints for the Bargain Hunter* that follow. You're probably already aware of the basic rules, but the caveat emptor rule cannot be overemphasized. I trust that your innate good shopping habits will caution you to comparison shop before buying and always to ask that number one, all-important question: "How can they sell it so cheap?" I've answered this question in most cases and have tried to lead you to stores that will give you an honest answer. But don't let your guard down—not for a minute!

Remember, too, that just because an item is cheap, it's not necessarily a bargain; and to turn the coin over, some merchandise is going to be expensive, even when priced at 20% or more under retail. Finally, nothing is a bargain if you don't need it. One of the biggest problems in shopping outlets and discount stores is the compulsion to buy everything simply because it all seems so cheap. I've had to learn self-restraint to avoid unjustified and unnecessary expenditures while being sorely tempted!

I have quoted specific prices in some listings to give you a clue to the kinds of bargains available at the various stores. The prices mentioned are based on research conducted in the winter and spring of 1982, but because of changes in the economy, those prices may be higher by the time you visit the stores. Still, chances are the ratio of the discount to the retail price will hold.

So, if you're determined to "beat the system", I'm with you. Once you get into the swing of buying at these prices, you'll soon discover that paying straight retail is for the unenlightened!

# Hints for the bargain hunter

It's difficult to make specific recommendations about where *you* should shop. Shopping is a highly personal activity and reflects many facets of your personality. Some prefer the tranquil atmosphere of the "better" stores, the sometimes higher quality product and the attentiveness of the personnel that go with it; others are name-brand afficianados and many are just plain budget-conscious. You'll discover that I've listed stores of every possible description; my own personal taste in bargain hunting is quite varied. I shop a chic apparel boutique one day and a bare-bones factory outlet the next. I adore rummaging in salvage and surplus outlets *and* relaxing in an elegant decorator's showroom. Limited facilities, goods, and services don't cause me to blink an eye; my goal is a *bargain*—and hang the tranquility. And if you've bought this book, you probably have one main objective in your shopping ventures: to get the most for your dollar.

# Questions to ask

Whenever an item is for sale to the public at 20-50% under retail, common sense tells you there must be a reason. I have tried in each entry to give you an explanation, and the answer generally falls into one or more categories described by the following terminology used in retailing:

• **Discontinued or manufacturer's close-out:** A product that is no longer being manufactured. In most instances this does not effect the merchandise, but where parts may need to be replaced, it could cause a problem.

• **Floor sample:** A model displayed in the store.

• **Freight damage:** Even if only one or two items in a shipment are broken, burned, chipped, marred, etc., for insurance purposes the entire lot is designated "damaged." This merchandise may be noticeably damaged; often, however, it is actually in A-1 condition but part of a shipment that met with physical mishap.

• **Irregular:** Merchandise with minor imperfections, often barely discernable.

• **In-season buying:** Most retailers buy pre-season, whereas a discounter will often purchase in-season, relieving the manufacturer of merchandise that is old to him but still new to the public.

• **Jobber:** A person who buys goods in quantity from manufacturers or importers and sells them to dealers.

• **Job lot:** Goods, often of various sorts, brought together for sale as one quantity.

• **Liquidated stock:** When a company or business is in financial trouble, the stock they have on hand is sometimes sold to merchandiser—often of the lot—at prices much lower than retail in order to liquidate the assets of the company.

• **Loss leader:** An item purposely priced low to get you into the store.

• **Odd-lots:** A relatively small quantity of unsold merchandise that remains after an order has been filled.

• **Open stock:** Individual pieces of merchandise sold in sets, which are kept in stock as replacements.

• **Overruns:** An excess of products, similar to surplus and overstocks, but generally due to a manufacturer's error.

• **Past season:** Goods manufactured for a previous season.

• **Retail:** The selling of merchandise directly to the consumer.

• **Returns:** Orders returned to the manufacturer by retail stores because they do not arrive on time. Fashion discounters are able to buy this merchandise below cost from the manufacturer, thereby helping him to alleviate his losses.

• **Samples:** An item shown by the manufacturer's representative to the prospective merchandiser/buyer for the purpose of selling the product.

• **Seconds:** Merchandise with more than minor flaws which may effect the esthetic appeal or performance of the product.

- **Surplus overstocks:** An excess quantity, over and above what is needed by the retailer.
- **Wholesale price:** Wholesale price refers to the cost of goods to the retailer, except in discount shopping when consumers can buy at or near this price.

In addition to the above, the business acumen of one retailer/buyer in purchasing merchandise may be superior to his competitors'; a better original buy generally is reflected in the price. Low overhead can also effect the price; stores in low-rent districts with few frills and little or no advertising can often undersell those in the high-rent areas. The necessity to keep goods moving sometimes forces a retailer into cutting prices—space is a problem in merchandising just as it is in your home...they're in it for the long haul, not for the quick profit. Bless them!

Once you have determined the reason the price is low, your next question should be: "Is there anything wrong with the item that will effect its performance or use to me?" Look for flaws before you buy. And if you find one, be realistic about whether you can repair it or have it repaired and still save money. If you've answered all these questions honestly and find the bargain value there...plunge, you've bagged a buy. Now you can relish that delicious feeling of beating the system ...you've earned it.

# Maps

In this edition I have included maps for areas of San Francisco where there are many outlets and resources for bargains in close proximity to each other. (See page 171).

# Timing

Many of the shops have specific days that new merchandise comes in. Knowing what those days are will enable you to get the pick of the new crop. When you find a store or outlet that sells merchandise that you're particularly interested in, be sure to ask if they have a mailing list and get on it. This will give you advance notice of sales and new arrivals. For many of these stores, mailing lists are their only form of advertising.

# How to use this book

*Bargain Hunting in the Bay Area* is arranged by categories, very much like the Yellow Pages of your telephone directory. Beneath the subject heading the name of each bargain shop and service is listed in alphabetical order. Also included is such information as address, telephone number, store hours, the means of purchasing, (cash only, cash or check, and which credit cards, if any, are accepted). The credit card code is

MC—MasterCharge, AE—American Express, FN—First National, and VISA. Also listed are the other cities in Northern California where a branch store or similar service is offered.

Because many stores sell a wide variety of merchandise I have not attempted the mammoth job of a complete cross-reference system. I have, however, made a limited number of cross-references where I felt they would be most helpful to the bargain hunter. Please be sure to look at the "also see's" when they appear under the main headings. Please consult the index at the end of the book:

**SUBJECT INDEX:** (see page 191)
Arranged by product or service supplied.
**ALPHABETICAL LISTING:** (see page 179)
**GEOGRAPHICAL LISTINGS:** (see page 183)
Arranged by the name of the city in which it is located.

I would be delighted to hear from other bargain hunters regarding new listings for future editions or other suggestions you may have. Please forward any comments to my publisher, *Wingbow Press*, 2940 Seventh St., Berkeley, Calif. 94710

*Sally Socolich*

# 1

# Almost All New, Sometimes Irregular, But Otherwise First Class Merchandise

# PPAREL

## Active Sportswear

(Also see **Sporting Goods**)

**FACTORY OUTLET — SKI & TENNIS APPAREL**
890 Cowan Road, Ste. E, Burlingame 94010. Phone: 692-7833. Hours: M-F 8:30am-5pm. Purchases: MC, VISA. Parking: Lot.

Italian sportswear is noted for its high prices. The lines sold by this distributor are no exception. The tennis, ski apparel and leisure apparel sold also reflect the sophisticated styling, high fashion and fine quality associated with the expensive imported lines that are carried by stores that cater to the 'best dress'. Fashions for men and women from the previous season, samples and returns are sold for wholesale prices, and in many instances, well below wholesale. The Italian sizes may throw you, but they can translate these into American sizes readily.

The selection of ski apparel is usually limited to 4-5 racks of jackets, bibs, pants and vests. Their accessories for the skier, i.e. gloves, apres ski boots and underwear offer some of the best savings. The tennis

selection is far more extensive, as is the room full of leisure clothing for men stocked with pants, shirts, jackets and warm-up suits. Finally, they have a room full of athletic shoes for men and women whether for tennis, running or all-around casual wear. These are usually priced a modest $5.00 over wholesale. All sales are final.

To find this outlet which faces the Bayshore Fwy., take the Millbrae offramp East, loop around to the right and return to the frontage road which is Cowan.

**FILA FACTORY OUTLET**
321 Industrial Road, San Carlos 94070. Phone: 595-1750. Hours: Tues-Sat 11am-5:30pm, Sat 10am-5pm. Purchases: VISA, MC. Parking: Lot.

I don't know if wearing expensive tennis clothes will improve your game, but if you're willing to try anything, consider the clothing at the *Fila Factory Store.* At this distribution center, a small factory store exists for the purpose of selling past season merchandise, samples, and some seconds that have been repaired.

I'm hard pressed to justify the high retail prices on Fila sportswear. In fact, I think they're outrageous, but there is no disputing the fact that they use quality fabric, they're well made and do wear well. At the factory store, prices are reduced approximately 50%, which makes them more affordable but still not inexpensive. Tennis skirts, men's shirts, warm-up suits, ski vests, sweaters, bathing suits, shorts and everything else they make are in this selection of clothing which is limited in styles and sizes, but changes frequently. Men's sizes range from 26-44 and women's sizes are 4-14. All sales final.

## L & L OUTLET (ADIDAS)

967 Contra Costa Blvd., Pleasant Hill 94523. Phone: 689-4150. Hours: M-F 11:30am-8pm, Sat 9am-6pm, Sun 11am-5pm. Purchases: MC, VISA. Parking: Lot.

If you have to have Adidas sportswear or athletic shoes you're going to get a price break at last! Instep which has several Adidas stores in the Bay Area has converted their former Pleasant Hill store into an outlet that is kept well supplied by Adidas with close outs, irregulars, and salesman's samples. All merchandise is reduced at least 30% off of original retail and a major part of the overall selection is reduced 50%. Everyone in the family can find bargains from infants (a few T-shirts), boys, girls, teens, and moms and dads. All the familiar shirts, jackets, shorts, tennis apparel, jogging suits, warm-up suits, bathing suits and everything else Adidas makes is usually in the store. Shipments from the factory arrive on a weekly basis so that the selection is constantly changing. Athletic shoes at 30-50% off are discontinued or have cosmetic flaws. Children's sizes start at size 3½ and go right through men's sizes 14. Basketball, tennis, jogging, football, soccer and all around athletic shoes are available. Sales on irregulars are final. These flaws are usually confined to a misprinted logo and are not associated with sizing or fabric imperfections. Returns on closeouts are allowed for exchange within

seven days. This store is at the intersection of Willow Pass/Taylor Blvd. and Contra Costa Blvd. right across from the Sun Valley Shopping Center.

## SF SKI/SPORTS FACTORY OUTLET

300 Brannan Street (2nd floor), San Francisco 94107. Phone: 543-5164. Hours: M-Sat 10am-5pm. Purchases: VISA, MC. Parking: Very limited street parking.

The *SF Ski/Sports Factory Outlet* opened in January, 1982, and is situated on a garment manufacturing facility. During ski season, their mainstay product lines are skiwear for men and women (parkas, vests, ski pants and bib overalls, one-piece cross-country suits and warm-up boots for indoor use). Many of the garments are manufactured in the plant which adjoins the outlet. These garments represent the top name manufacturers with whom they do business in their contract division. They also produce skiwear of their own design and manufacture which they sell only from their own outlet.

In addition to garments produced, they also have a variety of showroom and salesmens' line samples of skiwear, mountaineering and camping wear which they buy directly from manufacturers. All of their merchandise is first quality (no seconds or rejects) and is offered at prices that are from 30-60% below regular retail prices. The majority of all skiwear is about 50% off.

Velour warm-up suits for men and women are dominant in their summer and fall lines. Available in standard sizes, they also make a special group of skiwear and warm-ups for TALL men and women, a group which generally has a hard time finding stylish garments at any price that fit properly. Their down-insulated, fashionable full length coats for men and women are priced at half of what they sell for downtown. I hesitated in listing such a new store without being able to rely on a proven track record in times when stores close faster than new ones open.

# Children's Apparel

(See **Baby Furniture — New and Used**)

### ANDY'S DAD'S PLACE
903 Fifth Ave., San Rafael 94901. Phone: 457-2919. Hours: M-Sat 10am-5pm. Purchases: VISA, MC. Parking: Street.

A little discount is better than none at all, therefore these 20% savings on fine fashions for boys will satisfy customers who want the very best but not at top dollar. The selection in boys' clothing ranges from size 4-20 in their suits, sportcoats, slacks, jackets, shirts, pajamas and jeans. This is a delightful store for the fashion conscious mother.

### CLOTHES CIRCUIT
(See **Apparel — Women's Neighborhood**)

### CARY & MOUSEFEATHERS FACTORY OUTLETS
1235 A & C Fourth St. (at Gilman), Berkeley 94710. Phone: 527-6360, 527-7381. Hours: M-F 10am-2pm (recommend calling ahead). Purchases: Cash or Check. Parking: Very limited street parking.

Consider this a two-for-one opportunity. These two outlets are side by side. The lines are high priced and sold in fine department stores and specialty shops. The dresses and play clothes convey a very romantic and Victorian feeling. At the outlets prices are reduced about 40-50% on the samples, end-of-season and irregulars. If you want the current season merchandise, be prepared to pay full retail. There is very little available for boys except in a few infant and toddler styles. Sizes range from infant through size 10. Most of the garments are made in 100% cotton. Quilters and sewers will find the prices on left-over fabrics very enticing.
    Do call ahead before visiting: occasionally they rush off to make deliveries and handle other business. Also, take note that there is one other outlet in Berkeley. Why not give them all a looksee?

### CARTER'S FACTORY OUTLET STORE
2329 Buchanan Drive, Antioch 94509. Phone: 415-757-8623. Hours: M-Sat 10am-5pm, Sun 1pm-5pm. Purchases: Cash or Check only. Parking: Free Lot.

The *Carter's Outlet* store is large, beautifully merchandised and well stocked. You will find a complete selection of everything Carter's makes: infant and layette goods, diapers, bibs, rubber pants, blankets, crib accessories, etc., plus playclothes, special occasion clothing and even Christening outfits. You'll be pleased to discover all the other manufacturers who use *Carter's Outlet Stores* to dispose of their overruns and end-of-season merchandise. Osh Kosh, Jack Tar, Brittania, Tie-ups, London Fog, Calvin Klein, Gloria Vanderbilt and Wonderalls are just a few worth mentioning.

The discounts at *Carter's* are not as great as the 'outlet' title would suggest. By far the largest part of their selection is discounted a modest 20-30% off retail, while the rest is discounted 30-60%. Rather than discourage a visit, I am only trying to give a realistic expectation about what you'll find after making what, for many, is a very long trek to Antioch

Most of the clothing in the store is from the previous year's stock, but only a retail fashion buyer would know the difference. The *Carter's* irregulars are clearly marked and priced accordingly. Your best buys will always be found on their special clearance racks and tables, where there are bits and pieces and in-store clearance merchandise. Size-range encompasses infants (including preemie sizes) through size 14 in girls and up to 18-20 in boys. Some teen-sized merchandise is available in a smaller selection. For harried parents, the children's playroom, with toys and T.V., is a welcome addition. Reach the outlet by taking the Somersville offramp South from Hwy. 4 and turning left on Buchanan.

## THE CHILDREN'S CORNER
1147 So Saratoga/Sunnyvale Road (Huntington Village Shopping Center), San Jose 95129. Phone 408-257-5332. Hours: Mon-Thurs 10am-5pm, Fri 1pm-5 pm. Sat 10am-5pm. Purchases: Cash, Check. Parking: Lot.

You'll find new and nearly new brand name merchandise at 40-60% off retail at this children's consignment shop. Also children's furniture, dance and sports equipment, toys, games, books, and maternity clothes. Consignments are accepted on an appointment basis. Whether you're buying or selling, you'll come out ahead. Sizes in clothing range from infant to pre-teen.

## CHOCOLATE MOOSE
821 Petaluma Blvd. North, Petaluma 94952. Phone: 707-763-9278. Hours: Mon-Sat 10am-5pm. Purchases: MC, VISA. Parking: Street.

Sonoma County has few resources where residents can purchase clothing at close to wholesale, but this manufacturer's outlet will save some a drive into the 'City'. *Chocolate Moose* is a specialty line for infants through size 6x. Winter fashions are usually made in soft colorful velours while the summer clothing is primarily cotton knits or cotton wovens in sporty, casual styles appropriate for playwear. In addition to the Chocolate Moose line, the owner utilizes her connections with other manufacturers of specialty lines to extend the selection of merchandise to include precious party dresses, T-shirts and quilted infant goods. These are all sold at 30-40% discounts. The discounts reflect the fact that these are end-of-season, samples, and overruns. Clothing from other manufacturers extends the size range to size 14.

## FACTORY OUTLET

1509-A San Pablo Ave., Berkeley 94702. Phone: 527-7633. Hours: M-F 10am-4pm. Purchases: Cash, Check. Parking: Street.

Upstairs at this outlet for Sweet Potatoes, a designer line of children's clothes, you can save 30-60% on their seconds, overruns, samples and past season merchandise. Sizes range from infant to 6x. Even discounted these great little garments are not inexpensive.

## JAMBOREE

5630 Geary (Betw. 20th & 21st Ave.), San Francisco 94121. Phone: 751-9000. Hours: M-S 9:30-6pm, Sun noon-5pm. Purchases: BA, MC, VISA. Parking: Street, City Lot.

**Other Stores:** 5730 Newpark Mall, Newark; 204 E. 2nd Ave., San Mateo; 1649 Hollenbeck Ave., Sunnyvale; 1690 Locust, Walnut Creek.

If you like to see your children turned out in style but you can't cope with high prices, *Jamboree* is the place. A little paint and good taste goes a long way in making a discount operation look like a fashionable children's shop. Most impressive are the European and American designer labels on the clothing as well as the most desirable and appreciated better American brands. Savings range from 20-50% off retail prices. These are not seconds or irregulars or out-of-season clothes. The stock is plentiful! I'm always thrilled when I find fancy dress clothes for my children at double reduced clearance prices. When you know you'll give something away or pass it along before it shows signs of wear, the savings are appreciated even more.

Size ranges from infants through 14 in boys and girls clothing. Exchanges are allowed but no cash refunds. No children of your own? Give one of their gift certificates!!

## KID'S CLOTHING CO.

216 Northgate One, San Rafael 94903. Phone: 479-4932. Hours: M-Sat 10am-5:30pm. Purchases: MC, VISA. Parking: Lot.

This looks like any other children's store, but there's one important difference. All the very good quality, name brand merchandise is marked down at least 20%. The owners buy some samples, some overruns and take a smaller markup on other merchandise to offer discount prices. At their sales they take an additional 20-25% off so you want to get on their mailing list. Girls sizes range from infant to Preteen and boys: infant-size 7. This Northgate One Shopping Center is occupied by several discount stores, don't leave without giving each a perusal.

## MARSHALL'S
(See **Family Clothing**)

## NANCY'S FANCY'S (RECYCLED)
1389 Solano (off Ramona), Albany 94706. Phone: 525-1882. Hours: M-Sat 1pm-5pm. Purchases: Cash or Check. Parking: Street.

You can shop here all week long, but if you want to sell or place merchandise on consignment, you must bring in your quality "reusables" on Fridays between 1pm-4:30pm. It helps if you leave the spots, stains and wrinkles at home; they're really not interested in things that look like they've been through five children. The clothing section offers sizes infant-14 for both boys and girls and I've seen some pretty fancy duds, obviously worn on special occasions only. Their prices on clothing and toys are usually about half the retail price. Often there's some infant furniture — high chairs, strollers and the like. For those with children 'on-the-way' check out the recycled maternity clothes. Don't worry about coming away empty-handed, there are many delightful shops on this street to justify your outing.

## OUTGROWN
1417 Fourth Street, San Rafael 94903. Phone: 457-2219. Hours: M-Sat 10am-4pm. Purchases: Cash or Check. Parking: Street.

*Outgrown* has a fairly good selection of used children's clothing in sizes infant through size 12. Although they request that clothing be cleaned and pressed before they put it on display, I was slightly disappointed by the somewhat rumpled appearance of many garments on the rack that looked like they had come straight from the ironing basket. Everything is relative; if you can't afford the price of new clothes, this is a good alternative. Occasionally they have pieces of used baby equipment; if this is what you want, call first.

## SUCH A BUSINESS
5533 College Ave., Oakland 94618. Phone: 665-6641. Hours: M-Sat 10am-5:30pm, Thurs eve till 8pm, Sun Noon-5pm. Purchases: BA, MC. Parking: Street.

There are many reasons why I like this store. I can always find great little toys, the kind of toys you use just as a little surprise or pick-me-up for the unhappy child. I also appreciate the samples and irregulars of Buster Brown, Billy the Kid, Wrangler, Polly Flanders and others that I find on their racks at 30-40% discounts. First quality clothing at regular prices is also mixed in with the bargains, which can be confusing. Prospective parents will be delighted with the selection and prices on new and used infant furniture and equipment. You can also shop leisurely after depositing the kids in the play area. This shop is about two blocks from the Rockridge Bart Station.

**THE TREEHOUSE**
1815D Ygnacio Valley Blvd., Ygnacio Plaza, Walnut Creek 94596. Phone: 935-0827. Hours: M-F 10am-6pm, Sat 10am-5pm, Sun Noon-5pm. Purchases: BA, MC. Parking: Lot.

**Other Stores:** 201 No. Hartz, Danville; 5400 Ygnacio Valley Rd., Concord.

The ladies who own this store spend a lot of time dealing with sales representatives, buying sample merchandise for their charming children's shop. The samples in boys' and girls' clothing, from the best manufacturers, come in infant sizes through size 16. They also have nightgowns, bathrobes, Communion dresses, playclothes and gorgeous dress ensembles for the little ones' special occasions. Savings range from 20-40% off except during sales when reductions are greater.

# Family Apparel

(Also see **Men's** and **Women's Apparel, Sporting Goods**)

**CAPWELL'S BUDGET STORE**
Broadway at 20th St., Oakland 94612. Phone: 832-1111. Hours: M-S 9:30am-6pm. Purchases: Cash, Check, store charge. Parking: Street, pay lot.

A fun way to get to *Capwell's Budget Store* is to ride BART to the 19th Street Station, where you will exit directly into the store below street level. You'll find almost everything here but furniture, stationary supplies, home appliances, and decorator items. Your incentive for shopping here is high fashion at low prices; at the *Budget Store* you can buy today's "in" look at a fraction of the price you'd pay upstairs.

Special purchases of selected irregulars, samples, and seconds are made from name brand manufacturers in men's, ladies' and children's clothing. Labels are sometimes removed or stamped "irregular," but the experienced shopper will recognize the popular manufacturers. The linen and bedding department has a January White Sale going on all year long, and the yardage department offers super bargains on remnants and savings on an assortment of first-quality fabrics.

All regular store services are available in the *Budget Store.* Ads spotlighting special bargains appear three times a week in the Oakland "Tribune."

## CLOTHES DIRECT

3535 Industrial Drive, B-2 (adjacent to K-Mart), Santa Rosa 94501. Phone: 707-523-2730. Hours: M-Sat 10am-6pm, Thurs to 9pm, Sun Noon-5pm. Parking: Lot.

**Other Stores:** Petaluma, Santa Cruz.

*Clothes Direct* is a 4,000 square foot warehouse-type store full of clothing for men, women and children. They specialize in popular labels in sportswear with a special emphasis on Junior and young men's fashions. They offer few frills: concrete floors, open beam ceilings, simple dressing rooms and no 'salespeople' unless you request help. Most of the merchandise is categorized as first quality closeouts and overruns from Bay Area and national manufacturers, or seconds and irregulars that are repaired and priced accordingly. First quality merchandise is usually discounted from 30-45%. Clearance racks are always in evidence with drastic markdowns on merchandise that has been around too long. To outfit the whole family, especially teens, for casual clothing, i.e. tops, bottoms, jackets, you can't do better for discount prices in Sonoma County than a shopping expedition to *Clothes Direct.*

## HALF OR LESS

330 No. Capitol Ave. (at Capitol Ave. & McKee-Montgomery Wards Shopping Center), San Jose 95133. Phone: 408-258-6818. Hours: M-F 10am-7pm, Sat 10am-5:30 pm, Sun Noon-5pm. Purchases: MC, VISA. Parking: Lot.

J.M. McDonald's sends all of their rejects and leftovers to their clearance store in East San Jose. Most of the merchandise has already been marked down 2 or 3 times in the regular store. When it ends up at *Half or Less*, prices are about 50% off original retail. By this time the clothing may be past season, a little tired looking or even obviously worn and returned. Yet, you can pick and poke your way through the racks and find gratifying bargains. I especially liked the children's selection. In addition to clothing for men, women, children and teens, the bedding and linen departments, luggage section and accessory tables offer many potentially great buys.

## MACY'S FURNITURE CLEARANCE PLACE
(See **Furniture and Accessories**)

## MARSHALL'S

5160 Stevens Creek Blvd. (at Law. Expy), San Jose 95129. Phone: 408-244-8962. Hours: M-S 9am-10pm, Sun Noon-5pm. Purchases: BA, MC. Parking: Free Lot.

**Other Stores:** Newark, Pleasant Hill, San Jose.

At *Marshall's*, it's department store selection (minus atmosphere) with many brand names selling for less than retail. Their clothing departments for men, boys, girls, infants and women are the largest part of *Marshall's* inventory. Their shoe department has excellent buys and lo and behold, they even have a lingerie and robe department. 20-60% savings are offered on merchandise categorized as irregular, samples or overruns. Some labels are cut. *Marshall's* has a full money back refund policy within 14 days of purchase with a sales slip verification. That's nice! Not to be overlooked are the linen, housewares, and gift departments where you can purchase sheets, spreads, and dust ruffles etc., at prices that should make white sale ad-makers blush. Conveniently *Macy's Furniture Clearance Place* is next door — two great bargain places side by side.

## MONTGOMERY WARD CLEARANCE CENTER
(See **General Merchandise — Liquidators**)

# Men's Apparel

(Also see **Active Sportswear & Family, Women's Apparel and Sporting Goods**)

## ATHLETIC SHOE FACTORY STORE
(See — **Shoes**)

## BELMONT CLOTHES
915 Ralston Ave., Suite B, Belmont 94002. Phone: 591-8760. Hours: T-F 10am-5:30am. Purchases: BA, MC. Parking: Private lot, street.

Professional and career men who are interested in dependable, enduring fashion rather than the latest fads and trends will be impressed with the fine quality and modest prices at *Belmont Clothes*. Discreetly tucked away behind a bank, the store is immaculate and simply furnished with most available space taken up by racks of suits, sportcoats, and slacks. In fact, they only sell these three items. Each item has a letter code on the hang tag which you compare to their posted price list which reflects their reduced prices compared to a suggested retail price. With lower overhead, and minimal advertising expenses, they still make a respectable profit and their customers reap a tidy savings!

Suits range in price from $139-$269, sportcoats, $80-$219, and slacks, $19-$44. Most of the selection is obtained from well known American manufacturers. Their selection is very extensive in all three categories with hard to find sizes available in good quantities. At these prices it's understandable that they charge extra for alterations. Once you get on their mailing list you'll be kept informed of their latest shipments and special sales. Finally, their low-key, no pressure approach to selling is very refreshing and most appreciated.

## CLOTHING CLEARANCE CENTER

695 Bryant Street, San Francisco 94105. Phone: 495-7879. Hours: M-F 10am-8pm, Sat 9am-6pm, Sun 10am-5pm. Purchases: VISA, MC. Parking: Street—difficult.

**Other Stores:** 2995 Junipero Serra Blvd., Daly City; 2660 El Camino Real, Santa Clara; 255 El Portal Shopping Center, San Pablo; 442-A Blossom Hill Rd., San Jose.

The man who has never ventured out into the bargain environment for his clothing needs may feel skeptical when first entering the warehouse—no frills—atmosphere of *CCC*. If he stays awhile and objectively considers the merchandise, he cannot fail to be impressed by the selection of suits, sportcoats, pants, shirts, sweaters and ties, etc. He will be pleased at the quality and quantity of garments in even hard-to-fit shorts, portlies, longs and extra longs.

With savings that average a cool 50%, you may wonder how they do it. *CCC* is associated with 137 outlets throughout the U.S., all buying through one centralized buying office, April-Marcus. April-Marcus buys the overstock inventories of manufacturers and retailers throughout the country (oversupplies are on the increase as the recession clamps down) and these tremendous savings are passed on to their customers. Their success has been noted by articles in "Newsweek" and "Money" magazines in 1979.

Their salesmen are not on commission so you won't have jackets forced off your body by aggressive salesmen, and they will give you as little or as much help as you need. I think it's wise to ask for assistance. You'll save time as they can steer you to those manufacturers that have a cut that is suited to your body type. At these prices any alterations are extra. They can be done on the premises for a minimal charge with fast, reliable service.

All the merchandise is first quality with a fashion orientation geared primarily to the MOR (middle-of-the-road) customer. However, I've observed men from all income levels, age groups and with varying tastes doing business here. You are unlikely to spend more than $99 for a sports coat, or more than $199 for a suit. They have frequent special markdowns like the 3-piece corduroy suit special for $59.95. A great price for a young man with limited funds who is still growing.

## CLOTHES CIRCUIT
(See **Apparel, Women's—Neighborhood Store**)

## DESIGNERS LOFT
(See **Apparel, Women's—Neighborhood Store**)

## EXECUTIVE CLOTHES

520 Washington St., San Francisco 94111. Phone: 433-7818. Hours: M-F 9:30am-5:30pm, Sat 10am-3pm. Purchases: MC, VISA. Parking: Street or Pay Lot.

You're greeted at this store across from the Transamerica Building by a loud jarring buzzer as you open the gate into the sales area. After you've calmed your pounding heart and nerves you can start to appreciate the selection of men's suits, sportcoats, slacks, shirts, raincoats, belts, and ties. Most of the merchandise sports their private label making comparison shopping difficult. (I find this impediment very common in the area of men's clothing.) However, if you're familiar with the merchandise sold in other retail stores you will recognize at *Executive Clothes,* the same quality and fine tailoring, but at a much lower price. Their selection of three piece wool suits in the $160 price range is extensive, and the stylish camel hair sportscoats at $158 were excellent values.

Most of their merchandise is purchased from American manufacturers whose styles are designed for the professional or executive mien. They maintain a complete size range which includes many hard to find sizes. Alternations are extra, but they will have them done for you at a very reasonable cost.

**Fashions Unlimited**
(See Apparel—Family)

**KUTLER BROS.**
585 Mission Street, San Francisco 94105. Phone: 543-7770. Hours: M-F 9am-5pm, Sat 9am-3pm. Purchases: VISA, MC. Parking: Street or Pay lots.

*Kutler Bros.* has the most impressive selection of fine quality men's clothing offered at discount prices (30-50%) in the Bay Area. Although I can't mention specific brands or labels, be assured that you will see many of their designer suits, sport coats, slacks, and raincoats, along with dress shirts, sport shirts,

sweaters, ties and belts, selling in only the 'best' men's stores or departments. *Kutler Bros.* does most of its business with executives and professionals. Accordingly, a large part of their clothing selection may seem high priced even at discount pricing. That $425-$450 suit can be a bargain for one customer at $269-$289, and out of reach for the next who will choose among the more modestly priced lines. Their size range is extensive and includes the hard-to-fit in any dimension. Alterations are not included in the discount price, but are done at a minimal charge right on the premises. The new shoe department contains the best names in imported and domestic footwear at 25-40% below retail. They carry a full range of styles—from penny loafers to fine Italian dress shoes, from crepe soled casuals to wing tips. My one frustration at *Kutler Bros.* is that all their prices are coded to protect the manufacturer. Therefore, if you're on a tight budget, let the salesman know and he'll keep you in your price range.

In order for *Kutler Bros.* to acquire these fine lines and to sell them at reduced prices, they have an agreement with their manufacturers to exclude the public and to restrict their business to a select clientele which is based on personal referrals, or to employees of large companies that have had entry arrangements made for them. While I find it hard to believe they'd turn a prospective customer away, I've always been asked for my card and cleared before gaining entrance to the showroom. Check with your company to see customer privileges have been arranged. If they haven't, suggest that they do.

## KUPPENHEIMER FACTORY STORES

455 Paseo Grande (San Lorenzo Village), San Lorenzo 94580. Phone: 278-0213. Hours: M-F 10am-9pm, Sat 9am-6pm, Sun 11am-6pm. Purchases: MC, VISA. Parking: Lot.

**Other Stores:** 651 Contra Costa Blvd., Pleasant Hill, 687-8309; 797 E. El Camino Real, Sunnyvale, 408-732-9820; 81 El Camino Real, San Carlos, 592-4005.

*Kuppenheimer* is a division of Hercules Manufacturing, who for over 70 years, has been making men's clothing and selling it to retailers nationwide. Now they have eliminated the middleman and are selling directly to the public through their factory owned stores. Controlling retail overhead allows them to reduce prices by operating basic no-frills stores. They offer a wide selection of suits, slacks and sportcoats in a complete size range whether your build is trim, regular, tall or portly. I think *Kuppenheimer* stores are a good resource for men on a tight budget, or for those who wear suits only on special occasions. While they have some quality garments, I thought many of their suits were lacking in fine tailoring or quality fabrics. Alterations are not included in the purchase price be can be done on the premises.

**Marshalls**
(Apparel—See **Family**)

## MEN'S CLOTHING CO.

1684 Locust Street, Walnut Creek 94596. Phone: 935-3321. Hours: M-Sat 9:30am-6pm, Thurs till 9pm, Sun Noon-5pm. Purchases: VISA, MC. Parking: Street.

A selection of quality designer and famous brand menswear with savings from 25-50% off suggested retail prices are found in this converted garage in downtown Walnut Creek. The location affects their prices as well as their method of buying. They pay cash for their purchases or use shorter credit terms, which allows them to buy at better prices, and they also buy in-season merchandise as well as some closeouts. A nice selection of wool and wool blend suits, and sportcoats are available in sizes 38S-42S, 38R-46R, also 38L-46L. They stock a full range of men's clothing. Although this is intended to be a no frills operation, the service is excellent. There is a charge for alterations.

## MEN'S CLOTHING OUTLET

One Monterey Road, Monterey 93940. Phone: 408-375-7694. Hours: M-Sat 10am-5pm, Sun Noon-5pm. Purchases: Cash or Check. Parking: Lot.

This manufacturer is well known, sells to many Bay Area better stores, and prefers to retain a very low profile, so I can't mention the label. However, when visiting the Monterey or Carmel area, it would be a shame not to allow an extra hour for a short jaunt to their factory store which is located by the Monterey airport. The outlet is large, full of clothing displayed on two-tiered racks. Their seconds , overruns, and discontinued styles are sold for about 50% off. Jackets and sportcoats in wools, corduroys, suedes, poplins, and other fabrics are available in men's sizes 34-58 including Long and X-Long. They stock overruns from other manufacturers with down vests, shirts, slacks to round out the selection. For women they make a line of blazers in wools and corduroys that are also 50% off in sizes 6-16. The overall selection offers a lot of versatility. They can clothe you for the weekend rodeo or Monday's meeting with corporate stockholders. They provide rudimentary dressing rooms, but pass on alterations. All sales are final, so shop with care!

## MEN'S SHIRT AND SWEATER OUTLET

8200 Capwell Drive, Oakland 94621. Phone: 635-8400. Hours: M-Th 11am-3pm, Fri 11am-4pm, Dec. Xmas hours M-F 10am-4pm. Purchases: Cash only. Parking: Free lot.

A pleasing selection of men's ski sweaters, mod T-shirts, golf shirts, and sports shirts is available at this manufacturer's outlet for a well-known brand found in better men's stores and department stores.

Finding the outlet takes all your investigative skills, since it is obscurely located at the side back corner of the building. A small hand-lettered sign saying "Open" is the only indication of the treasure trove of men's wear within. Merchandise is neatly arranged on tables or racks in sizes S to XL. There are dressing rooms. Exchanges are permitted, but no cash refunds or credit slips.

## MEN'S WEARHOUSE

5353 Almaden Expressway #39 (Almaden Plaza), San Jose 95118. Phone: 408-723-1900. Hours: M-F 10am-9pm, Sat 10am-6pm, Sun Noon-5pm. Purchases: MC, VISA. Parking: Lot.

**Other Stores:** 2550 West El Camino Real, San Antonio Center, Mt. View; 508-K Contra Costa Blvd., Pleasant Hill.

The Houston based *Men's Wearhouse* has twenty stores. Most of their merchandise bears their own private label. However, they select the fabrics and styles for their stores and have them made by such well known manufacturers as Pierre Cardin, Johnny Carson, Botany 500, Cartier, Nino Cerruti, YSL, Givenchy and Adolfo. Because they deal with these manufacturers on a volume, cash basis, they buy 'right' and can pass on considerable savings to value-conscious men. Additionally, they do purchase regular inventory from these and other manufacturers. Overall the discounts range from 20-40% off retail prices on their suits, sportcoats, ties, shirts, sweaters, raincoats and belts. A smaller section of the store is devoted to women's clothing (career oriented apparel) within the same discount range. Sizes in men's clothing ranges from 36S-52X Long. Alterations are not included in the purchase price but often can be done while you wait depending on the complexity of the job. Alterations are guaranteed to fit to your satisfaction. Full refunds will be given on unaltered merchandise if returned within 30 days accompanied with a receipt. I liked their prices and their quality.

## MERCHANDISERS, INC.
343 Golden Gate Ave., San Francisco 94102. Phone: 864-0515. Hours: M-F 9am-5:30 pm, Sat 10am-4pm. Purchases: Cash, check. Parking: Street.

**Other Store:** 43 Stockton (upstairs), San Francisco.

This business grew like Topsy from a wholesale distributor who opened an outlet to accommodate his friends to what is now a successful retail operation that can accommodate just about any sportsminded man. It's very accessible to the businessman in the Civic Center district who makes this a regular lunchtime outing.

The merchandise in both stores consists of 50% clothing and 50% sporting goods with an emphasis on clothing from October to December. Name brands currently featured in both men's clothing and sporting goods include Jantzen, Munsingwear, Izod, John Weitz, Glen Oaks, Pierre Cardin, Roger Keith, Nike, Addidas, Converse, Wilson, Dunlop, Spalding Ektelon, Voit and others. Merchandise carried includes sportcoats, slacks, casual pants, dress shirts, ties, sport shirts, jackets, sweaters, raincoats, swimwear, and all clothing accessories such as socks, underwear, pajamas, etc. Sporting goods items include any type of athletic clothing and all types of athletic shoes for men and women from the top brands, tennis rackets and equipment, racquetball, camping, backpacking and team sport equipment. Everything is marked on a cost plus basis, which is considerably less than the markup of a full service store. Savings range from 20-45%.

## THE SAMPLE SELL
310 Linda Lane, Danville 94526. Phone: 837-3550. Hours: M-F 10am-9pm, Sat 10am-5:30pm, Sun Noon-5pm. Purchases: BA, MC. Parking: Street.

The *Sample Sell* has a slightly different merchandising angle. They sell samples of men's sportswear for wholesale plus $2.50. You might well wonder how they can possibly survive with this pricing system; it should be obvious if you stop and think about it. They're buying this merchandise for less than the wholesale price; nevertheless, your savings are considerable. These samples are all first quality. Brands they carry include Levi, John Henry, Christian Dior, Lord Jeff, Farah, Oscar de la Renta, Cresco and about 80 other labels! Pants come in sizes 30-38, suits and jackets in 40 regular (mostly) and shirts in small, medium and large.

## SHEEPSKIN OUTLET
68 Coombs St. (off Imola), Napa 94559. Phone: 707-253-0923. Hours: Daily 10:30am-4:30pm. Closed Tues & Wed. Purchases: VISA, MC. Parking: Lot.

Sawyer of Napa does very well as a by-product industry. That is, turning sheepskin from lambs grown on the Western slopes of the U.S. for food consumption into beautiful coats, vests, jackets and car seat covers. Their fine quality apparel sells in Harrods of London, Bloomingdales, Lord And Taylor plus many other fine stores. The outlet store which is open fall through spring each year is the repository of samples, discontinued styles, overruns, and occasionally seconds—all sold for approximately 40% off retail.

Be prepared for the prices: even at 40% off, a quality full length woman's coat can range from $480 up. Men's jackets start at $210 and vests are $66-$130. If you're a Perry Ellis customer, you'll be delighted over the prices on his exciting coats and jackets which he designs for Sawyer. To maximize profits, leftover sheepskin is made into hats, golf club covers, booties, purses, etc. and also sold for discount prices. Sold for $70 a pair, their car seat covers are popular.

Sheepskin can last for 25 years if properly cared for. The high cost of these garments can be attributed to the 65 processes involved in taking raw skin and turning it into a perfect finished product. Sizes in women's garments range from 4-16, men's sizes are 34-50. Exchanges are accepted within 30 days of purchase.

**Sportique**
(See **Apparel, Women's—Neighborhood Stores**)

**Western Fur Traders Outlet**
(See **Apparel—Women's Factory Outlets**)

## WESTERN HAT OUTLET
Hunter's Point Naval Shipyard, Building 351 (3rd floor) San Francisco, 94124. Phone: 822-1277. Hours: Wednesday Only 10am-3pm. Purchases: Cash or Check. Parking: Lot.

This manufacturer makes men's and ladies modified Western fashion hats in pigskin leather. Many are in luscious earth tones but they also have hats in mauve, white, blue, tan and other fashion colors. At retail, prices range from $60-$100, but at the factory, all the salesman's samples, overruns, discontinued styles and irregulars are reduced to wholesale or below. Sizes in men's hats (the biggest part of the selection) are XS (6¾) to XL (7½). There are approximately 100 hats on the clearance racks most of the time.

Ladies have an extra bonus, a tantalizing selection of very trendy (as opposed to classic) casual, unstructured, soft body leather handbags. These are made from chamois or glove leathers and are designed to add the perfect high fashion touch to expensive sportswear. At retail these bags sell for $60-$90, and at the outlet, $15-$45. Note that the hours are limited to Wednesday's and you must obtain a pass and map to the building at the entrance to Hunter's Point Naval Shipyard.

# Women's Apparel

(Also see **Family Apparel**)

With 72 separate listings for women's clothing I divided the listings into three categories. Hopefully, this will enable you to locate the resources that best suit your shopping needs, while saving time, gas and money.

**Factory Outlets:** Stores owned and operated by a clothing manufacturer, usually located on or near the manufacturer's plant. Most of these stores elect to keep a low profile, and depend on word-of-mouth advertising. Most prefer to go nameless or choose an innocuous name like "Factory Outlet" or "Factory Store" which makes it difficult sometimes to figure out who they really are and what labels they sell. Factory outlets rarely take credit cards and may have unconventional hours.

**Chain Stores:** Stores with two or more locations. Multiple stores do not necessarily mean better stores; however, they often have greater buying power and the savings at these stores can be as substantial as those found at factory outlets. You may find a greater diversity in fashion selection since in addition to fashions from local manufacturers, they offer fashions from manufacturers around the country. These stores sell overruns, samples, close-outs and factory irregulars. They usually take advantage of in-season buying (larger retail stores place their orders far in advance of the season) relieving the manufacturer of merchandise that is old to him, but still new to the public. Make a point of getting on their mailing lists . . . first one at the sales, usually gets the best buys!

**Neighborhood Stores:** Fashion discount stores have mushroomed throughout the Bay Area. In the interest (necessity!!) of saving gas, it's to your advantage to take note of those stores that are convenient to you, that lie in the path of daily commuting, or near excursions you take in your car. It's not my intention to give each of these stores equal status—some are noticeably better than others, a clue is the space I've given to the listing. In the final analysis, your personal taste, fashion orientation and budget will determine which stores will find a spot on your winner's list.

## Factory Outlets

**BETTER DRESS OUTLET**
777 Florida Street, San Francisco. Phone: 821-4423. Hours: M-Sat 10am-5pm. Purchases: BA, MC. Parking: Street (difficult).

If you find that better dresses that sell at retail between $70-$150 are a little much for your budget, try this outlet where the prices are approximately 40% off retail. This manufacturer is well known for the fine quality silk, wool and cotton dresses that are available in sizes 4 through 14 in updated and contemporary styles. These dresses are perfect for dressier occasions and also for the career women. Along with the dresses they have a smaller collection of separates that are equally popular.

Finding this outlet is not easy. Drive down Florida, stop and park just before 20th Street, and look for the iron gate with the address overhead. Proceed through the gate and down the walk behind the building, go in the back door and huff and puff up three flights of stairs. Your reward is several racks of samples and overruns to choose from. On special sale days, the selection is even better so get on their mailing list!

## BLUXOME FACTORY OUTLET

173 Bluxome (3rd Floor), San Francisco 94107. Phone: 974-1250. Hours: Sat only 9am-1pm. Purchases: Cash or Check.

Carol Miller spent years designing fashions for another manufacturer before setting out on her own. Her enterprise has been rewarded as her line is selling well in many better stores and specialty shops. Her line includes the basics for the more conventional as well as more fashion forward styles that will appeal to those who consider themselves 'trend setters'. Prices on her related separates, at wholesale, range from $16-$45. On Saturday, you have a chance to buy the end-of-season overruns and closeouts if you fit sizes 4-14. Typical of better quality, higher priced garments, sizes run larger and lengths are more adequate for taller

gals. Bluxome is an alley-type street sandwiched between Bryant and Townsend, off 5th Street. Once through the bright blue door, follow the maze of stairs up to the 3rd floor. All sales final.

## THE COMPANY STORE

1903 Fillmore St., San Francisco 94115. Phone: 921-0365. Hours: M-Sat 10am-6pm. Purchases: BA, MC. Parking: Lot.

This cozy little neighborhood store located in a renovated Victorian building offers less than retail prices to the larger than average lady. Primarily, this is an outlet for a San Francisco manufacturer who specializes in modestly priced clothing for career women. In addition, she has brought in other lines of sportswear and casual clothing. Some of the garments are irregular, others are overruns, samples or special make-up orders just for the outlet of their best selling designs. The size range in sportswear goes from 32-44, dresses accommodate sizes 15-25 or 14½ to 24½, and tops range from 36-46. The dresses usually retail from $44-$64 but 30-40% reductions will help those pocket books ravaged by inflation. The styles are appealing, sophisticated and up-to-date. You won't find the mundane fashions that have prevailed in larger fashions for so many years. In the corner they pile fabrics that are left over from the factory. Dressing rooms are available. All sales are final.

## EMERYVILLE CLOTHING & FABRIC OUTLET
1711 64th St. (Next to Fwy 80), Emeryville 94608. Hours: M-F 10am-3pm. Purchases: Cash or Check. Parking: Street.

This is the outlet for the Krist Gudnason line which caters to the younger Missy size market in sizes 6-18. Their racks are filled with caftans, street dresses, and skirts that are samples, overruns, and irregulars. Savings are 40-60% off retail. Fabrics from their sewing room and design department as well as notions (zippers, buttons, cording and trims) are available in a good selection at give-away prices. Bags of quilting scraps are super buys. This outlet is hard to find. From Freeway 80 take the Powell offramp East, turn right on Christie, and right again on 64th St.

## END OF THE LINE
275 Brannan, San Francisco 94107. Phone: 989-0234. Hours: M-Sat 10am-4:30pm. Purchases: BA, MC. Parking: Street:

Rosani for Misses, Rags and Rag A Muffins for Juniors are the labels sold at this outlet for 40-50% off retail. Their dresses and blouses range in size from 6-14 to 5-13. This is a moderately priced line at retail so at the outlet dresses are usually priced between $15-$35 and blouses from $10-$16. These fashions are usually executed in cotton blends or synthetics and have an updated look. They've provided a communal dressing room and a nice seating area for weary husbands or boyfriends. Parking in this area is grim during the week: check the pay lot down the street, or better yet, wait till the weekend when the area is free of workers.

## SUSANNA ENGLAND DESIGNS
10855 San Pablo Ave., El Cerrito 94530. Phone: 235-4660. Hours: Subject to owner's schedule. Call ahead. Purchases: Cash or Checks. Parking: Street.

Susanna England designs very special outerwear for fashionable boutiques. You might call her garments 'limited editions'. Jackets, vests and coats are quilted with fabric appliques, all in natural fibers. Because of their unique 'art in wearing' qualities, the garments are not inexpensive even at her factory store. Factory prices range from $40-$200 and represent discounts from 20%-50% off retail. Her 'little' store has very limited hours and a limited selection of garments. At any one time there are no more than 100 pieces on the racks. Sizes range from 6/8 to 12/14. The selection changes weekly.

## ESPRIT FACTORY OUTLET
901 Minnesota St., San Francisco 94107. Phone: 821-2000. Hours: M-F 10am-6pm, Sat 10am-5pm. Purchases: VISA, MC. Parking: Very limited street parking.

The opening of the *Esprit Outlet* was a dream come true for the many teens and women who delight in their fashions. They are often viewed on the fashion pages of "Seventeen" and "Mademoiselle". Even more surprising is the care and planning that created such a pleasurable outlet to shop in. The high tech display units, vibrant colors and background music give an air of razzle-dazzle to the whole environment. They even provide mini shopping carts to load up your bargains!

For the uninitiated, *Esprit* has several apparel and accessory lines which include: shoes, belts, blouses, handbags, sweaters, pants, jackets, blazers, dresses, related separates, sweat pants and shirts, well, just about everything. If you order their catalog from one of their magazine advertisements, you can get a peek at what 'may' be coming into the outlet, but always a few months behind the retail stores. The clothing at the outlet is classified as seasonal overruns, returns, production samples and seconds.

Their production samples are very intriguing. Some are originals that never made it into mass production. They're usually sold for 50-60% off what the anticipated retail price would have been. Bargains in seconds can be like the $5.00 corduroy culotte skirt with a broken zipper I snatched from a bin. Did I feel smug! Overall the discounts range from 20-60% off retail. If you think their prices are higher than other outlets, bear in mind that *Esprit* is a higher priced line, therefore outlet prices are higher proportionately. The *Esprit* line encompasses sizes 3-13. Security is very tight at the outlet; you have to leave your purse at the checkstand and the guards keep everyone honest. Be careful in making your selections, all sales are final. Be sure to get on their mailing list for special unadvertised sales for preferred customers. One last note: by the fall of 1982, merchandise from their new girls line (sizes 8-14) should be on sale in the outlet.

## FACTORY OUTLET
4th & Alice, Oakland 94607. Hours: M-F 11am-6pm, Sat 11am-4pm. Purchases: Cash only. Parking: Street.

Overruns and closeouts, in first quality Junior fashions that appeal to the "Seventeen" reader are sold at prices close to wholesale. These dresses and blouses are moderately priced at retail and many sell under the Eber label. This is a small outlet and the selection is haphazard at times.

## FARR WEST
560 College Ave., Palo Alto 94306. Phone: 494-3325. Hours: Tues-Fri 10am-4:30pm, Sat 10am-2pm. Purchases: Cash or Check. Parking: Street.

*Farr West* is a manufacturer of lingerie which includes slips, camisoles, panties, robes, hostess pajamas, elegant and Tom Boy types of sleepwear and coverups. Their little factory store in the blue and white cottage west of El Camino Real has the leftovers, irregulars and samples at reduced prices, usually 40-50% off retail. Some visits are very rewarding, some are disappointing. Like most outlets, timing is everything. Leftover fabrics, velours, jerseys, terry cloth, lingerie fabrics and trims are sold in pieces at wholesale prices.

## THE GREAT BLOUSE & SEPARATES OUTLET
208, 218 and 244 Fremont St., San Francisco 94105. Phone: 986-3800. Hours: M-S 10am-3:45pm. Purchases: Cash. Parking: Street (limited).

I cut my teeth on bargain hunting at these outlet stores. The labels, Fritzi (Misses sizes), You Babes, and That's My Babee (Junior sizes) are very popular with Bay Area bargain sleuths. There is a dressing room at the main store at 244, but none at the other two outlets. The amenities are nil—racks so close together you can hardly move between them to check out the skirts, dresses, blouses and pants.

   The long popularity of these outlets can only be attributed to the low prices, 40-70% off on their seconds, irregulars and overruns. At the 218 store they frequently have drastic sales and you'll find blouses and sweaters for $5-$7. You may end up buying clothes you don't really need just because the prices are so irresistible. Flaws are usually marked with masking tape and sometimes I've had the price marked down further when I've found one they had missed. Get on their mailing list so you can participate in their end-of-season and overstock sales. All sales are final, so check garments carefully before buying.

## GUNNE SAX FACTORY OUTLET
524 2nd Street (2nd floor), San Francisco 94107. Phone: 495-3326. Hours: M-Sat 9am-4:30pm. Purchases: Cash, Check. Parking: Street (limited).

This is where all my younger friends go to buy long party dresses, prom dresses, etc. These dresses have also been popular for weddings, both for the bride and bridesmaids. *Gunne Sax* is a Junior line in sizes 5-13. Fathers are delighted at the savings. Irregulars, samples, overruns are approximately 50% off, sometimes 75% or more on very irregular garments. Often a handy seamstress can repair those irregularities, then glow over her super bargain. There are blouses and short dresses in the same general styles and fabulous buys on fabrics (laces, cottons, and voiles in lovely colors). You can't return these dresses, so be sure you can fix (or live with) the flaws before taking your purchase home. Note: They are now carrying delectable little girls dresses, blouses and skirts.

## HOUSE OF LARGE SIZES — OUTLET STORES
207 El Portal Drive (El Portal Shopping Center), San Pablo 94806. Phone: 236-3618. Hours: M,T 9:30am-6pm, W, Th, F 9:30am-7pm, Sat 9:30am-5pm, Sun Noon-5pm. Purchases: MC, VISA. Parking: Lot.

**Other Stores:** Fremont Fashion Center, 39141 Civic Ctr. Dr., Fremont; Foothill Square, 10700 MacArthur Blvd., Oakland.

*House of Large Sizes*, which has ten retail stores in the Bay Area, also has three large outlet stores to take all the leftovers, past season and special purchases they acquire from several manufacturers. These outlet stores are well stocked with separates, coats, sweaters and a smaller offering of dresses. Brand names include Levi, Koret, Mr. Alex, Rejoice, Catalina, Ecco Bay,

Peronsal and California Maker. Sizes at these stores range from 38-52 or 14½-32½. When the leftovers are sent to the outlet stores are they reduced by 33%. After arrival they are continuously marked down until they're sold. Get on the mailing list for their last chance sales.

## JEANNE-MARC FACTORY OUTLET

1821 Powell Street, San Francisco 94133. Phone: 397-5722. Hours: Tues-Sat Noon-6pm. Purchases: VISA, MC. Parking: Street.

One stands out when wearing a *Jeanne-Marc* design. Most of their fashions are trend-setting, distinctive, sometimes dramatic, and always project the fine quality that is associated with expensive designer apparel. If you subscribe to two or three high fashion magazines, you're probably a potential *Jeanne-Marc* customer. This line is always sold in the designer section of better stores at 'high prices'. At their outlet, you won't see the same fashions you're seeing in the stores, but you may find something you admired but couldn't afford last season. Samples, a few irregulars and end-of-season overruns describe the selection at the outlet. There are jackets, vests, dresses, separates, active sportswear and jumpsuits in sizes Petite through Large which will fit sizes 4-16 depending on the garment or the style. Prices are reduced at least 50-60% off former retail and range at the outlet from $5 for shorts and accessories to as much as $150 for a full length coat. If you can, go on Wednesday when they have their red tag markdowns. Selected garments are tagged for a 50% markdown on that day, or hit them on Thursdays when new merchandise is received. Before leaving the area, check the fabric outlet next door. You may find additional fabric to make a related garment to match a jacket, blouse, skirt etc. you bought at the outlet. All sales are final.

## LADIES JEAN OUTLET

380 Swift Ave. No. 1, South San Francisco 94080. Phone: 589-4335. Hours: M-F Noon-4pm. Purchases: MC, VISA. Parking: Street.

This jean manufacturer is not well known for their own line (Cougar) because their pants are sold primarily under the private labels of major stores. Other labels they distribute in pants, novelty pants and jackets are Sasson and Simone Pereire. These pants at the factory are overruns, samples, seconds and discontinued styles. Prices range from $10-$30. Sizes range from Junior 3-15 and Missy 8-18. Their hours change frequently, so call before visiting.

## LILLI ANN FACTORY OUTLET

2701 16th St., San Francisco 94103. Phone: 863-2720. Hours: Sat 9am-1pm. Purchases: BA, MC. Parking: Street.

This factory store for a leading name-brand ladies' coat and dress manufacturer (Lilli Ann and Adolf Schuman) offers irregulars and seconds at wholesale prices. The styles are truly elegant, more suited to the mature woman who desires that expensive look. The coats, with their fur trims, capes and fancy fabrics are a little much for the casual, suburban way of life, but fine for more formal lifestyles. There are many coat and dress ensembles with exquisite design and tailoring, as well as many bright-colored all-weather coats in vinyls and suedes, plus sophisticated sportswear.

This manufacturer sells his lines in only the most exclusive stores and shops. You probably won't find anything here for under $75, and that's the wholesale price!

In a separate room you'll find damaged clothing for up to 75% off. 'Damaged' means that some clothing may be soiled, flawed or sized improperly. Of course, selection and size are limited in this room, and no exchanges or returns are accepted. The fabric room offers elegant pre-cut fabrics, clearly labeled as to fiber content and length, at wholesale prices.

## TERRY McHUGH OUTLET
425 Second Street, (Fifth Floor), San Francisco 94107. Phone: 495-7590. Hours: M-F 10am-3pm. Purchases: Cash or Check. Parking: Street (very limited).

Terry McHugh manufactures a neat line of dresses that are perfect for career dressing. At the factory she has set aside the 'turquoise' room to display and sell current overruns, the few irregulars and past season garments. Sizes are S-M-L and fit sizes 6-14. Her specialty for fall and winter fashions are the woolblend jersey dresses that last from year to year with a change of accessories. These retail around $100 but sell at the outlet for $30-$50. Her spring and summer fashions include knits and cotton wovens, some suitable for the office, others perfect for vacation or resort apparel. When you browse through the racks, keep in mind that most of her styles must be worn to be appreciated. Do try them on for full effect. All sales final.

## THE OUTLET STORE
221 So. Maple, South San Francisco 94118. Phone: 761-1467. Hours: T-Sat 9am-4pm. Purchases: VISA, MC. Parking: Lot.

You really have to go out of your way to find this Albee factory outlet so I'm including directions on how to get there. Take the Bayshore Fwy. south to Grand Ave., turn west, turn left on Linden, right on Victory and left on South Maple. The outlet is adjacent to the factory.

Moms and teens can shop here together if they're between sizes 6-16. Pants, skirts, sweaters and blouses predominate in the selection of samples and overruns from the factory warehouse. There is a rack at the back with irregulars at super low prices. Occasionally, when I've wanted something in a different color the salespeople have been able to round it up from their stockroom. Most of their fashions, made in synthetics and cottons, are seen prominently displayed in retail stores.

## OLGA FASHION FABRICS & OTHER THINGS

12200 Saratoga-Sunnyvale Rd., Saratoga 95070. Phone: 408-253-2780. Hours: M-Sat 10:30am-6pm. Purchases: BA, MC. Parking: Free Lot.

*Olga,* known for beautiful lingerie, undergarments and loungewear, has opened an outlet in Saratoga. I was impressed with the large selection of discontinued and irregular styles in nightgowns (petite-38), panties (4-9), bras (32-38), slips, camisoles, leotards, body slips, suits and bathrobes, with even a few racks of *Olga* sportswear. Most garments marked irregular appear to be perfect. Garments marked as seconds have the flaws flagged with tape for easy evaluation. The discounts range from very modest to sensational. For instance, the best selling *Olga* bra, regularly sold retail for $10, was discounted 20% and priced at $8. Some lovely gowns were reduced from $35-$27. I didn't turn cartwheels at these discounts, but I was favorably impressed with the girdles for $5, the leotards marked down from $17-$8 and another rack of gowns in a slow selling color priced to clear at $10. Their seconds are usually about one half off and are often the best values if you can overlook the flaws. I'm told the way to get the maximum savings at the outlet is to get on their mailing list. Once a month, rain or shine, they have a sale where selected types, styles or certain colors of merchandise are drastically reduced. Mailing list customers get advance notice and a preferred shopping day before the newspaper ads run in local papers.

Like most outlet stores this is a self service operation, although the staff will assist with measurements and fitting if requested. The very modest will have to wait in line for the one private dressing room. Others can 'bare all' in the communal dressing room.

Ladies devoted to stretch and sew will be delighted with an assortment of fabrics and laces from the *Olga* factory at great savings. The Olgalon fabric, 100% breathable polyester, cannot be purchased in most fabric stores. To find the store look for West Coast Federal Savings and drive to the back of the building where the outlet is located. Note: there are no exchanges or refunds.

## RAINCOAT OUTLET

543 Howard Street (2nd floor), San Francisco 94105. Phone: 362-2626. Hours: M-F 8am-4pm, Sat 7:30am-11:30am. Purchases: Cash or Check. Parking: Street.

Proceed with caution when shopping at this outlet. The careless and inconsiderate shopper who throws and drapes clothing on racks and chairs is not appreciated; in fact, she'll be sharply reprimanded! You're also well advised to schedule your visits on Saturdays when there is the time and the staff available to help you.

This is my favorite resource for raincoats and velvet blazers with coordinating skirts and vests. This manufacturer enjoys a good reputation for the quality and classic styling that prevails in her line. Check first before you start rummaging through the racks, many are off-limits. You can choose from samples and overruns in sizes 4-24. There is one small mirror and no dressing room. The very modest retreat into a corner and hide behind a rack of clothes. You can expect a 40-50% savings, but forget the service, they simply are not set up to pamper your ego.

## THE SAN FRANCISCO MERCANTILE COMPANY
2915 Sacramento St., San Francisco 94115. Phone: 563-0113. Hours: M-Sat 10am-6pm, Sun Noon-5pm. Purchases: VISA, MC. Parking: Street.

If you're enchanted by those Victorian inspired nightgowns and robes made by Queen Anne's Lace but put off by their high prices, stop by their factory owned boutique and take advantage of discount prices that will save you 30-50% off retail. The gowns in soft cottons and flannels, noted for their tucks and ruffles, in 100% cotton, are all first quality, but will be past season. Sizes range from petite to large, or 3/4 to 13/14.

   The Rio sportswear line and Aileen West dresses are usually well represented. These fashions seem to bridge the generation gap, appealing to women of all ages. They tend to be very feminine with many styles in soft cotton or natural fibers. Dressing rooms are provided at this elegant little store. Note: Occasionally they will have some merchandise that is not discounted, however, this constitutes a small percentage of the total selection.

## SILKY WAY
953 Mission St., San Francisco 94103. Phone: 957-1731. Hours: M-Sat 10am-5:30pm. Purchases: VISA, MC. Parking: 5th St., downtown garage.
**Other Stores:** 709 Clay St., San Francisco; 451 Saratoga Ave., San Jose.

One way to justify the dry cleaning costs for silk garments, is to save money on the initial cost of your clothing. At *Silky Way,* the outlet stores for an import firm, blouses, skirts, pants, and dresses in silk are sold for discounts of 30-50% off comparably priced merchandise in other stores. Some of their blouses and dresses are very nice, especially when considering the price. A few lines are made in polyester and have a lower price. Don't be put off by the wrinkles in some of the clothes, handsteaming of garments is just not part of the outlet milieu. You'll have no problem pressing out the wrinkles yourself. Sizes are 4-14. All sales final.

## WESTERN FUR TRADERS OUTLET
1400-A Howard Street (at 10th Street), San Francisco 94103. Phone: 626-1940. Hours: M-F 9am-5pm, Sat 10am-4pm. Purchases: VISA, MC, AE. Parking: Limited street parking.

If you have allergies, beware! At this basement outlet, sheepskin shearling is being cut into coats, jackets, vests, car seat covers, bags, mittens, slippers and hats. You're invited to take a look around and watch the fur fly! This manufacturer makes shearling products for resale in retail stores throughout the country and also distributes fur jackets from the Orient for several major importers. These fur jackets and coats are made from mink, red fox, blue fox, oppossum, coyote and black fox. At the factory store you can buy the apparel and accessories for 20% above wholesale, and during their frequent sales you can buy at wholesale prices. Of special interest is the possibility of having a coat or jacket made to your design or size specifications for a nice discount price. All their shearling garments are made from U.S. tanned skins. Prices range from $10-$900. The garments are fully guaranteed. While they do not give refunds they will allow for exchanges or credit.

# CHAIN STORES

The following stores have more than one location in the Bay Area. Generally they have greater buying power and more diversity in their clothing selection.

### THE CLOTHES CIRCUIT
120 Petticoat Lane, Walnut Creek 94596. Phone: 933-0300. Hours: M-F 9:30am-9pm, Sat 9:30am-6pm, Sun Noon-5pm. Purchases: BA, MC, VISA. Parking: Private Lot.
**Other Stores:** 7216 Regional St., Dublin, 828-5544. 30 Golf Club Rd., Pleasant Hill, 689-7465.

If you need a dress for church or an important daytime occasion and you're lucky enough to wear sample sizes 8-12, go no further: this is the place! *Clothes Circuit* obtains the salesmen's samples from the 'Who's Who' of apparel makers. Prices are reduced about 30% from the retail price on these garments. For the girls and ladies in sizes 6-16 in Juniors and Misses there is quite a selection of coordinated sportswear. The men's section is well stocked with casual pants, shirts, sweaters and jackets. *Clothes Circuit* also has a few racks of merchandise that other stores don't seem to bother with; namely, ski pants, powder pants, ski jackets for the whole family, swimwear, jogging suits, warm-up suits, tennis togs and golf clothes. I've had good luck finding children's parkas and jackets from the best manufacturers (Pacific Trail, White Stag) and have really appreciated the 30% discount. They have very good sales during January and July and will mail advance notices to customers who request this info. You won't miss this store if you look for *Lipperts Ice Cream Parlor* first and then look further back to the parking area.

### CLOTHES CITY
861 4th Street, San Rafael 94901. Phone: 456-0860. Hours: 9:30am-6pm, Thurs eve till 9pm, Sun Noon-5pm. Purchases: VISA, MC. Parking: Street.
**Other Stores:** 190 Northgate One, Terra Linda, 415-499-0999; 42 Petaluma Blvd., North, Petaluma, 707-762-8133.

*Clothes City* has undergone a metamorphosis since my last edition. From far out and funky, it has become more traditional and more fashion oriented to the suburban woman. The prices have also changed because they are no longer just buying irregulars and end-of-season merchandise. Most of their merchandise is very current and therefore they are not able to offer great discounts. On some styles you may have to be content with a minimal 10-15% discount while on others you can still realize a hefty 30-40% savings. Fashion brands include Calvin Klein, Sasson, Chemin de Fer, Bill Blass and Gloria Vanderbilt. Along with pants, they carry blouses, sweaters and jackets — all discounted.

## CLOTHES ENCOUNTER
217 Kearny Street, San Francisco 94104. Phone: 788-1747. Hours: M-F 10am-5:45pm, Sat 11am-5pm. Purchases: BA, MC. Parking: Pay Garage.

**Other Store:** 2348 Mission St., San Francisco.

Imagine a discount store that validates! Just one block from the Stockton-O'Farrell garage they'll give you one hour's free parking with a purchase. If that isn't incentive enough consider the merchandise: Joshua Tree, Judy Knapp, Jack Mulqueen, Diane Von Furstenberg, First Glance, Jonathan Martin and others, all at 33⅓-60% off regular retail. You're really in luck when you chance upon their additional 20% off sales. They also carry accessories like hats, bags, belts, scarves, pins and jewelry along with the clothing. The store manager is very helpful if you're having problems pulling a special look together. In the hustle and bustle of downtown shopping you could easily pass right by . . . but don't.

## CLOTHES RACK
255 Kearny St., San Francisco 94108. Phone: 781-0630. Hours: M-Sat 10am-6pm. Purchases: BA, MC. Parking: Street & Pay Lots.

**Other Stores:** Berkeley, Burlingame, Davis, Daly City, Napa, Oakland, Sacramento, San Rafael, Citrus Heights, Santa Rosa, Walnut Creek.

With new ownership the *Clothes Rack* has undergone a major transformation. They're aiming to be a bit more high class than their competition by offering the younger career woman top value for her clothing dollar with contemporary designer fashions that represent better quality and a sounder investment. Many of their new lines are the type that you build your wardrobe around and expect to wear more than one season. Value is what they're trying to provide, and with reductions of 25-60% on their current, first quality merchandise, value is what you get. Sizes in their pants, skirts, blouses, blazers, dresses and coats are geared towards the woman who fits in the 5/6 to 13/14 range. Along with clothes for the working girl, there are clothes for leisure time activities and just plain loafing.

You may want to visit more than one store since each store is merchandised to suit the needs of the customers in the area.

## FASHIONS UNLIMITED
5100-5 Clayton Rd. (Vineyard Shopping Center), Concord 94521. Phone: 825-3874. Hours: M-F 9:30am-

9pm, Sat 9:30am-6pm, Sun 11am-5pm. Purchases: MC, VISA. Parking: Free Lot.

**Other Store:** 7352 Greenback Lane, Citrus Heights.

Bobbie Brooks, Huck-A-Poo, Modern Juniors, Villager, Levi's, Faded Glory, Funny Girl, Ecco Bay, Crazy Horse and Tom Boy are just a few of the prominent manufacturers represented in the selection of Juniors and Misses clothing at this 4,000 sq. ft. store. All the labels are left intact on this first quality merchandise which includes dresses, separates, blazers, raincoats, and ski clothing.

The greatest strength of this store is the selection of clothing from manufacturers throughout the country, which offers shoppers a refreshing choice in making their purchases. Careful buying enables the owners to pass on savings of 30-60% off retail prices. Dressing rooms, exchange privileges, and a sparkling fresh decor spell success for the owners and their value conscious customers.

## GARMENT DEPOT
977 Moraga Road, Lafayette 94549. Phone: 284-2600. Hours: M-Sat 10am-6pm, Sun Noon-5pm. Purchases: BA, MC. Parking: Lot.

**Other Stores:** 5400 Ygnacio Blvd. (Clayton Valley Shopping Center) Concord.

These nicely appointed stores are conveniently located in small shopping centers. They carry junior sized 3-13 and missy sized 6-16 sportswear and dresses at 25-40% discounts. Their selection of dresses is small compared to the selection of Levi's and Chemin de Fer pants. I can always find a top, blouse, sweater, or T-shirt from their well-stocked racks. They have a fashion accessory selection with belts, scarves and some costume jewelry, helpful for putting a whole look together. The large communal dressing room has plenty of mirrors; you can see yourself from every angle, and of course, that can be depressing!

## THE GOLD HANGER
56 Bayfair Mall, San Leandro 94578. Phone: 278-4653. Hours: M-F 10am-9pm, Sat 10am-6pm, Sun 11:30am-5pm. Purchases: BA, MC. Parking: Lot.

**Other Stores:** Campbell, Castro Valley, San Jose, Newark.

If you're a petite 4'11" and your best friend is a robust 5'10" you probably have trouble shopping in the same stores. At Gold Hanger you can both shop successfully. The emphasis here is depth. Sizes range from 5 to 18 in small, med and tall lengths. Regardless of your height or girth you're bound to find something in their proportioned sizes.

There is a large selection of casual clothing (tops and bottoms) in current, popular fashions in all the 'in' colors. The merchandise is unbranded (which means this is budget merchandise for budget clothing stores) but they take a lower mark-up and their prices are 15-25% less than other budget stores. Even though these are budget brands I found the selection very pleasing and regardless of the price the clothes look like they cost more. They had some great prices on belts. I often find that these little items put the biggest dent in my clothing budget. Unlike so many bargain stores they will provide a box and bow — nice for gift giving — and also make exchanges.

## HARMONY & LOTUS

638 San Anselmo Ave., San Anselmo 94960. Phone: 453-0940. Hours: M-F 11:30am-5:30pm, Sat 11am-5pm. Purchases: VISA, MC. Parking: Street.

**Other Stores:** 513 Fourth Street & 4213 Montgomery Drive, Santa Rosa; 115 San Jose Ave., Capitola; 34 Sunnyside Avenue, Mill Valley.

The five *Harmony and Lotus* stores are unique for their emphasis on natural fiber clothing. You can buy an outfit for a country picnic or an elegant dinner party and everything in between. The blouses, skirts, pants, sweaters, and dresses are first quality and discounted about 30-50% off the retail prices of other stores. The sweaters are suitable for men or women. Many styles are imported while others are made especially for their stores. They also carry several lines from popular manufacturers who utilize natural fibers in their clothing. All five stores have a charming boutique appearance. The clothing will appeal to those with fairly conventional taste as well as those who like a touch of the exotic. Sizes are 3-14.

## LOEHMANN'S

75 Westlake Mall, Daly City 94015. Phone: 755-2424. Hours: M-Sat 10am-5:30pm, Wed 10am-9:30pm. Purchases: Cash, Check. Parking: Lot.

**Other Stores:** 1651 Hollenbeck Ave., Sunnyvale 94087; East Bay: Fall 1982.

*Loehmann's* has been famous for over 55 years on the East Coast for quality fashions at great savings. Yes, they are a branch of the *Loehmann's* in New York City and Boston. They've been so successful that they now have 55 stores across the United States. Their clothing is the better designer-type; many are samples and overruns.

Their Daly City store has a no frills appearance that is in direct contrast to the exciting selection of clothing sold here. There are all types of "mood" clothes — cocktail, dressy, furs, in-between, sportswear; and those of you clever enough to recognize designer clothes without a label will find fashions from Geoffrey Beene, Adele Simpson, Bill Blass, Ann Klein and others of equal renown.

Inflation fighters will want to sharpen their nails and develop their aggressiveness to hang on to their "finds". Their communal dressing rooms always seem a bit hectic (like a dressing room for a dance company with two minutes to change for their next number). You can be sure that you'll save at least ⅓ off the retail price, and often 50% or more. There are no returns or refunds: buy wisely.

## MARSHALL'S
(See **Family Apparel**)

## MY FAVORITE CLOTHING STORE
825 Francisco Blvd. West, San Rafael 94901. Phone: 453-4195. Hours: M-Sat 10am-6pm, Sun 11am-5pm. Purchases: Cash Only. Parking: Lot.

**Other Stores:** 33 Drumm St. & 2544 Mission St., San Francisco; 1608 Sir Francis Drake Blvd., San Anselmo.

I keep going back to this store even though some visits are very disappointing. Because they buy closeouts and overruns from manufacturers like Santa Cruz Imports, Carol Little, Pronto, Pacific Blue and St. Tropez, the selection at times looks a little 'old'. On the other hand, I'm delighted with a summer dress I bought last fall for $10 and three tops for $5 each. Their super savings are the 'as is' racks that have clothes with missing buttons, snaps or slight flaws for savings that are 70% off retail. You'll usually find an extensive selection of blouses, pants, skirts, blazers, T-shirts, accessories, swimwear and other active sportswear. The Drumm St. store also features fashions for the working woman in the financial district.

## PATTI QUINN'S
505 Mission St., San Francisco 94105. Phone: 541-0413. Hours: M-F 10am-6pm, Sat 10am-3pm. Purchases: VISA, MC. Parking: Street or Pay Lot.

**Other Stores:** 1585 No. 4th St., San Jose, 408-288-9179; 215 So. Ellsworth, San Mateo, 344-2589. Extended Hours: M-S 10am-6pm, Sun Noon-5pm.

*Patti Quinn's* rates a high mark on the basis of their wide selection of fashion merchandise for Juniors and Women with a price range that gives everyone a chance. These are overruns and closeouts, arriving in mid-season after the retail stores have stopped buying. Savings are 30-60% off. Each store has a small shoe department where discounts of 15-50% prevail on current and past season's shoes. The Mission Street store caters to working women with more suits and fancy blouses, while the suburban stores have a bigger selection of casual sportswear. What sets *Patti Quinn's* apart from all the other discount stores is the quality of their selection with brands like Evan Piccone, Ellen Tracy, Condor, Villager, Ann Klein, Sir for Her, Expresso, Adolfo and others. Sizes range from 4 16 or 5 15.

## PIC-A-DILLY
1847 El Camino Real, Burlingame Plaza, Burlingame 94010. Phone: 697-9846. Purchases: Cash, Check.
**Other Stores:** Antioch, Belmont, Campbell, Capitola, Cupertino, Concord, Daly City, Dublin, Fairfield, Fremont, Hayward, Larkspur, Los Gatos, Menlo Park, Milpitas, Modesto, Mt. View, Oakland, Petaluma, Redwood City, Richmond, Salinas, San Anselmo, San Francisco, San Jose, San Lorenzo, San Mateo, San Rafael, Santa Clara, Santa Cruz, Santa Rosa, Stockton, Sunnyvale, Union City, Walnut Creek.

*Pic-a-dilly* buys overruns of current fashion apparel, the same fashions you buy in the big stores. Their New York buyers are "in the market" every day. Fashions are shipped direct to the Bay Area for distribution in their 35 stores. Of course, they cut some labels to protect the manufacturer, but do you really care if you can save $$$? The savings are gratifying, 30-50% off, and they are marked down even more the longer they hang on the racks. Quick turnover is a must to maintain low prices. Stop in frequently when you're shopping for blouses, dresses, swimwear, skirts, pants, raincoats, ski jackets, even tennis togs. Their fashion range has appeal from the most mod gal to the basically conservative matron. Among my friends who shop there is my 16-year-old babysitter and a 57-year-old neighbor! The stores are all self-service, simple and clean.

## RAGSMATAZZ
2036 Union St., San Francisco 94123. Phone: 563-1398. Hours: M-Sat 11am-6pm, Sun Noon-5pm. Purchases: BA, MC. Parking: Street.

**Other Stores:** 382 Park St., Moraga, 376-5395; 1120 First St., Napa, 707-255-0404; 1994 Mountain Blvd., Oakland, 339-2316; Petaluma Plaza, Petaluma, 707-763-8934; 270 Golf Club Rd., Pleasant Hill, 827-4575; 910 Sir Francis Drake Blvd., San Anselmo, 456-5907; 2036 Union St., San Franciso, 563-1398; 3024 Taraval St., San Francisco, 566-2066; 254 Clement St., San Francisco, 221-2854.

Don't think you have the wrong place just because this store doesn't look like the typical bargain store. It is uniquely located on a lower level, next door to the Delancey Street Restaurant. Most of the clothing is categorized as manufacturers' overruns. All are first quality, popular brands like Malibu, Foxy Lady, Phase II, Colours, East Side Clothing Co. and First Glance to name just a few. The prices are great! About 40% off on dresses, pants, blazers, gowns, blouses, sweaters and T-shirts. Junior sizes only 3-13. You can exchange within 7 days. Parking at their Union Street store is always a problem. Good luck!

## S & R FASHION CENTER
2058 Mission Street, San Francisco 94110. Phone: 626-0856. Hours: M-Sat 11am-6pm, Sun 12am-5pm. Purchases: Cash, Check. Parking: Street.

**Other Stores:** 960 Geneva, San Francisco.

Only the most dedicated bargain hunters will enjoy shopping at *S & R*. This is a last post outlet for many Bay Area manufacturers. You'll find out of season, overruns, irregulars all jammed onto racks in such a manner that few have the patience to look for that super buy amidst the clutter. The prices are an inducement to persevere: up to 70% off on their range of fashions that will suit juniors through matrons. Parking can be a problem at this Mission Street location. I've picked up a few parking tickets when my five minute excursion lasted an hour or longer.

## SOMETHING SPECIAL

1299 4th St., San Rafael 94901. Phone: 457-4616. Hours: M-Sat 10am-6pm, Fri till 7pm, Sun Noon-5pm. Purchases: BA, MC. Parking: Street.

**Other Stores:** 1113 Burlingame Ave. (Downtown), Burlingame, 343-3993; 1855 El Camino (Burlingame Plaza), Burlingame, 692-1267; 182 No. 1 Northgate Plaza, Northgate, 472-6823; 255 University Ave., Palo Alto, 328-7361; 332 Walnut St., Redwood City, 367-1200; 3130 Fillmore St., San Francisco, 922-2662; 3415 California St. (Laurel Village), San Francisco, 221-5960; 31 Bovet Rd., (Borel Square), San Mateo, 574-7771; 1299 Fourth St. (Downtown), San Rafael, 457-4616.

Your impressions of this chain may vary appreciably depending on which store you choose to visit. The San Francisco stores are geared to the career and working women, with many nice suits, silk dresses and classy coordinates from better quality manufacturers. The suburban stores wisely feature more clothing for casual lifestyles. Prices at all stores are 25-50% off retail pricing on their first quality merchandise. Styles are updated in sizes 3-13 and the stores are more fashionably decorated so they look less like a discount store and more like a retail store. Some of the brands carried are Larry Levine, Paul Stanley, Foxy Lady, Sir For Her, Jonathan Marten, Sasson, Collage, Lopez and Malibu Media.

## TAGGS

1670 So. Bascom Ave., Campbell 95008. Phone: 408-377-7544. Hours: M-F 10am-9pm, Sat 10am-6pm, Sun Noon-5pm. Purchases: MC, VISA. Parking: Lot.

**Other Stores:** Westlake Mall, Daly City; Calvares Plaza, Milpitas; San Lorenzo Shopping Center, San Lorenzo.

If you can curb the impulse to buy the latest new fashions as they appear in full service retail stores, then you may be able to save money at *Taggs* when those offerings hit their racks several weeks later. Lines like Jack Winter, Liz Claiborne, Evan Piccone, Cardessa, Campus Casual and Gloria Vanderbilt are indicative of the quality level at these stores. Sizes range from 4-16 and include Junior and Misses. *Taggs* is trying to provide the career oriented woman with a choice of sportswear and coordinates that will help project that 'professional' image, but at an affordable price.

# NEIGHBORHOOD STORES

These stores are excellent local resources for fashion discounts. Circle those in areas where you frequently shop. The size of the stores and the depth and quality of selection varies greatly, an indication is the space I have given to each store listing. Please remember to use the geographical index in the back of the book to easily locate stores in neighboring communities.

## ADDED DIMENSIONS

1355 No. Main Street, Walnut Creek 94596. Phone: 939-8623. Hours: M-Sat 10am-5:30 pm, Th 10am-7:30pm. Purchases: BA, MC. Parking: Street or Lot.

Over 22 million women in the U.S. wear size 16 or over. Unfortunately most retailers choose to ignore this statistic. Larger women who are searching for fashionable sportswear with an updated image will be delighted with this store. The owner, who has an extensive background in fashion buying and retailing, took a look at the marketplace and realized there was a great need for a fashion outlet that was geared just for the larger woman. The size range in dresses is 16-16½ to 24-24½. Pants range from 30-46, tops from 36-46. This store barely qualifies for a listing because most fashions are discounted a minimal 10%. If you're lucky enough to find something on the sale racks in the back of the store you may save as much as 40%. While I wish that the discounts could be greater, I know ladies in this size range will be gratified by the quality, the fashionable styles and the selection.

## CLOTHES HOUND

3127 Stevens Creek Blvd., Santa Clara 95050. Phone: (408) 247-2970. Hours: T, W, Sat 10am-6pm, M, Th, F 10am-9pm, Sun Noon-5pm. Purchases: VISA, MC. Parking: Lot.

Evan-Piccone, Gant, Austin Hill, Country Set, Diva, Dudley, Hunter Haig and others are all owned by the corporate giant that also owns the Clothes Hound.

This store serves as a discount clearance center for all these companies that have overruns, discontinued fashions, store returns, and irregulars. The bargains for men and women are a tempting 40% off on the better quality separates. For women there are skirts, blazers, blouses, dresses, pant-suits and suits, plus a line of wedding dresses. For men there are suits, sportcoats, shirts, ties, underwear and sweaters. A portion of the merchandise has obviously been around for a while, but the rest is in-season, top quality, and just what you're looking for. Sizes in men's suits and sport coats range from 36-60, Short to X-Long and women's sizes are 4-16 and styles are geared to the working woman with a mature fashion orientation. There is also a boys department with 'church or special occasion clothes' sizes 6-20. Prices at their "end of season" sales will knock your socks off!

## CRACOLICE'S HOUSE OF FASHION

2145 Morrill Ave. (at Landress), San Jose 95132. Phone: 408-262-9230. Hours: M-F 10am-8pm, Sat 10am-6pm, Sun Noon-5pm. Purchases: VISA, MC. Parking: Lot.

**Other Store:** 123 So. Main St., Milpitas.

If you like the fashions from Eber, Bobbi Brooks, Byer, U-Babes, Ocean Pacific and Ship and Shore, you'll find these plus more at this discount store. Geared to the Junior market, everything appears to be reduced approximately 30-50% off retail on their separates and sportswear. There are a few racks of dresses but overall this is a good place to pick up a blouse, a pair of pants to fill the gaps in your wardrobe. Note: They have a fairly good selection of teen boys' and men's-sportswear.

## DANBURY LTD.
120 East Prospect Ave., Danville 94526. Phone: 837-3777. Hours: M-Sat 10:30am-5pm. Purchases: BA, MC. Parking: Street.

This obscure little boutique offers casual and career fashions. It's patronized particularly by women in their 30's who like the look of class and sophistication. *Danbury* is a sample shop with the biggest selection in sizes 8-10. Some 10's in their better lines fit 12's beautifully.

Their selection changes frequently, often they get sample merchandise before it's shown in local prestige and hi-fashion stores. I've seen fine designer lines on their racks like John Meyer, Austin Hill and Patty Woodard, great for career-conscious women. They also have samples in lingerie and bathing suits.

They keep a mailing list for active customers who want to be the first to know when new designer merchandise has arrived. Savings on samples are approximately a third.

## DANDELION
250-A Magnolia Ave., Larkspur 94939. Phone: 924-6211. Hours: T-Sat 10am-5pm. Purchases: BA, MC. Parking: Lot.

You'll get a lift just visiting this store, the crisp, cheerful, lattice decor with bright yellow awnings is very refreshing. The merchandise speaks for itself . . . some of the very best classic sportswear manufacturers are found in sample sizes (8-10). Evan Piccone, Ellen Tracy, Intuitions, Breckenridge, Patty Woodard and John Meyer labels are the reason why many women leave their names so that they can be called when something new and just right comes into the store. Winter lines have wool skirts, pants, blazers, and sweaters; and summer lines include the bright colors and comfortable fabrics associated with the season. These samples are priced 1/3 off prevailing retail; reason alone that so many Marin value-conscious shoppers have frequented this store for the past nine years.

## THE DESIGNER LOFT
991 Mission St. (2nd floor) San Francisco 94105. Phone: 495-6600. Hours: M-F 10:30am-5.30pm, Sat 10am-5:30pm. Purchases: MC, VISA. Parking: Pay Lots or street.

When you get to the corner of 2nd and Mission look for the pair of inflated pants that wave from the window of this second floor store. All of the better designer lines in mens and womens pants are sold for a solid 25% discount. These are current styles and the same that you see downtown for a lot more. Sizes for men are 28-38, women to 22, misses 4-16 and juniors 3-13. Calvin Klein, Jordache, Sergio Valente, Cacharel, Sasson, Liz Claiborne and Gloria Vanderbilt are typical of the brands carried. Prices are kept low by the obviously bare bones, no frills approach to merchandising. Dressing rooms are available and exchanges can be made. There are no cash refunds.

## FACTORY STORE
145 West Santa Clara, San Jose 95110. Phone: 998-3066. Hours: M-Sat 10am-5pm. Purchases: BA, MC. Parking: Lot.

People who confine themselves to shopping centers in the San Jose area will miss this store which is located downtown amidst the banks and office buildings. The working women in the area are finding their lunch hours are just not adequate to fully explore the fashion possibilities and discount prices. Most of the clothing originates from Los Angeles jobbers and manufacturers; some clothing is bought from fashion boutiques and may be coming in at the end of the season. Some clothing also looks a little "tired." Sizes range from 6-16, all sales are final.

## FACTORY-STORE (OUTERWARE)
520 3rd St., San Francisco 94107. Phone: 495-5956. Hours: M-Sat 10am-5pm. Purchases: VISA, MC. Parking: Street.

The name would suggest that this is a factory outlet but it's not. Rather it is a discount store that features raincoats, jackets, windbreakers, car coats, ski wear, parkas, and all weather coats at reduced prices. All the merchandise is first quality and generally manufacturers' overruns and closeouts. Some brands may seem familiar while others are unknown import brands. The prices are very good especially if you don't mind last season's colors or styles when you hit the ski slopes. There is a good selection for men, women and younger teens. There are no dressing rooms, but that's okay; for this type of clothing you don't need them. All sales are final.

## FASHION EXPRESS
590 Howard Street, San Francisco 94105. Phone: 495-4180. Hours: M-F 10am-5pm, Sat 9am-2pm. Purchases: VISA, MC. Parking: Street.

This discount store caters to both juniors (3-13) and women (6-18) in their selection of separates, coordinates and dresses. Merchandise is first quality, in-season overruns from moderate to higher priced manufacturers. Since they are located near several factory outlets in this part of town, a visit will fit right into your itinerary.

## FASHION-AIRE
1375 Blossom Hill Road, San Jose 95118. Phone: 448-2500. Hours: M-F 10am-9pm, Sat 10am-6pm, Sun Noon-5pm. Purchases: MC, BA. Parking: Lot.

Working primarily with jobbers and manufacturers in Los Angeles, *Fashion-Aire* has stocked their store with budget fashions that they offer at reduced prices. Most of the garments in their sportswear selection for Juniors are priced around $15. Even though the prices are definitely budget, they've attempted to surround you with more than a budget environment and even round out their selection with a few accessories like scarves, gold jewelry and belts.

## FASHION FACTORY
10730 San Pablo Ave., El Cerrito 94530. Phone: 525-3733. Hours: M-S 9:30am-5:30pm. Purchases: BA, MC. Parking: Lot.

*Fashion Factory* features hundreds of women's garments in sizes 8-20. The styles are up-to-date but with appeal primarily to mature women, not much for Junior-sized "mod" ladies. The brand names are well known (Koret, Tan-Jay, Goldic, Catalina and Graff, etc.) and the garments are in excellent condition (no seconds or irregulars). Of special interest to travellers is the availablity of hard-to-find end of season clothing when other stores have already cleared their racks of seasonal goods. The store is clean and well organized with dressing rooms and exchange privileges. Savings average 35% and go up 50% during 'end of season' sales. What really sets this discount operation apart from most others is the quality of sales help. They are experienced, helpful and willing to give personalized service.

## GOIN' IN STYLE
1024 Magnolia Avenue, Larkspur 94939. Phone: 461-1558. Hours: Tues-Sat 10am-5pm. Purchases: Cash or Check. Parking: Lot.

You have two reasons for visiting *Goin' In Style*. First, you may want to *sell* your wedding gown, bridesmaid dress, formal gown or evening dress, or anything that relates to more formal, special occasion kind of attire. These garments must be cleaned before they can be placed on consignment. The selling price is usually set at about ½ the retail cost, then you split that with the owner which yields a 25% return on your initial outlay. Not bad on something you plan never to wear again. Secondly, if you want to buy any of the above, you'll find a choice selection of lovely formal garments that still look like new. The wedding gowns are exquisite, and from time to time, they'll have a complete set of bridesmaids gowns. I'm not sure how often it works that your group will match sizes with what they've got but it's worth a try. Additionally, they have new bridal veils, wedding accessories, even shoes. Finally, many high school girls find lovely prom dresses at prices dad will love.

## THE GOOD BUY SHOP
5353 Almaden Expressway, No. 19 Almaden Fashion Plaza, San Jose 95118. Phone: 408-265-1111, ext 249. Hours: M-Wed 10am-6pm, Th-F 10am-9pm, Sat 10am-6pm, Sun Noon-5pm. Purchases: Cash or Check. Parking: Lot.

After the sales and markdowns at the 20 Northern California *Emporium-Capwell* stores, women's clothing that is still left on the rack is dispatched to their own clearance center just five doors down from the San Jose *Emporium*. At this last chance disposal site,

Misses (6-18) and Juniors (3-13) apparel is marked down yet again. Many items are sold below cost just to get rid of them. Keep in mind most of these garments are one season behind . . . which according to my calculations is just about right for those of us who prefer to buy the clothes we wear in season. I think this will be just the place to buy a bathing suit in September or October when they have vanished from other stores.

You can find clothing that originated in their budget departments as well as expensive and appealing higher priced merchandise from their high fashion departments. Considering the many different types and qualities of merchandise they're sending here, they do an admirable job of keeping it all in neat and good order. You won't be treated, or feel, like a discount shopper. You have to be a good sport, too. Obviously with a merchandising concept like this, they won't have all styles, or sizes; there will be many one-of-a-kind garments. Unlike the department stores, all sales are final and you will forego some of the amenities, but not dressing rooms. If you have an *Emporium* credit card, you can have a field day . . . they will take that!

## JEAN HARRIS' DESIGNER DISCOUNT BOUTIQUE
100 No. Hartz (corner Prospect), Danville 94526. Phone: 837-3600. Hours: Tues-Sat 10am-5:30pm, Sun Noon-4pm. Purchases: MC, VISA. Parking: Lot.

Jean Harris, owner of two distinctive clothing stores, has transformed one into a Designer Discount boutique. Her customers can now take advantage of the discounts which have become available to her. After years of business she has made friends with many designers and manufacturers, and they have agreed to let her have first crack at their showroom samples, their off-season merchandise and even designer one-of-a kinds. These lines at greatly reduced prices are discerningly selected. Quality, craftmanship, color and good design are basic in the selection process of these fine garments. If one word could describe her apparel it would be "distinctive". Prices are reduced from 30-70% off retail and range from very modest to $200-$300. A visit to Danville with its quaint restaurants and charming antique shops becomes a perfect time to stop in to see the latest arrrivals. Sizes are 4-16 in the dresses, suits, sweaters, pants and sportswear. Her jewelry and accessories are very unique!

## INA'S SAMPLER
60 Middle Rincon Road, Santa Rosa 95405. Phone: 707-538-0982. Hours: M-Sat 10am-5pm. Purchases: MC, VISA. Parking: Lot.

Look carefully for this little house set back from the street where you'll find a nice collection of better brands in ladies clothing. J.G. Hook, Evan Piccone, Intuitions, John Meyer and Breckenridge are a few of the brands that are usually available at 30-50% discounts. Some merchandise is as current as that on the racks of downtown stores and represents samples the owner has purchased with her 'connections'.

Overall the size range is 4-12. Sonoma County is limited in discount fashion resources so don't miss this one. If you drive Hwy. 12 from Santa Rosa to Napa you'll be passing right by!

## K & E DEPARTMENT STORE

2226 Taraval Street (Between 32nd & 33rd Ave.), San Francisco 94116. Phone: 731-3221. Hours: M-Sat 9am-6pm. Purchases: BA, MC. Parking: Street.

Plan to spend some time at K & E or forget it! It's a real hodgepodge of ladies' and younger women's clothing. The racks are simply jammed with merchandise and the chaos can be unnerving. You'll find bathing suits, lingeries, aprons, leisurewear, bathrobes, jogging suits, skirts, dresses, pants, blouses and accessories. Sizes range from 30-54 women's, 6-20 misses and 3-13 juniors. Some of the merchandise is irregular and priced accordingly. For all the chaos there seems to be many faithful shoppers who don't mind weeding through the racks to dig out those super buys that reflect savings of 40-70% off. K & E carries a full line of square dance dresses, accessories and square dance shoes for approximately 30% off.

## KUTLER BROS.

(See Apparel — Men)

## LUSTY LADIES

137 Tunstead Avenue, San Anselmo 94960. Phone: 456-7860. Hours: M-Sat 11am-5pm. Purchases: BA, MC. Parking: Street.

*Lusty Ladies* has an eclectic selection of fashions popular with students at the College of Marin. For the sophisticate, they have blouses, dresses, sweaters and blazers that are from manufacturers and designers who are fashion-forward rather than safely conventional. They usually have a good selection of Sticky Fingers pants along with many other good brands. Prices are usually reduced 40-50% off retail on their Junior fashions.

## M.C.O. OF SAN FRANCISCO

360 Florida Street, San Francisco 94110. Phone: 552-3550. Hours: M-Sat 10am-5pm, Sun Noon-5pm. Purchases: MC, VISA. Parking: Lot.

For many years this was the location of the Koret factory outlet. It is now privately owned. You will still find some overruns and irregulars from Koret, but by far the largest part of the selection is from other well known manufacturers. Evan-Piccone, Stanley Blacker, Givenchy Sport, Modern Juniors, Prestige, Calvin Klein, Ann Klein and many others provide a nice range of fashions for both Juniors and Misses in casual sportswear and career dressing. There is a small shoe department with 'leftovers' from a local shoe chain, also bags, hats, belts and other accessories. Discounts range from 30-60% off retail. Get on their mailing list to catch their super sales!

## MADELLE'S

1270 Newell Ave. (Newell Hill Place — behind Capwells), Walnut Creek 94596. Phone: 945-8404. Hours: M-Sat 9:30am-6pm. Purchases: MC, VISA. Parking: Lot.

Many of our discounters cater to the Junior market or what I call the 'bubble gum crowd' rather than the mature, career-oriented woman who is seeking better quality and classic styling. If you're in the latter group, and you're trying to build an 'investment wardrobe,' *Madelle's* in Walnut Creek is worth a trip. Buying directly from New York, they comb the market for in-season closeouts that will serve the fashion needs of their customers. Labels like Evan-Piccone, Oscar de la Renta, Bethany, Ann French and St. Emilion in blouses are beautifully merchandised in their lovely store. While discounts of 20-40% prevail, the atmosphere is more akin to expensive speciality shops. Sizes are 4-16 in Misses sizes. All the fashions are first quality and bear labels. Unlike other discount operations, you won't have to weed your way through the rejects to find the choicest buys — everything is choice. *Madelle's* is tucked away in a small shopping center one block behind the Capwell's parking lot.

## MAGNARAMA (JOSEPH MAGNIN)

#2 Stonestown Shopping Center (second level of Joseph Magnin Store), San Francisco 94132. Phone: 772-2457 or 772-2475. Hours: MTSat 10am-6pm, WThF 10am-9pm, Sun Noon-5pm. Purchases: VISA, MC, AE. Parking: Lot.

At the *Magnarama* department at the Stonestown Joseph Magnin store, all the 'leftovers' from other stores are banished. Feel sorry for the clothes — they were rejected by buyers at their original retail prices — but feel happy for yourself: you reap the savings! These ultra-fashionable clothes have already been on sale once in the regular JM departments, but were relegated to the *Magnarama* racks when they didn't sell. So prices have been slashed once, twice, thrice, as the price tag shows. Each time the price is reduced they cross out the former one, which delights me — I'm always much more pleased with a bargain buy when I can compare the sale price with the original. There's a certain amount of ego satisfaction at having beat the system.

You'll find the savings amount to a whopping 50-75%. Examine the goods before purchase: there may be a missing button, belt, snap, pulled or ripped seam, or some other flaw (then again, lots of the clothes are in perfect condition). All sales are final; there are no exchanges or refunds.

## MARSHALL'S
(See **Family Clothing**)

## MANUFACTURER'S OUTLET STORE — M.O.S.

344 California Ave., Palo Alto 94061. Phone: 321-4385. Hours: M-Sat 10am-5:30pm. Purchases: BA, MC. Parking: Street.

For ladies with conventional good taste here is a little shop just for you. Coordinated sportswear is the specialty with several popular well-known brands represented. Sizes range from 6-20 in Misses and 5-15 in Junior selections. Regular merchandise is reduced 25%, irregulars (a small proportion of the total selection) are 40% off, and manufacturers' overruns are usually 30% off. They have sales in January and August — don't miss them!

## MEN'S WEARHOUSE
(See **Apparel — Men**)

## MERCHANDISERS INC.
(See **Apparel — Men**)

## N.A.N.C.Y'S FASHION CLEARANCE
4220 Broadway, Oakland 94611. Phone: 547-2202. Hours: M-F 10am-6pm, Sat 10am-5:30pm. Purchases: BA, MC, VISA. Parking: Street.

East Bay ladies will be delighted with the selection of clothing displayed at this store. Merchandise is made available through special purchase from many manufacturers; most are overruns. They also carry close-outs from local department stores and there is a wide range of styles and qualities represented. I saw many prestigious labels among the clothes. The biggest selection can be found in their separates; however, they do have some dresses and suits. There is a limited selection of children's clothing. The savings range from 40-75% off retail prices. There are dressing rooms available and the atmosphere and decor is certainly posh compared to most outlet stores. Size range in ladies clothing is 6-16.

## DONNA PILLER'S
(See **Shoes**)

## PRIVATE LABEL
110 Town & Country Village, Palo Alto 94301. Phone: 326-4686. Hours: M-Sat 10am-6pm. Purchases: VISA, MC. Parking: Lot.

**Other Stores:** 695 Veterans Blvd., Redwood City, 363-1177; Sweater Connexion, 3648 The Barnyard, Carmel, 408-624-2172.

*Private Label* is one of the best kept secrets on the Peninsula. First impressions would suggest that this is just another posh boutique common to this shopping center. However, the discerning woman of fashion sophisticate will recognize the label and also note the discount prices. This quality line of ladies separates and sportswear is made in the Orient and distributed throughout the U.S. to stores like *Lord & Taylor* and *Bloomingdales* from their distribution warehouse in Redwood City. In major stores this line would be found in better sportswear departments where retail prices range from $59-$150 on individual separates. Sizes are 2-14 or Petite through Large.

The fashions in this line are made from natural fibers. The silks are 16 mummy (the same weight used by exclusive design houses), wool gabardines and velvets are used in the fall and winter collections of pants and skirts, cashmere and hand knit silk sweaters are very lovely, plus the cotton and linen, spring and summer, fashions are delightful! Prices are the best news: at all three stores current season merchandise is discounted approximately 30% off retail, while end of season fashions are 40-60% off. Savvy customers head right for the markdown racks where occasionally a second or an irregular may be found. If you can live with the flaw, you'll love the price. This is one of the few factory outlet stores that offers better quality to women with careers who want to look well dressed or to women who are willing to spend $30-$75 on separates to achieve a quality image.

## REFLECTIONS
1115 Magnolia, Larkspur 94939. Phone: 461-4522. Hours: T-Sat 10:30am-4:30pm. Purchases: BA, MC. Parking: Lot.

Contemporary fashions for Juniors and Misses in sizes 3/4 to 13/16 are crowded into this small discount boutique. Silk fashions and quality knits are always conspicuous in the selection at 40-50% discounts. They carry a limited selection of better children's (girls') clothing at 30-50% off.

## THE SAMPLE CELL
150 N. Hartz Ave., Danville 94526. Phone: 837-1558. Hours: M-F 10am-9pm, Sat 10am-5:30pm, Sun Noon-5pm. Purchases: BA, MC. Parking: Street.

At *The Sample Cell* the original wholesale tag is left on the salesmen's samples; you add $2.50 to arrive at your purchase price. Most garments are size 10. This should not discourage 8-12's or junior sizes 7-11 from giving them a try. Sample sizes can run large or small depending on the manufacturer. You'll get advance notice of what the next season will look like because many shipments of samples arrive well in advance of retail stores' new merchandise. Don Kenny, Happy Legs, Koret, Modern Juniors and Gloria Vanderbilt are some of the manufacturers spotted on their racks. In addition to separates and coordinates, *The Sample Cell* has some very nice dresses.

## SAMPLE VILLAGE
2226 So. Bascom Ave., Campbell 95008. Phone: 337-6083. Hours: M-Sat 10:30am-5:30pm. Purchases: BA, MC. Parking: Lot.

Salesmen's samples of separates and dresses sell for 25-35% off. Size range 5-13.

## SECRET HANG-UPS
645 E. Blithedale (upstairs) Blithedale Plaza, Mill Valley. Phone: 383-1204. Hours: M-Sat 10am-6pm, Sun Noon-5pm. Purchases: MC, VISA. Parking: Lot.

The atmosphere is more 'boutique' than discount at this charming little upstairs store in Mill Valley. You can save about 30% on the blouses, skirts, dresses, suits, etc., from manufacturers like Modern Junior, Jonathon Martin, String Bean and Esprit de Corps. Sizes range from 5-12 but are predominately junior sizes and fashions. Getting help is no problem, they love to help you organize a total look.

## SHAZAM

254 Clement St., San Francisco 94118. Phone: 221-2854. Hours: M-Sat 10am-6pm. Purchases: BA, MC. Parking: Street.

The ambiance of this store is right out of a disco dance club, complete with flashing lights and vibrating background music. Savings of 15-30% are possible on the chic collection of the latest fashions for the younger fashion-minded woman. Dresses and separates in Jr. sizes will help you create that 'foxy look,' perfect for weekend happenings.

## SOFT TOUCH FACTORY STORE

501 Bryant, San Francisco 94107. Phone: 495-5940. Hours: M-Sat 10am-5pm. Purchases: BA, MC. Parking: Street.

Some of the fashions in this store come from fancy boutiques, which accounts for their good quality and the fact that they may be slightly past season. Other in-season merchandise represents successful buying ventures from Los Angeles jobbers and manufacturers. These prices must account for the popularity of the store with working girls in the area, who also find that their updated fashion orientation in dresses, skirts, pants, jeans, blazers, tops and sweaters in sizes 8-16 is very enticing at savings 40-60% off. Throw in dressing rooms, restrooms and enough room to move around in, and you'll want to add this store to your weekend shopping forays. All sales are final . . . naturally.

## SPARE CHANGES

170 Woodside Plaza, Woodside Road, Redwood City. Phone: 363-1088. Hours: M-Sat 10am-6pm, Thurs till 9pm. Sun Noon-5pm. Purchases: MC, VISA. Parking: Street.

*Spare Changes* has many of the same labels that are prominent in the factory outlets in San Francisco. Those on the Peninsula who just can't get to the City, Fritzi, Esprit, Santa Cruz, Foxy Lady and other brands are priced just a little higher than the outlets, and sometimes a little less. Junior and Misses sizes are available in the selection of separates, dresses and sportswear that are fairly current to almost obsolete in styles that will suit those from twelve to sixty.

## SPORTIQUE FASHIONS

2310 Homestead Rd., Foothill Plaza, Los Altos 94022. Phone: 735-8660. Hours: M-F 10am-9pm, Sat 10am-6pm, Sun Noon-5pm. Purchases: BA, MC.

Consider shopping at *Sportique* a family outing. Not only do they have a substantial selection of Juniors and Misses sportswear, they give men, infants, toddlers and pre-teens a fair shake. They buy from approximately 300 manufacturers, local and nationally-known favorites. Their savings range up to 60% below prevailing retail and best of all they don't cut their labels. Prices almost compare to the factory outlets in the City. Sifting through the racks takes some time but with 21 dressing rooms there's no waiting to try on. They offer a reasonable exchange or refund policy except on final sale merchandise. *Sportique* buys only first quality garments. I'm sure if I lived closer I'd be a regular.

## THE WEDDING TRUNK
1478 University Ave., Berkeley 94705. Phone: 548-3269. Hours: Wed-Sat 11am-5:30pm. Purchases: Cash or Check. Parking: Street.

Here's an old idea with a new twist: a recycling center for wedding dresses. This charming little shop stocks approximately 100 'once worn' wedding gowns that date from 1920. Most of the dresses are contemporary, that is, dating from 1965-1980. The older, vintage gowns are more limited in supply but in greater demand. You may find elegant, sophisticated, demure and old-fashioned gowns in satins, silks, organza's, voile's and lace starting at $50 and going as high as $325. The average price of a new gown is $400, so it's possible for the prospective bride to buy a gown here that she could otherwise never afford. They have a very large dressing room and the prospective bride is treated with all the consideration and attention that she would expect at the poshest bridal salon. These gowns have been cleaned and are in excellent condition. For the bride who is short on time, another advantage is that there is no delay while the dress is ordered and made-up at the factory (a process that can take 2-4 months).

The owners of this store are interested in purchasing gowns; they particularly appreciate the larger sizes and older gowns from the 30's, 40's and 50's.

## WOMEN AT LARGE
39102 Fremont Hub, Fremont 94538. Phone: 792-1292. Hours: M-F 10am-9pm, Sat 10am-5:30pm, Sun 10am-5pm. Purchases: VISA, MC. Parking: Lot.

Don't go here to buy a dress, they don't have any. However, if you need casual sportswear or separates, and you're concerned about price, you'll be pleased to discover this store. *Women at Large* is a descriptive name for the size range 36-52 in tops, and 30-40 in pants. Better yet, their clothing is geared for the younger woman and her tight budget. Everything is discounted at least 30%. These fashions are closeouts, odd lots and overruns but not old and outdated. Many popular manufacturers are well represented in the selection.

# APPLIANCES

(Also see **Furniture and Accessories—Catalog Discounters, Warehouse Sales; General Merchandise—Catalog Discounters**)

**A & B Premiums**
(See **Cameras**)

**CVB (CENTRAL VOLUME BUYERS)**
1815 So. Monterey Rd. (Betw. Tully & Alma), San Jose 95112. Phone: 998-2906. Hours: T-Sat 10am-6pm. Purchases: MC, BA.

Don't be put off by the potholes in the parking lot, the quonset-hut-look of the yellow building or the freight depot appearance of the interior—what really count are the savings! My price comparisons on name-brand TV's, Video Tape Recorders, and kitchen and laundry appliances prove CVB fulfills its claims and offers the lowest prices in the area. Most appliances are in the original factory crates, ready for delivery. Others are uncrated for your inspection. CVB offers a 30-day trade-in policy, so if you get a lemon (that can happen anywhere) they'll gladly exchange the item for you. Additionally, you have the manufacturer's warranty on all merchandise—double protection. Their 30-day written price-guarantee allows you a refund of the difference if you can find the same merchandise sold elsewhere for less. Now that's laying it on the line! Delivery is nominal: $24.00 from San Jose to Salinas. Take note—they will not quote prices over the phone.

**CHERIN'S**
727 Valencia Street, San Francisco 94110. Phone: 864-2111. Hours: M-F 10am-6pm, Sat 10am-5pm. Purchases: Cash or Check. Parking: Street.

A great source for home appliances in every category. This store has a good selection of refrigerators, freezers, washers, dryers, TV's, vacuum cleaners, microwave ovens, VTR's, Cuisinarts, and SCM typewriters, etc. Contractor prices prevail for everyone. Their business is mostly referral. They rarely advertise their low prices which I found in my comparative shopping to be about the lowest anywhere. Don't expect them to quote prices over the phone if they don't know you.

**FILCO**
1433 Fulton Ave. (Filco Plaza), Sacramento 95825. Phone: 916-488-8484, 488-8471. Hours: M-Sat 10am-7pm. Purchases: VISA, MC. Parking: Free Lot.

In the Sacramento area Filco's prices are hard to beat! Working with a very minimal markup, they offer an extensive selection in the camera and home appliance areas. Most major brands of 35mm cameras, accessories, and instant picture cameras are in stock at terrific prices. Kodak film is sold at *cost*. This is their loss leader and certainly lures customers who often leave with more than film once they see all the other bargains. Kodak processing is always 30% off. JennAir, Kitchen Aid, Panasonic, Whirlpool, Litton, Amana, Sony and GE are a few of the major brands represented in the appliance and home entertainment divisions. Their prices on video game cartridges are usually lower than those better-known 'discount catalog stores'. Call ahead to check availability on popular cartridges: when they're hot, they don't last long.

## GENERAL ELECTRIC SERVICENTER
1727 No. First Street, San Jose 95112. Phone: 408-298-4203. Hours: M-Sat 8:30am-5:30pm. Purchases: BA, MC. Parking: Private Lot.

One of the very best ways to replace an old or broken General Electric small appliance is through the exchange program offered at the *General Electric Servicenter*. It is possible to trade in that old iron, coffeepot, or toaster oven for another and save approximately 30% off the suggested retail price. On price comparisons I made, the trade-in price was lower than any discount store or catalog discount house.

On display here are reconditioned appliances that carry the following description: "Reconditioned appliances generally represent appliances that have been used in displays or that failed in initial use. They have all been carefully reconditioned by trained GE technicians using new GE replacement parts where required. They have been carefully tested to assure that they meet operating standards required of new appliances and carry the same warranty as new products." On these you can save 30-35%. If what you want isn't on display, be sure to ask—it may be on hand in the storeroom.

## HOUSE OF LOUIE
1045 Bryant St. (near 9th), San Francisco. Phone: 621-1901, 621-7100. Hours: M, Tues, F, Sat 10am-6pm, Thur, 10am-8pm, Sun 1-5pm. Purchases: Cash or Check. Parking: Free lot on side of building.

At this warehouse operation you can get some of the best buys available on appliances and home entertainment needs. Most of the items, such as refrigerators, dishwashers, stoves (including built-ins), stereos, washers, dryers, VTR's, televisions, and kitchen cabinets are available on a cost-plus 10% basis. You can choose from famous name brands on floor display or from manufacturers' catalogs. On special orders, all sales are final.

Also on display is a wide selection of home furnishings in the low to moderate price range, including chairs, sofas, formal dining room furniture, dinettes, baby furniture, and imported Chinese Modern pieces. Savings are from 20-30%. The better goods can be ordered too, with savings of about 20%. Delivery is free within the city of San Francisco; installation is extra.

## KEN LUFF APPLIANCES

Phone Orders Only: 837-0125. Hours: Recommended calling between 2pm-6pm daily. Purchases: BA, MC.

Many of my Contra Costa friends have purchased their appliances the "lazy way", over the phone. Of course you have to know what you want: brand, name, model numbers, etc. Mr. Luff has the merchandise delivered from the manufacturer's Bay Area distribution warehouse directly to your home. His sources for major appliances include many of the best manufacturers, with all categories of kitchen and laundry appliances. If there's any problem, he'll put you in touch with the manufacturer's authorized repair representative. Doing business this way is unconventional, but I've heard only positive reports from his customers and found my own conversations with Mr. Luff to be not only helpful and informative but very pleasant as well. His prices usually reflect a cost of 10-12% above wholesale.

## L & Z PREMIUMS

1162 Saratoga Ave., San Jose 95129. Phone: 408-985-7918. Hours: M-F 10am-8pm, Sat 10am-6pm. Purchases: MC, VISA. Parking: Lot.

*L & Z* is not a typical appliance store. They have some appliances on the floor but offer a greater selection from their manufacturers' catalogs. Prices reflect a very minimal markup and delivery charges are reasonable. Most major brands of TV's, VTR's, kitchen appliances like microwaves and refrigerators, laundry appli-ances, car stereos and expensive radios can be ordered. Delivery is usually within a few days.

About half of their business is devoted to photographers with a complete selection of major brand cameras, accessories, dark room equipment, chemicals, papers etc. sold for pleasing discounts. Kodak processing is 30% off and Kodak film is sold at their cost.

## PJ'S TELEVISION & APPLIANCE

2232 Mission Street, San Francisco 94110. Phone: 626-1920. Hours: M-Sat 9am-6pm. Purchases: VISA, MC. Parking: Street.

When you see the full page ads that *PJ's* runs in the San Francisco "Advertiser" you'd expect to find a huge store full of merchandise. Instead this immaculate store in the Mission District has a compact showroom full of home appliances, home entertainment products, even car stereos. Their prices leave little room for profit so they try to make their profits on volume sales. It's unlikely that you'll leave this store without placing an order: I suspect they'll go as low as necessary to make the sale. It's safe to say that all the important, major brands are carried. I almost hate to mention how great their prices are on video game sets and cartridges; in fact, they come in and go out so fast, you should call for availability before driving into the City. They will quote prices over the phone. They charge for delivery (doesn't everyone?) and handle any problems that arise. If you're interested in a home or small office computer, talk to them about it, they have 'connections'.

## REED SUPPLY CO.

1328 Fruitvale Ave., Oakland 94601. Phone: 436-7271. Hours: T-Sat 10am-5pm. Purchases: Cash or Check. Parking: Street.

The outward appearance of this squatty, drab-looking store is deceptive. People who are involved in remodeling projects will make many visits if they appreciate good prices. Even with the restaurant lighting (very dim) the appliances, kitchen cabinets, bathroom vanities, fireplaces, custom countertops, Green house windows, waterheaters, central heating sheet metal products, special plumbing fixtures and faucets can be special ordered from sample catalogs. Just about everything for the kitchen or bathroom is attainable. Delivery can be arranged and charges will be according to the distance involved. Working on a low markup they have a legion of satisfied customers who are more than willing to forsake the typical retail atmosphere.

## SUNBEAM APPLIANCE CO.

655 Mission St., San Francisco 94105. Phone: 362-7195. Hours: M-F 8:30am-5pm. Purchases: Cash or Check. Parking: Free Lot.

**Other Store**: 2100 De La Cruz Ave., Santa Clara 95050.

It's not too exciting to have to spend good money on a new iron, mixer, or coffeepot, so bargain hunters will really appreciate the nice selection of 'as is' Oster and Sunbeam merchandise available at the *Sunbeam Appliance Company*. 'As is' items were once display models, salesmen's samples, discounted models, or factory closeouts; all pieces are perfect, both mechanically and electrically, and are guaranteed to perform satisfactorily even when they may have small flaws on the finish or trim. If you have a very old appliance for which there are no longer replacement parts available, you may exchange it for a new model for less than you would pay anywhere else (though colors and models of exchange merchandise are limited). You may also locate some hard-to-find appliances such as egg cookers, large juicers, or meat grinders. They will special-order any new item for you and, of course, can provide or order any Sunbeam or Oster replacement part.

# ARTS, CRAFTS, AND HOBBY SUPPLIES

## ARTISTS' CO-OPERATIVE OF SAN FRANCISCO

1750 Union Street, San Francisco 94123. Phone: 885-2052. Hours: Daily 11am-6pm. Purchases: BA, MC, VISA. Parking: Street or Pay Lot.

Artist-owned and artist-operated, the gallery has exhibited the original art of Bay Area painters, sculptors, printmakers and ceramists since 1955. The Co-op's founding intention was to provide an exhibiting forum for the area's new talent and offer the public works of contemporary artists at a reasonable price. Additional savings are possible because the salesman's salary and commission is eliminated by volunteer staffing of member artists. The commission structure differs from privately owned galleries and therefore the artist does not have to price his work as high to receive a fair compensation for his creative efforts. It's possible to purchase works of emerging artists and then find pleasure in watching your art appreciate as subsequent works sell for higher and higher prices.

## CANDLE OUTLET

460 Du Bois, San Rafael 94901. Phone: 453-9320. Hours: M-F 8am-4pm. Purchases: Cash or Check. Parking: Lot.

The biggest difficulty you'll have in doing business with the *Candle Outlet* is in finding the place. Once you locate Du Bois, drive to 444 and turn into what appears to be an alley of sorts, then drive down the row of buildings until you reach #460. The outlet section is off of the reception area in a corner of the warehouse. These name brand candles are sometimes seconds but mostly are just left overs or discontinued colors. The prices are extremely low; taper and twists are sold by the pound, columns such as a 2" x 6" are 70¢ each. All prices were at least ½ off. I have to emphasize that the selection is not always reliable. At times the shelves are well stocked. But if the stock is depleted, and the warehousepeople are busy, they may not restock immediately. This outlet falls in the hit or miss category. Along with the candles you will occasionally spot wreaths, candle holders and other candle accessories at discount prices. The color assortment is often very limited with dozens of one color and just a few of another. Last, this is definitely not a place for lunch hour shoppers. They close down during lunch and lock the doors. Everything considered. Good Luck!

## BLUEGATE CANDLE FACTORY OUTLET
(See **Late Additions**)

## THE CANDLE SHOP

3020 Middlefield Rd., Redwood City 94063. Phone: 365-7650. Hours: M-F 9:30am-5pm, Sat 10am-4pm, Sundays — Nov. and Dec. Purchases: BA, MC. Parking: Street.

Our holidays wouldn't be special if we didn't have candles to mark the occasions. Candles, like everything else, seem to be rather expensive luxuries these days, and that's why The Candle Shop is a must on your list of bargain places. This is an outlet for a Peninsula manufacturer, and you'll find a fantastic assortment of just about every kind of candle made in their selection of store returns or seconds. Seconds in candles usually mean that the color wasn't true to the manufacturer's standards or they were bruised or chipped in handling. These flaws won't bother you when you compare the prices at The Candle Shop to other retail stores. Savings run 50-75% off. A 12" spiral is just 12¢ compared to 45¢ in a popular brand. You can buy tapers, spirals, novelties, German import, bulk candle wax for your own candle making project along with all the other supplies you may need. There is always a selection of Christmas wreaths and candle holders. Don't pass up the bargains on B.I.A. Cordon Bleu gourment cookware up to 60% off and imported hand cut crystal from Germany at 30% off. This is one place where just a few dollars will go a long way!

## FANTASTICO

559 6th Street, San Francisco 94103. Phone: 982-0680. Hours: M-F 8:30am-5:30pm, Sat 8:30am-1pm. Purchases: Cash, Check. Parking: Street, Lot.

Fantastico is the retail subsidiary of Angray, the wholesale supply house for nurseries and florists. Their warehouse has just about everything for all you craft-oriented people. The selection in dried and silk flowers is overwhelming. They stock all those exotic specimens you see in beautiful arrangements in fancy stores, plus all the makings to put them together: tapes, wires, ribbons, foam, etc. My favorite is florist ribbon that I buy in rolls for gift wrapping at 1/3 the cost of the Hallmark types. One roll usually lasts me about a year. For holiday decorations and ideas, this is the place to come. They also have baskets, plastic flowers and fruits, doll houses, crates, ceramics, terrarium bottles, plant stands and many accessory items. Prices to the general public are usually 10-30% lower than anywhere else. An exception is in their paper and party supply section where retail prices prevail except on quantity purchases.

## FLAX'S WAREHOUSE

1699 Market (corner Valencia), San Francisco 94113. Phone: 864-FLAX. Hours: M-F 9am-5:30pm, Sat 10am-5pm. Purchases: BA, MC, VISA. Parking: Free Lot.
**Other Store:** 510 East El Camino Real, Sunnyvale.
You don't have to be a starving artist to find the savings and good values at Flax's Warehouse appeal-

ing. They've trimmed their operating cost by using a self-service approach: eliminating services like gift certificates, deliveries, store charges, etc.; and they've chosen a low rent location.

Basic stocks of leading brands of fine art supplies are discounted 20-50% off the list price. Items like Grumbacher oil colors are 20% off, Bellini oil colors are 30% off, brushes, pastels, watercolors, stretched canvas, pre-cut mats, plain and fancy frames, paper and other paraphernalia are discounted appreciably. Periodically, closeouts of selected merchandise are displayed with near wholesale prices. Unfortunately, graphic artists won't find much in the selection for their needs.

## JEFFREY KRIGER FRAMING
156 Russ Street, San Francisco 94103. Phone: 621-4226. Hours: M-F 10:30am-5:15pm, Sat 11am-2pm. Purchases: VISA, MC. Parking: Very limited.

If you don't like the do-it-yourself frame shops because you don't like to do the work yourself and their prices don't seem to be that much of a bargain, you'll be pleased to do business with Jeffrey Kriger. First, he does the work himself, and second his prices are often less than the do-it-yourself shops. You can even elect to save more just by buying all the framing materials, i.e. glass, mats, backings, frame, fasteners etc. and then doing the work at home. Your one limitation is that he only sells aluminum framing yet when you see the many frame styles, finishes, and colors you won't think this

is so limiting. His labor charge on most jobs ranges from $4.50-$7.50. Savings do add up if you do-it-yourself when you have many pictures to frame or if you're an artist with a show to get ready for. Additionally, he has reasonable rates for vacuum dry mounting. He offers several qualities of materials for framing that allow you to frame a magazine picture with inexpensive materials or to frame a fine work of art with museum quality mats and backings. The studio is located in an offbeat alley-type street south of Market. Russ St. is between 6th and 7th Streets and between Howard and Folsom. Parking is alway at a premium!

## MASLACH ART GLASS STUDIO AND SECONDS STORE
(See **Dinnerware and Accessories**)

## NERVO INTERNATIONAL
650 University Avenue, Berkeley 94710. Phone: 848-6464. Hours: T-F 9am-5pm, Sat 10am-4pm. Purchases: BA, MC. Parking: Lot.

Nervo is a nationwide distributor of stained glass and stained glass supplies. Although most small stores sell scraps, you usually cannot find the selection of scraps or the large scrap pieces that are always on sale at Nervo. Discounted catalog items like lamp parts or zinc cane are frequently included in the sale bins. Like all distributors, mistakes occur, goods are damaged, and bargain hunters get the rewards. Retail priced merchandise is discounted 20% on Saturdays only. The business is located directly beneath the University Avenue overpass.

## NEW COLONY LIGHT WORKS FACTORY OUTLET
20 Galli Drive #4, Novato 94947. Phone: 415-883-2366. Hours: M-F 9am-4:30pm. Purchases: MC, VISA. Parking: Lot.

This candle manufacturer produces a completely handmade candle using specially blended wax that promotes a slow burning, dripless, smokeless candle with a wonderful glow. These decorator candles, which are turned on a lathe to achieve a unique layered look, sometimes end up with a chip or dent or may be slightly off color. They are then banished to the reject tables where the prices are reduced 35-50% off retail. They recommend calling before a visit because their outlet hours are subject to the demands of their business.

## SAN FRANCISCO MUSEUM OF
## MODERN ART RENTAL GALLERY
Fort Mason Center (Corner of Buchanan & Marina), San Francisco 94123. Phone: 441-4777. Hours: Tues-Sat 11:30am-5:30pm. Closed month of August. Purchases: MC, VISA. Parking: Free Lot.

The *San Francisco Museum of Modern Art* operates a rental gallery at Fort Mason, Building A, where you can rent a painting, sculpture, graphic or photograph for a two-month period, with the option to extend the rental time for another two months. If you decide to buy the work, half the rental fee applies toward the purchase price. The rental fees are set up on a sliding scale. For example, an art work with a purchase price of from $50-$99 rents for $10 for two months. Something costing $800-$899 would rent for $50. The goal of the gallery is to give new artists exposure. Before showing at the gallery, their work is juried which indicates that the quality of the work at the gallery is high. Many of these new artists have not shown in galleries before, but they are very good. This is an excellent chance to take part in the beginning of an artist's career—at a very low cost. I particularly like the trial period option in buying a work of art that you hope to keep forever.

## ABE SCHUSTER
2940 West St., Oakland 94608. Phone: 653-3588. Hours: M-F 8am-5pm, Sat 9am-3pm. Purchases: BA, MC. Parking: Street.

This warehouse operation, which vibrates with the noise of cutting saws, offers spectacular savings on lucite acrylic sheets for skylights, desk tops, wind breaks, picture frames, furniture, and any other do-it-yourself projects you may have in mind.

You can save 50% off on factory seconds with barely perceptible flaws. Their regular stock of plastic and plastic-related materials such as plastic letters, corrugated fiberglass, resins, and finishes are priced about 24-40% lower than at other retail stores. They cut sheets to size for a small charge. Green thumbers take note! You can purchase Filon home greenhouse panels for the lowest prices around.

## SUPER YARN MART
4525 Stevens Creek Blvd., Santa Clara 95050. Phone: 243-2012. Hours: M-F 9:30am-9pm, Sat 9:30am-5:30pm, Sun, 11am-5pm. Purchases: BA, MC. Parking: Free lot.

**Other Stores:** 5200 Mowry Ave., Fremont, 793-1712; 24046 Hesperian Blvd., Hayward, 785-9384.

There are more than 16 branches of this store in the Los Angeles area alone. Their volume buying of carload mill shipments allows them to offer truly fantastic bargains—well, it's almost hard to believe. Lucky Bay Area—we can now save too. The place is a maze of colors; tables piled with yarn here, bins overflowing there, cones hanging neatly on a wall. Whatever kind of yarn you want—cotton, wool, mohair, nylon, or acrylic—you'll find it here. You'll also find novelty yarns, imported and domestic yarns, mill surplus yarns (still on cones), and bulk yarns sold by the pound or ounce. All for sale at reduced prices, up to 50% off the original retail price. Besides knitting and crochet supplies, they also have all the needlepoint and embroidery accessories you could wish for at discount prices. For the less adventurous there are many different kinds of kits (the same ones you see in fancy department stores) for "substantially" less.

## TALLOW TUBE
1014 Howard, San Mateo 94401. Phone: 347-0554. Hours: M-F 10am-5pm, Sat 10am-2pm except summer. Purchases: Cash, check. Parking: Street.

You'll be greeted by smiling faces at this informal candle shop and factory. Besides taking the seconds, off-colors and overstock from several candle manufacturers, they also make their own. You can catch glimpses of this process going on in the back room. When their own candles come out too long, or too short, or too whatever, they're sold along with the other rejects at 30-60% off. Approximately 80% of the inventory is in the "reject" category. The selection includes tapers, spirals, molded rounds, and decorative candles. Around Christmas time you can buy big blocks of candle wax to use in making your own candles or even waxing your water skis.

## UNITED SURPLUS SALES
198 11th St., Oakland 94607. Phone: 893-3467. Hours: M-Sat 9am-5:30pm. Purchases: BA, MC. Parking: Street, Free lot.

This store is well organized, spacious and airy, with a great variety of things for sale. Up to 20% off retail is offered on all purchases of leading brand-name artist's paints, brushes, and supplies. A large selection of frames is available, including inexpensive, unfinished raw oak frames. (A five-day exchange on frames is allowed). Streched canvas and pre-cut mats are available at the same savings, though there's no exchange or refund on the latter.

Wall-hung rolls of upholstery yardage are sold for 50% off retail with selected seconds occasionally available at even greater savings. All sizes and quantities of foam can be found, and it will be cut to size for you (you'll appreciate this service if you have ever tried to cut a 4-inch slab of foam yourself).

They also sell camping equipment, as well as occasional bargain-priced soft goods such as camouflage pants, etc. when they get it through special purchase.

## UP AGAINST THE WALL
1349 East Taylor St., San Jose 95133. Phone: 408-287-4821. Hours: M-F 9am-5pm. Purchases: MC, VISA. Parking: Lot.

If you want to know where to save money on framing, ask a starving artist. I did, and several directed me to this unlikely operation obscurely located in San Jose. This is not a do-it-yourself frame shop. Catering to artists and interior designers, *Up Against the Wall* uses aluminum frames exclusively. These aluminum moldings are of the highest quality in three sizes: Slim, Graphic, and Canvas. Each size is available in ten finishes. The hardware is heavy duty, single piece metal with pre-started screws. This is a super time saver of special value to artists who may be framing a number of pieces at one time for a show or fair.

If you have works to frame you have two options: first, you can take your picture and have the job done from start to finish; second, you can opt to do the work yourself at home, after purchasing all the materials. They will cut the glass, the matts, the backings, etc. You assemble. Artists from outside the Bay Area do all their business by mail, sending measurements, color choices for matts and receive the materials by UPS. This is worthwhile because prices on materials are much lower than other outlets including the You-Frame-It operations. You can buy matts, corrugated backing, glass, plexiglass or foam core and arrange for vacuum dry mounting or shrink wrapping. On fine art or expensive works of art, conservation mounting will be done by request. You can write for a price list of materials and service charges. Be sure to call for directions or you'll never find them.

## YORK CANDLE COMPANY
21 Duffy Place (Corner of Duffy Pl. & Irwin St.), San Rafael 94901. Phone: 457-3610. Hours: M-Sat 9am-5pm. Purchases: BA, MC. Parking: Free lot.

This candle factory is located in the industrial section of San Rafael right next to the *Bargain Box Thrift Shop*. You may find your senses overpowered with the combined fragrances of the 14 different scents used in their candle production. Because the candles are made on the premises you can buy wholesale. All their candles are made with domestic ingredients and they claim that they outburn all the imported ones they've tested. They are also dripless and smokeless. Occasionally they may have specials when a wheel runs off-color or some color proves unpopular and they slash prices to clear their inventory. A very nice accommodation is their special order department. They will make to order special anniversary, wedding or block candles.

# Automobiles and Trucks

## General

**AVIS INC.**
200 El Camino, San Bruno 94066. Phone: 877-6763. Hours: M-Wed 9am-7pm, Th, F 9am-9pm, Sat 9am-6pm, Sun Noon-5pm. Purchases: Cash, Certified Check, Financing available. Parking: Lot.

**Other Lots:** San Jose, Oakland, Sacramento.

At Avis they sell current-model travel rental cars that have been completely re-conditioned. They rent and sell primarily General Motors models. Usually cars are deluxe models with air conditioning, power brakes, power steering, and custom accesories. Since Avis has already made their money on rental services, you'll find lower prices than in used car lots with comparable models. Inventory changes constantly, so sooner or later they are bound to have the car you have in mind.

## BROWN-CLARKSON, INC.

365 Convention Way, Redwood City 94063. Phone: 364-7410. Hours: M-F 9am-6pm, Sat 9am-1pm. Purchases: No financing available. Parking: Street.

If you don't like to haggle or negotiate car prices, or feel that you're always being manipulated by skillful sales personnel, then you can avoid the whole scene by dealing with an auto broker.

In California, anyone engaging in the sale of automobiles must be licensed by the State of California, Department of Motor Vehicles. To obtain a dealer's license in California one must submit to an investigation of his background, including fingerprinting which is checked by the State and the FBI. He must have a suitable place to do business, subject to all the financial and bonding requirements of DMV, and the Board of Equalization, which is the agency collecting the retail sales tax. So, an automobile broker is a licensed automobile dealer. The primary difference is that the automobile broker handles all makes of cars, whereas the automobile dealer handles only one make. Automobile brokers sell brand new cars and trucks to individuals who are referred to them by personnel managers of large companies, clubs, credit unions or friends. Because of the lack of radio, TV, newspaper advertising, sales commissions and no 'flooring' on inventory, the cost of doing business obviously is much lower and therefore the prices for these cars are substantially lower. Consumers obtain correct and direct information relative to the cost of new cars. The "Kelley Wholesale New Car Price Manual" with which they operate, as do all leasing companies, banks and most credit unions gives the actual factory invoice cost of every new car. The 'factory invoice cost' is the amount of money a new car dealer must pay his factory to purchase that car.

All cars sold by *Brown-Clarkson* are brand new, covered by the Manufacturer's warranty that is good in all 50 states and may be serviced at any dealership you choose. *Brown-Clarkson* registers the car with DMV, handles the sales tax and pink slips. Because they do not stock cars, *Brown-Clarkson* recommends that consumers test drive and make car selections before coming to their office. Then you can discuss the specifics, i.e. make, options, color and price. On American cars at this time, you are quoted a price that is $395 over actual factory cost. Foreign cars are quoted with the lowest price that they can obtain for you. This amount includes all the dealer preparation, mechanical service, polishing, etc. The price usually reflects a savings of a few hundred to a few thousand dollars depending on the make and model. Cars may be obtained from the lots of local dealers or directly from the factory. One major ingredient of this transaction must be handled on your own, that is the financing. Most people tend to utilize the services of the credit unions where they work. Finally, many people have expressed their satisfaction with the savings and service that were obtained from buying a car in this manner without haggling or negotiating. Consider this option the next time you buy a new car: it may save you $$$$$$$.

## DOLLAR-A-DAY-RENT-CAR-SYSTEMS

1815 Old Bayshore Hwy., Burlingame 94010. Phone: 697-5780. Hours: M-F 7am-Midnight. Purchases: Cash, check. Parking: Free lot.
**Other Lots:** San Francisco, San Francisco Airport, San Jose, Oakland Airport, Palo Alto.

If you need a compact car you can save a lot of money on one here. *Dollar-a-Day* sells current model used rental cars that have been reconditioned. These are primarily Ford products whose condition is at least comparable to that of any vehicle you would find at a used car lot. All cars will have limited warranty covering engine, transmission, drive train and differential for 12 months or 12,000 miles. Since *Dollar-a-Day* is not out to sell cars but to dispose of capital equipment, their prices are lower than most lots. The cars are sold between October and March, according to their schedule for replacing rental stock. These cars have all been serviced regularly and are in good to excellent condition. A car will be held for you for several days while you arrange financing. If it takes longer than several days you will be asked for a small deposit, refundable if you change you mind. If you're in the market for a car, you can check on *Avis* and *Dollar-a-Day* at the same time since they're in the same vicinity.

## HERTZ CAR SALES

300 E. Millbrae Ave., Millbrae 94030. Phone: 877-3737. Hours: M-F 8am-7pm, Sat & Sun 9am-6pm. Purchases: Cash, cashier's check, financing available. Parking: Street, free lot.

**Other Stores:** Oakland Airport, San Jose Airport, Hayward, Concord, Sacramento and Fresno.

*Hertz* selects and sells only the finer cars from its rental fleet. Every *Hertz* used car that is offered for sale has a record of service and maintenance that you can check *before you buy. Hertz* backs every car with a Limited Warranty covering the engine, transmission, drive shaft and differential for 12 months or 12,000 miles. All *Hertz* cars look terrific and are priced to sell. You can expect all the features you're probably looking for: air conditioning, automatic transmission, power steering and brakes, radio and radial tires. Because of their limited driving life, rentals usually have less wear-and-tear on them. They've had more T.L.C. too. Telephone them for more information. They are very helpful over the phone.

## HIGHWAY PATROL CAR SALE

3601 Telegraph Ave., Oakland. Phone: 050-9111 for information. Hours: Announced. Purchases: Certified or cashier's check only.

Need a good car for towing a boat or house trailer? The *Highway Patrol* retires all their cars when the mileage approaches 90,000 miles, when the performance required for high-speed pursuits may become too demanding. Most cars returned for this reason have many years of good use left for the conventional driver. They also have many desirable special features not normally found in used cars, such as heavy-duty equipment for touring or towing, automatic transmissions, air conditioning, and heavy-duty disc brakes. All cars are safety-checked, smog-certified, and compression-checked. They handle beautifully!

When enough cars are accumulated, an auction is held. A minimum bid is placed on each car, along with a description of any mechanical problems that may require attention. Sealed bids are taken and forwarded to Sacramento; holders of winning bids are notified. Some cars are sold in their original black-and-white paint, while others have been painted in bright colors (these cost more). Most cars will be sold for under $1,300 and are usually two years old. Look for notices of these sales in the classified section of major newspapers.

### POLICE AUCTIONS
(See **Part II—Auctions**)

### THRIFTY RENT-A-CAR
111 98th Ave. (corner Airport Dr.), Oakland 94603. Phone: 568-1220. Hours: Daily 8am-5pm. Purchases: Certified Check. Parking: Lot.

*Thrifty Rent-a-Car* sells their cars when they are 12-18 months old and usually have less than 24,000 miles. These American cars, compacts, full size sedans, station wagons, and occasionally vans are well maintained with service records available for your perusal. Prices are lower than at used car lots and include warranties. If you're not interested in cars, but you're going to 'Fly Oakland', be advised that their rates for short or long term parking from their Park 'N' Fly lot will save you a

tidy sum. Their shuttle bus is always there before you've had a chance to put your luggage down, even if you're coming in from one of World's midnight landings.

## Auto Parts

(Also see **General Merchandise—Catalog Discounters, —Discount Stores**)

### 4-DAY TIRE STORES
390 East Gish, San Jose 95112. Phone: 293-8323. Hours: W, Th, F, 8:30am-8pm, Sat 8:30am-5pm. Purchases: BA, MC.

**Other Stores:** 1050 Marina Blvd., San Leandro; 2151 Marconi, No. Sacramento; 4320 Fruitridge Rd., So. Sacramento.

*Four Day* has a unique but plausible merchandising approach: they are open only during the most efficient selling hours of the week, which allows them maximum sales with one-shift overhead. Their stock is large, and they say they can fit any type of car (or driver). Their ad in the San Jose "Mercury" every week lists practically every cut-price tire they sell; it gives the regular retail price, their credit price, their cash price, their cash and carry price, and the federal excise tax on each tire (as you can imagine, it's a big ad). The brands they sell include Lee (U.S.-made), Bridgestone

(Japan), Dunlop, Pirelli, Veith, Semperit, Ceat, Fulda (Germany), Michelin, Metzeler and *Four Day*'s own brand. They have their own special guarantee: if one of their tires fails due to workmanship or road hazards or wears out before you have received the guaranteed mileage, you can return the tire and the guarantee and they will give you credit (or mail you cash) for the unused miles (the percentage of unused miles multiplied by the price).

# BEAUTY SUPPLIES AND COSMETICS

Anyone who buys beauty supplies at retail prices these days just isn't economy-minded. In most communities around the Bay Area there are stores which sell to the public name-brand retail and professional brands of bleaches, frosting supplies, permanents, hair sprays, setting lotions, conditioners, relaxers, and so forth for substantially less than retail (often at savings of as much as 40%). Many items they carry are simply not sold in your corner drug store. Some brands aren't in their usual retail store packages (complete with instructions), so it behooves you to have had some experience in this do-it-yourself approach to hair styling or to stick with brands that do have instructions. Check with the beauty supply stores in your area to see what products are available for your use.

**NICCOLE'S COSMETIC OUTLET**
3121-D Crow Canyon Place (Crow Canyon Commons Shopping Center), San Ramon 94583. Phone: 838-7610. Hours: M-Sat 10am-5pm. Purchases: VISA, MC. Parking: Lot.

The owner of this cosmetic store has put her years of experience in the cosmetic industry to good use by creating her own line of cosmetics called Private Label. She sells these products without the massive and expensive advertising campaigns that add so much to the basic cost of every namebrand cosmetic or skin care product that is purchased by consumers. Also missing is elaborate and ornate packaging.

The skin care products, i.e. moisturizers, collagen elastin cremes, masques, facial scrubs, cleansing gels, etc. and various bath products are priced at 50-70% off the prices of comparable products. I've tried several and they seem to do the job just as well as the national brands I've used. The cosmetics like lipsticks, blushers, eye shadows, foundations, powders etc., are ordered from many of the same color laboratories that manufacture these products under many different labels for the industry 'giants'. The difference between one product and another is often only a matter of packaging and marketing.

At the Cosmetic Outlet, the regular lipsticks sell for $1.25 rather than $5.50-$6.25 for comparable brands. Slimline lipsticks are $2.50 rather than $5-$9.50. Eye shadows are $2.40 versus $7.50-$9.00, and the foundations are a modest $1.75. Similar foundations sell for $12-$25. All of these products can be sampled at their cosmetic bar before purchasing. If you'd like cosmetics at a reasonable price and you want to forego the costs of marketing and advertising that are inherent in name brands, then the Private Label concept is one you should investigate.

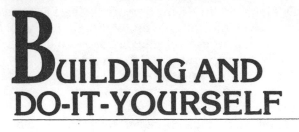

# BUILDING AND DO-IT-YOURSELF

(Also see **General Merchandise—Liquidators; Part II: Surplus Stores; Wrecking and Salvage Yards**)

## General

**BEST BLOCKS, INC.**
34840 Alvarado-Niles Rd., Union City 94587. Phone: 471-1966. Hours: M-F 7:30am-5pm, Sat 8am-4pm. Purchases: BA, MC, VISA.

It's really not necessary to rip-off construction sites for building blocks because at this manufacturer's yard there are blocks for everything from hi-rise buildings to back yard barbecues. Best of all, there is always a selection of seconds and off-color blocks at savings of 15-50%. On their top quality overstock blocks you can save by buying directly from the source and on quantity purchases you can save even more. You can choose from sump blocks, stepping stones, patio tile (including seconds), garden blocks, 'pavelock' concrete pavers, tree rings and decorative rock. They have over 600 sizes, styles and shapes. Whether you're building a tile patio, or installing your own fireplace or heatstove, they can tell you how to do it, what you will need, and what it will cost. Delivery service available at reasonable charge; technical and design literature available at no cost. All you need is the muscle to do the job!

## S. DE BELLA BARREL CO.
1176 Harrison St., San Francisco 94103. Phone: 861-1700. Hours: M-F 8am-4pm. Purchases: Cash, check. Parking: Street.

*Salvatore De Bella* is one of the biggest importers and manufacturers of barrels in the nation. His barrel factory is a perfect setting for a shoot-it-out scene from one of the popular TV detective series (I was ready to take cover as soon as I heard a shot). There are mountains of barrels, about 3,000 of them, stacked 30 feet high. When you come in you may see the coopers (barrelmakers) at their noisy work; I was fascinated by their skill and precision.

The imported used barrels may have held Irish whiskey, French cognac, Kentucky bourbon, or West Indian rum. The barrels are cleaned and restored for use as planters, tables, stools, cradles, dog houses or what have you. Best of all, a used 50-gallon barrel sells for only $20.00, a half barrel for only $9.50. Spigots and barrel stands are also available. If your taste runs to the exotic, you may be interested in the handmade hand-carved oval oak barrels, a *De Bella* specialty.

## KEN'S GLASS
2784 Monterey Road, San Jose 95111. Phone: (408-578-5211). Hours: Daily 9am-5pm. Closed Wed & Sun. Purchases: Cash, Check. Parking: Lot.

The do-it-yourselfer will need to develop a strategy to take advantage of the cheap, cheap prices at this glass and mirror shop. Ken is able to offer these prices because he cuts corners. No secretary, virtually no overhead, no delivery, no installation, no cut-outs on glass or mirrors (although he will trim edges to size), and a cash and carry basis. Ken stocks first quality glass and mirror, also seconds with a substantial price differential, in all sizes and shapes. He always has a good selection of precut sizes of glass and mirrors for shelving, picture frames, and rounds for table tops. Check the bargains in all nine rooms of this old house before deciding, you'll find many options pricewise (30-80% discounts) whether you're covering an entire wall with mirror or simply replacing a broken window.

## LUNDY'S WOOD PRODUCTS
36 Simms, San Rafael 94901. Phone: 454-0130. Hours: M-F 7:30am-5pm, Sat 8:30am-1:30pm. Purchases: VISA, MC. Parking: Lot.

*Lundy's* may not be a household word mainly because they do most of their business with cabinet shops and contractors. However, many fellows involved in various woodworking projects have reported that after extensive comparative shopping they end up at *Lundy's*. Unlike other lumber companies that advertise extensively to the consumer market offering a wide selection of woods for exterior and interior use, *Lundy's* offers a choice selection of finished products used in furniture making and cabinets. For example: Sanded fir plywood, hardwood plywood with veneers, hardwood moldings, hardwood lumber, veneers, marine plywood and softwood plywood and moldings. A friend reported saving $20 on a 4 x 8 skin of walnut! Exterior siding is available by special order as are the Andersen Window Walls (the double insulated wooden sash windows). They also carry oversized 5' x 9' plywoods for ping pong table tops and 4' x 10' sizes in fir plywood. Where their prices on woods are substantially less you can assume that they have been able to buy 'right' from their suppliers. *Lundy's* is directly across the street from Marin Surplus.

## MCINTYRE TILE CO.
55 West Grant, Healdsburg 95448. Phone: 707-433-8866. Hours: M-F 9am-5pm. Purchases: Cash or Check.

*McIntyre Tile* is not displayed in any Bay Area distributors' showrooms, but rather sold directly through architects and interior designers. It is expensive, about $7 a sq. ft., and is handmade, high-fired stoneware. It is very appealing for it's natural look and many neutral shades. Before making a trip to Healdsburg, call first and request a selection of samples in your color range. If you see one you like, then inquire about their seconds, which are ½ price and may be off color, slightly warped, but otherwise structurally sound. The 'thirds'

are $5.00 per box. They prefer that you make an appointment, before coming in to see them, many days their production schedule is so heavy they don't have time to spend with customers who want to pick and poke through the seconds selection. Note that they are closed on Saturdays.

## NISSAN TILE
697 Veterans Blvd., Redwood City. Phone: 364-6547. Hours: M-Sat 8am-5pm, Th 8am-9pm, Sat 9am-4:30pm. Purchases: BA, MC, VISA. Parking: Street.

**Other Store:** 1226 So. Bascom Ave., San Jose.

You can't possibly imagine the potential for beauty, design and interest in your home until you contemplate the selection of tile at *Nissan*. Their showroom floor is a patchwork of exotic and different tile patterns; in fact I could hardly bring myself to walk across. *Nissan* claims they are the biggest importer of ceramic tile in the Bay Area. They distribute to tile contractors and retail stores. They have Italian, Japanese and domestic tiles. You can save 30% on tile sold under the *Nissan* label and on odd lots left over from custom jobs. They have supplies for do-it-yourselfers and all the free advice you need.

## SKY, LIGHT & SUN
2019 Blake St., Berkeley 94704. Phone: 841-2323. Hours: M-F 9am-5pm. Closed between Noon-1pm. Purchases: Cash or Check. Parking: Limited street parking.

If you're building or remodeling and contemplating a passive solar system design for energy savings, chances are you may need insulated tempered glass. *Sky, Light & Sun* stocks and sells tempered glass in three sizes. These panels of glass are available in single panes of glass or in sealed insulated units. This material is best described as factory-seconds or factory surplus glass, a designation that refers to minor, non-structural, cosmetic scratches or blemishes. Intelligent design work utilizing these three sizes can greatly reduce the cost of a greenhouse, solar collector, or other building project. Your savings: about 50%. It is important to know building code restrictions regarding installations, so it sometimes better to have your contractor do the buying for you. In any case, check the availability before framing. They sell tremendous quantities of these seconds, but occasionally a contractor will buy their entire inventory leaving their cupboards bare until the next shipment.

## STONELIGHT TILE
1651 Pomona Ave., San Jose 95110. Phone: 292-7424. Hours: M-F 8am-4:30pm, Sat 8am-12noon. Purchases: Cash, check. Parking: Lot.

*Stonelight Tile* is a glazed tile with an unusually dense body like those made in Europe for centuries. The fact that it is made chiefly of natural clays instead of talc, as is most commercial tile, means that Stonelight tile will have a 'natural' look and contributes to its great popularity among architects and designers. Made locally in San Jose, their outdoor yard has stacks of tiles

that are left over from custom jobs or have been judged as seconds because of surface irregularities, color imperfections, or have been chipped. People are welcome to browse and hand pick those tiles that they need for their own remodeling projects. The savings are considerable. Seconds sell for $1.80 a sq. ft. and overruns at $2.50 a sq. ft. Normal retail for these tiles is in the neighborhood of $3.50-$5.00 a sq. ft. You may have to pay a full price for trim pieces if they are not in the seconds or overrun selection. The best time for shopping is during the week, when the selection is the best, and preferably in dry weather. Boxes for packing are provided. This is a friendly place, they will give you instructions, and can sell you the mastic, grout, coloring agents, and spreaders necessary for installation. There's nothing like getting the best for less!

# Tools

## BLACK AND DECKER MANUFACTURING CO.
15206 E. 14th, San Leandro. Phone: 276-1610. Hours: M-F 8am-5pm, Sat 9am-1pm. Purchases: MC, BA, VISA. Parking: Street.

**Other Stores:** San Jose, South San Francisco.

If your husband is a 'Handy Andy' and loves to buy new tools for his own garage workshop, make sure he checks *Black and Decker* before investing any money in tools. The reason is simple: there are many 'reconditioned' tools available here at great savings, such as sanders, saws, drills, even lawn edgers and lawn mowers. These reconditioned tools may have been returned by their owner within 90 days because of performance failures. They have had a trip back to the factory and are now provided with all new parts and the same one-year guarantee as new tools. Some other tools are box-damaged or were once salesmen's samples.

The savings range from 20-30% off regular retail. Because the supply and availability of these tools may vary, you should call them about what you want; they will gladly take your name and notify you when your tool is available.

## PORTER-CABLE TOOL CENTER
3029 Teagarden Street, San Leandro 94577. Phone: 357-9762. Hours: M-F 8am-4:30pm. Purchases: VISA, MC.

**Other Store:** 2305 De La Cruz Blvd., Santa Clara.

The Rockwell line has become Porter-Cable. The name may be different but the product is the same. Like other service centers you can buy reconditioned portable electric tools for about half the retail cost.

## POST LIQUIDATORS
328 12th Street, Oakland 94607. Phone: 893-7275. Hours: M-F 8am-5pm, Sat 8am-2:30pm. Purchases: BA, MC. Parking: Street.

**Other Stores:** Sacramento, Santa Rosa.

Oakland business people spend many lunch hours picking through the bargains at this liquidation store. Buying in tremendous quantities, from major tool manufacturers, both American and foreign, and buying up liquidated merchandise and government surplus, they are able to offer great discounts for tools and supplies that people require for their projects. You will usually find drill presses, bench grinders, hand tools, jacks, vises, wrenches, socket sets, electric tools, air tools, electric saws, lathes, and tool boxes. Everything is fully guaranteed and comes in the original factory packaging. In addition to the tool selection, they have an eclectic assortment of miscellaneous merchandise like cutlery sets, camping knives, starter cables, etc. The only drawbacks are the stores cramped quarters that lends itself to a slightly disordered feeling.

## SKIL POWER TOOL SERVICE CENTER
1170 Burnett Ave., "D," Concord 94520. Phone: 827-1427. Hours: M-F 8am-5pm. Purchases: BA, MC. Parking: Street, free lot.

**Other Stores:** 2130 De La Cruz Blvd., Santa Clara.

If you have a broken electric home shop tool, you're lucky if it's made by *Skil Power Tools,* for you can probably trade it in for a new one if reconditioning is too expensive. On a trade-in you save about 30% on the less expensive and up to 50% on the more expensive tools. (Not every tool in the *Skil* line is included in their exchange program, however.)

There are three categories of tools available with savings up to 25%. All are specifically labeled with special tags which state: "To assure the controlled high quality required for sale at a *Skil Service Center*, Rebuilt Power Tools, Discontinued Models, and Factory Appearance Rejects are tested for conformance to original equipment standards. Factory Trained Repair Technicians have performed a complete Detectron diagnostic examination of the tool. All repairs and/or parts replacement have been made as required to effect a like-new operative condition. Each of these tools is guaranteed against defects caused by faulty materials or workmanship." These tools carry the same guarantee as their other retail tools.

The *Skil* line includes weedeaters, sanders, drills, jig saws, hand saws, and Recipro saws. Occasionally they have discontinued industrial tools. They will gladly try to locate a reconditioned tool at one of their other service centers for you if what you want is not on display. You can call in advance for information on the availability of a special tool.

## WESTERN HARDWARE & TOOL COMPANY

450 Bryant Street, San Francisco 94107. Phone: 781-1088. Hours: 8:15-5pm, Sat 9am-4pm. Purchases: BA, MC. Parking: Street, very limited.

This is truly handy-man's heaven! If you have a heavy duty job and need a heavy duty tool, this company is for you. They are a major industrial supplier of tools for linemen, electricians, auto mechanics, carpenters, iron and steel workers, and manufacturing or industrial plants in Northern California. These are not always the same products that you will find in the neighborhood hardware or building supply store. They have industrial ratings and sometimes may cost a bit more, even at a discount, than a home rated product. Even so, the prices on their tools are substantially discounted from the manufacturer's published price list. On products that serve for both the industrial and home shop market, like Stanley tapes, vice grip sets, block sanders, saws, hammers, and other hand tools, your savings may range from 15-40% off prevailing retail prices.

Don't be concerned when you walk in the door and don't see any tools, they're in the back warehouse where you're welcome to browse. They have no sales gimmicks, loss leaders etc., just low dealer prices everyday. Don't plan on a lunch hour visit, they close down. Parking, too, can give you gray hairs. During the week people circle around like sharks hoping to spot a space and many take a chance and double park in desperation.

# Cameras

(Also see **General Merchandise—Catalog Discounters —Discount Stores**)

## A & B PREMIUMS PHOTO & APPLIANCE CENTER

4375-D Clayton Road, Concord 94521. Phone: 415-827-3373. Hours: M-F 9am-8pm, Sat 9am-6pm. Purchases: MC, VISA. Parking: Lot.

The value conscious 'aspiring' photographers that I know in this area all shop for their photo needs at this unlikely store. All Kodak processing is done for a 30% discount all year long. To be sure, Kodak processing is quite expensive, but for those who want superior quality and assurances of good results, their prices are about the best. Kodak film is sold for cost! (This is their loss leader to create traffic, good idea.) Additionally, cameras, accessories such as lenses, filters, flashes, tripods, etc. plus dark room equipment, papers and chemicals are sold at super discount prices. Another aspect of their business is related to small and large home appliances and entertainment needs. Washers, dryers, dishwashers, compacters, refrigerators, TV's, and radios are sold for a minimal markup. Their prices on video game units and cartridges are very good and usually beat any competitor in Contra Costa County.

## ALAMEDA CAMERA SWAP

2540 Santa Clara Ave., Alameda 94501. Phone: Info: 521-2177 or 522-3336. Hours: Sundays 9am-2pm. Purchases: Cash or Check. Parking: Lot.

The *Alameda Camera Swap* is held each Sunday in the Grand Ballroom of the Alameda Hotel, at the corner of Santa Clara and Broadway. Anything photographic is fair game in this indoor flea market that always has a good selection of cameras, camera accessories, books, images, lenses, dark room gear and paper prints, merchandise that appeals to both the collector and the photographer. At the camera swap there are no dealers for new merchandise, no stores represented. The average Sunday swap has approximately 40 dealers with tables of merchandise. Many dealers have been coming regularly for years and enjoy a reliable reputation. This is a very legitimate operation, all items with serial numbers are checked out by the Alameda Police Department. Most of the dealers will guarantee their equipment. Be sure to ask for a guarantee and a receipt for your purchase.

If you have equipment you'd like to sell, you should go to the swap on Sunday morning at 8:30am to reserve your table; the charge is a nominal $3.50. There is a 50 cent admission charge to the public, children under twelve are free. The swap is a great place to meet and talk with photographers, collectors and others seriously interested in all aspects of photography or photographic collectibles. Most dealers are very willing to give you the benefit of their expertise.

## FILCO, L & Z PREMIUMS
(See **Appliances**)

## SAN JOSE CAMERA

1600 Winchester Blvd., Campbell 95008. Phone: 408-374-1880. Hours: M-Sat 10am-6pm, Thurs pm till 8pm. Purchases: BA, MC.

Photo-buffs who are interested in the more sophisticated, exotic and usually more expensive cameras and accessories will feel right at home in this camera shop. Most major brands are carried: Leica, Cannon, Nikon, Olympus, Vivitar, Rollei, Minolta, Pentax, Hasselblad, Mamiya, Konica, Beseler Enlargers, Kodak carousel projectors, Gossen exposure meters and Halliburton cases.

I would suggest that you do some research regarding your needs and selections before coming here because their staff is limited and they're usually very busy. They simply don't have the time to give you lengthy demonstrations or sales talks. If you can tell them what you want, they'll probably be able to give you the lowest price in the Bay Area. They are very good about standing behind their merchandise or handling any problems; however, they have a strict policy regarding exchanges, all sales are final! San Jose Camera is located at Hamilton & Winchester, take Hamilton offramp from Fwy. 17.

# CARPETS AND FLOOR COVERINGS

(Also see **Furniture—Catalog Discounters, Warehouse Sales**)

Comparison shopping is essential when bargain hunting for carpeting and other floor covering. Some stores give you a lower price on the carpet but make up for it with their installation and padding costs, while others charge a slightly higher price for the carpeting but toss in the installation and padding for free. The variance in price is the only constant. Always remember to price the carpet and padding separately, since there are different weights and quality to consider in padding. When comparing the total cost among the stores, be sure you're comparing the same quality carpeting, padding and installation. Ask how they plan to arrange the carpet seams and how they will be joined. Ask also what kind of stripping will be used when soft and hardcover floor coverings meet. Be sure to tell the salesman what you expect of the carpet (how long you expect it to last, the kind of traffic it will bear, its exposure to strong sunlight, etc.). He will be better able to advise you.

The cunning and expertise of the retail carpet store buyer will greatly affect the price you pay. One carpet store may pull a coup in a big buy, enabling them to sell that stock at a lower price than its competitors. Two months later a different store may make the best buy, and then sell at a lower price. Carpet "wholesalers" abound throughout the Bay Area, and they are able to offer good buys because of their different business styles. Some stores specialize in buying overstocks and closeout patterns and colors. Others buy room-size remnants or pieces in off-color dye lots. Some specialize in bankrupt stocks. For these many reasons you can save on your carpeting dollar. Remember that it's a changing market. Always take your time, comparison shop, and consider all the factors.

# General

### LAWRENCE CONTRACT FURNISHERS
470-B Vandell Way, Campbell 95008. Phone: 408-374-7590. Hours: M-F 8am-5:30pm. Purchases: Cash or Check. Parking: Lot.

For South Bay shoppers *Lawrence*'s is one of the best resources for carpeting, vinyl floor coverings, hard wood flooring kits, draperies, wallpapers and many fine furniture lines. The showroom is small, mostly stocked with wallpaper books, carpet and flooring samples. It's almost too much to take in all at once. Installation of flooring and carpeting will be provided (of course you pay for it) but I've found their prices to be lower than most other places. They can't provide decorator services at these prices, but they enjoy a re-liable reputation. To find this out-of-the-way showroom from the San Tomas Expressway, take the Winchester offramp in Campbell, go West to Hacienda, turn left, and turn right on Dell. *Lawrence* is on the corner of Vandell and Dell.

### MONROE SCHNEIDER ASSOCIATES
274 Wattis Way, South San Francisco 94080. Phone: 871-6276. Hours: M-F 8am-5pm by appt. Evenings & Weekends by appt. Purchases: Cash or Check. Parking: Lot.

This firm specializes in working with developers to design and furnish the interiors for model homes, and then works with new home buyers who are making selections of carpeting, flooring, wallpaper, and window coverings that will go into their new homes. With all these resources they're willing to provide the same service to the general public at considerable savings. Their carpeting prices are excellent; the installation and padding is also arranged. One nice extra is the design assistance provided by their staff. It is important to make an appointment before coming in so a member of the staff will be free to help you. Along with carpeting, you can order other home furnishings from their catalogs at noteworthy savings.

### S & G DISCOUNT OUTLET INC.
505 S. Market St., San Jose 95113. Phone: 292-8971. Hours: M-F 9am-6pm, Sat 9am-5pm, Th eve. till 6pm. Purchases: BA, MC. Parking: Free lot.

One of the largest selections of linoleum I have ever seen, for 10-30% less than regular retail, *S & G* carries Armstrong, Mannington, Congoleum, and other brands of floor coverings. Indoor-outdoor carpeting is by special order only.

*S & G* supplies to the trade, and the pace is sometimes pretty busy. When you go, know what you want and have with you the measurements of the floor you want covered (for one thing, you might find just what you need among their remnants). They had a fairly large selection when I was there, but turnover is brisk.

## TRADEWAY STORES WAREHOUSE
350 Carlson Blvd. (next to Blue Chip Stamp Redemption Center), Richmond 94804. Phone: 233-0841. Hours: M-Sat 10am-5:30pm, Sun Noon-5pm. Purchases: BA, MC. Parking: Free lot.

Other Otoroni El Cerrito.

If you're looking for bargain prices on carpeting, this warehouse for the *Tradeway Stores* offers a tremendous selection of carpeting that has been written off as an insurance loss. Name-brand carpet mills also dispose of overruns, excess inventories, seconds, and off-color carpeting here. You will feel as if you're walking on the bottom of the Grand Canyon—carpeting is stacked in rolls 20 feet high, and higher. If you want to see a particular piece, a man will get it for you with a special forklift.

Savings are usually about 30% though on unusual or novelty carpeting you may save as much as 70-80%.

This is strictly a case of "what you see is what you get." There are no special or custom orders. Padding is sometimes available at below wholesale prices. They do not install, but will refer you to installers. All carpet on display is conveniently ready for immediate delivery, though you will save additional money if you take the carpet home yourself, or have your installer pick it up.

Not to be overlooked are the second and third floors of this warehouse. They are jammed, piled, and stacked with distressed furniture, also representing manufacturers' fire and insurance losses. On some pieces you can actually see where the flames left their mark, although this is unusual. Many well-known manufacturers are represented in this selection of furniture for any room in the house at savings of as much as 40%. Delivery is free on large pieces, although your price will be reduced if you carry it off by yourself. All sales are final.

# Remnants

## CARPET CENTER
921 Parker Street, Berkeley 94710. Phone: 549-1100. Hours: M-Sat 9am-5:30pm, M & Th till 8:30pm. Purchases: BA, MC. Parking: Street.

Located in the low rent industrial district of Berkeley, this huge warehouse has one of the best selections of carpet remnants and area rugs in the East Bay. Even better, they have an accommodating price range in carpets to choose from, from budget to the best! They can provide the padding and installation at an extra charge.

## CARPET REMNANTS UNLIMITED
1145 Jordan Lane, Napa 94588. Phone: 707-252-6695. Hours: M-Sat 9am-5pm. Purchases:MC, VISA.

Discontinued patterns from Walter's Carpet Mills are sold here in remnant pieces or off the roll. Nothing is priced over $11.00 a yard, a hefty savings most of the time, when you consider many of Walter's carpets sell in the neighborhood of $15-$30 a yard. Some of their rolls are large enough to carpet a whole house. They won't do the installation, but will refer you to installers that they feel do a reliable job.

## FLOORCRAFT
470 Bayshore Blvd., San Francisco 95116. Phone: 824-4056. Hours: M 8am-9pm, TWTHF 8am-5:30pm, Sat 8am-5pm, Sun 10am-5pm. Purchases: BA, MC.

They always have about 400 remnants in stock priced from $3.99-$8.50 per yard. Your best prices are always on the "weird" sizes, because it's harder to sell a piece 7' x 20', than a standard 10' x 12'. Installation is provided, keep in mind the cost for a small room is disproportionately high when compared to doing a whole house or several rooms.

## MACY'S FURNITURE CLEARANCE PLACE
(See **Furniture and Accessories**)

## REMNANT WORLD CARPETS
5160 Stevens Creek Blvd. (At Lawrence Expressway), San Jose 95129. Phone: 984-1965. Hours: M-F 10am-9pm, Sat 9am-6pm, Sun Noon-5pm. Purchases: BA, MC. Parking: Lot.

**Other Stores:** 2730 Story Rd., San Jose; 3058 Almadden Expressway, San Jose.

They're really set up for the do-it-yourselfer. If you buy your carpet from them they'll lend you a tool box with all the tools necessary, including the knee-kicker (carpet stretcher), and give you plenty of free advice. Their remnants come from mills like Apollo, Coronet, Woodcrest, El Dorado, and Western, all well known carpet brands. Their prices are good and if you lack the fortitude to lay it yourself, they'll install if for you.

# CHRISTMAS DECORATIONS

## DISPLAY DIMENSIONS
1169 Mission Street, San Francisco 94102. Phone: 861-6300. Hours: M-F 10am-5pm *Month of November*. Purchases: Cash, Check. Parking: Street.

Every year for one month *Display Dimensions* opens its doors to the public. Those elegant and clever decorations, fixtures and accessories you see in store displays are often designed and sold by this outfit. How often have you seen just the right thing and then been told that it was not for sale but for display only?

During their month-long sale you can buy Xmas decorations, ornaments, seasonal decorations, garment racks, fixture hardware, baskets, trim items, home furnishing items, one-of-a-kind designs and decorative accessories. All merchandise is priced slightly above their cost. This is not the place to take children! I usually lose myself in contemplation of all the treasures for at least an hour before making my selections. *Display Dimensions* is also an excellent resource for small stores with a limited decorating budget.

## FANTASTICO
(See **Arts, Crafts and Hobby Supplies**)

## FLOWER TERMINAL
(See **Flowers-Plants-Pots**)

# DINNERWARE AND ACCESSORIES

(Also see **Furniture and Accessories—Catalog Discounters; General Merchandise—Catalog Discounters; Giftwares; Jewelry and Diamonds**)

## General

**S. CHRISTIAN OF COPENHAGEN, INC.**
225 Post Street, San Francisco 94108. Phone: 392-3394. Hours: 9:30am-6pm. Purchases: MC, BA, VISA. Parking: Pay Lots.

**Other Stores:** 1001 Front, San Francisco; Town & Country Village, Palo Alto; Town & Country Village, San Jose.

Make a beeline for the best buy in the store—the crystal table with Rosenthal seconds and irregulars priced at least 60% below retail. The flaws are very slight—tiny bubbles in the glass, a size difference among pieces of a set, a few swirl marks. They do not, in my estimation, affect the magnificence of this marvelous hand-blown glassware in the least. You might want to con-sider the special prices on their Collector's plates and dining room sets while you're looking around.

**THE CANDLE SHOP**
(See **Arts, Crafts, and Hobby Supplies**)

**COST PLUS IMPORTERS**
(See **General Merchandise—Discount Stores**)

**DANSK II**
Ocean Ave. & San Carlos, Carmel 93921. Phone: 408-625-1600. Hours: Daily 10am-6pm. Purchases: Cash or Check. Parking: Street.

When manufacturers update their lines periodically it's logical that something else has to go. All discontinued merchandise from *Dansk* is sent to *Dansk II* in Carmel and is sold at 33-66% savings. Shoppers who appreciate contemporary and functional wares will be delighted with the selection of Kobenstyle Cookware and nonconforming items: teakwood trays and salad bowls, china, stemware and bar glasses, plastics, stainless steel items, candles and candleholders. Carmel not only has charm, it has bargains!

**HEATH CERAMICS INC.—FACTORY STORE**
400 Gate 5 Road, Sausalito 94965. Phone: 332-3732. Hours: Daily, 10am-5pm. Purchases: MC, VISA. Parking: Lot.

A visit to Sausalito is a Must for the tourist, an outing for Bay Area residents. The *Heath Factory Store* in

Sausalito could well be the focal point of the trip. Bargain hunting in this pleasant environment is a unique experience. Overruns and seconds of tile for flooring, counters, and walls are available in extraordinary colors and textures at very worthwhile savings. Their dishes and heat-tempered cookware that do not pass their high standards during inspection are sold for 40% below retail prices. This does not mean that they're chipped or cracked, just little flaws that the untrained eye can hardly discern. Bargain hunting in the *Factory Store* can become habit-forming. With these savings from regular retail prices, you are apt to find yourself returning, to round out your dinnerware set, to buy gifts, to purchase tile for a remodeling project, or just to introduce a friend to the experience.

## MARJORIE LUMM'S WINE GLASSES
112 Pine St., San Anselmo 94960. Phone: 454-0660. Hours: M-F 9:30am-5pm. Weekends by appt. Purchases: VISA, MC. Parking: Municpal Lot.

Marjorie Lumm runs a nationwide mail order wine glass business, carrying probably the most extensive selection of classic wine glasses to be found anywhere. Formerly located in Sausalito, her warehouse is now in San Anselmo, where she has tables of seconds. Marjorie's wine glasses are handblown, good quality glasses of medium weight. The glasses are made in West Virginia, the center for fine glassmaking in the United States. Wine enthusiasts prefer glasses that are made from clear glass, with no color or cut designs to impede the evaluation of color and clarity. Her all-purpose wine glass sells for $6.15 in her catalog and is reduced to $3.05 as a second. All seconds are reduced 50% in price. These glasses are not chipped but may have small bubbles or swirl effects in the glass which you can barely discern. Certainly your guests will never spot the flaws. You can obtain one of her catalogs by writing to P.O. Box 732, Sausalito, 94966, and then determine from the pictures if these glasses are in keeping with your tastes and whether a visit is warranted. You can buy two or twenty, suit yourself. Sometimes they may not have just the pieces you want or in the quantities you need, so you might call ahead first.

## MASLACH ART GLASS STUDIO & SECONDS STORE
44 Industrial Way, Greenbrae 94904. Phone: 924-2010. Hours: T-Sat 11am-5pm. Purchases: BA, MC. Parking: In front.

Original glassware, where each piece is handblown into contemporary designs, is perfect for people who are looking for something just a little different. You'll save 50% off on their pieces of stemware, bowls, bud vases, hurricane lamps and egg-shaped paperweights. Marble collectors will love rummaging through their seconds and will surely find a choice original. Their newest look is stemware in iridescent colors that suggests an art nouveau look. While browsing you can watch their master glassblowers at work. A goblet classed as a second, which may have minute cosmetic flaws, sells for about $15-$30. There are good quantities of many pieces. You can buy a whole set or just a few. The store is located 1 block north of Cost Plus.

# Restaurant Supply Stores

### COMMERCIAL FOOD EQUIPMENT CO.
501 E. 12th St., Oakland. Phone: 893-2736. Hours: M-F 8:30am-5pm. Purchases: Cash, Check. Parking: Street.

Restaurant supply stores are truly a boon for families with fumbly-fingered young children (or couples who fight a lot). A magnificent assortment of sturdy dishes is available in the back room of this establishment. While restaurant dishes may not have the graceful look of your regular china, they will probably last a lot longer. Both new and used dishes are priced by the dozen here; for quantities of less than a dozen, 10% is added to the price. On used dishes, savings are about 50%, and all they need is a little soap and water to become useful additions to your kitchen.

### FOOD SERVICE EQUIPMENT INC.
710 E. 14th St., San Leandro. Phone: 568-2922. Hours: M-F 8am-5pm, Sat 9am-2pm. Purchases: BA, MC. Parking: Street.

This is the nicest restaurant supply store I've found so far. It's spacious and attractive, with merchandise beautifully displayed. On the main floor there are always specials on discontinued merchandise, with many one-of-a-kind items. The upstairs back room is stacked high with sturdy restaurant dishes in many colors and patterns (or plain, even). Here there are used dishes and kitchenware at savings of about 50%, discontinued lines of dishes, and new dishes that have been returned to the store. Dishes are priced by the dozen.

### ROYAL SUPPLY CO.
501 15th Street (Corner San Bruno), San Francisco 94103. Phone: 626-1700. Hours: M-F 8:30am-5pm. Purchases: VISA, MC.

The closeout room of this major distributor is a bonanza for anyone shopping for good quality glasses, barware, stemware or sturdy restaurant china at super low prices 50% off list. These items can be purchased in any quantity from the closeout room. At these prices I couldn't resist a dozen Bloody Mary or Ice Tea glasses at $2.10 and with a few extra I don't have to worry about breakage. New items are added to the closeout room on a regular basis. Many of these glasses would make lovely gifts. Your bargain gift will make you look positively magnanimous!

# DRAPERIES

## Fabrics

(Also see **Fabrics—Drapery and Upholstery Yardage and Supplies**)

## Ready Made

### AMERICAN DRAPERIES

1168 San Luis Obispo, Hayward 94544. Phone: 489-4760. Hours: Announced in Bay Area Newspapers. Purchases: BA, MC.

American Draperies makes draperies for homes and apartment houses. Twice a year they clear out their warehouse of miscellaneous stock, discontinued fabrics, production overruns, and odd sizes, most priced between $12.00 and $35.00. Bring your rod sizes and lengths required. The draperies are on hangers in panels or pairs. The fabrics are sold for 39¢-99¢/yard. Their sales are announced in Bay Area newspapers and usually occur on the first weekend in May and November. All sales are final. For the best selection be there when the doors open; however, at 2:30 in the afternoon, an additional 20% discount is applied to the sale merchandise. If you really don't want to miss this sale, call and ask to be put on their mailing list.

### FOOTHILL DRAPERIES

3121 Story Road, San Jose 95127. Phone: 408-258-7599. Hours: M-Sat 9am-5:30pm. Purchases: BA, MC. Parking: Private lot.

**Other Stores:** 897 Blossom Hill Rd., and 454 El Paseo de Saratoga, San Jose.

This custom drapery store has found a way to cut losses and keep their overhead down. They utilize all left-over fabrics by making up ready-made draperies in standard window sizes. They have about 1,000 of these leftovers in their three showrooms. Most are one-of-a-kind and there are some customer returns. You can buy custom quality at 30-40% off. Bring your measurements and choose from satins, brocades, open weaves, linens, patterns and sheers.

### ROBERT'S DRAPERIES

998 Bidwell Ave., Sunnyvale 94086. Phone: 736-6560. Hours: M-F 8am-5pm. Purchases: Cash or Check. Parking: Street.

This is basically a family operation that has been in existence for 22 years. What makes it unique is that all the work is done in their converted garage, and much of the selling takes place in their home. When you drive up and realize the business is actually conducted at this house, you may feel uncomfortable; but gradually you'll feel right at home. They specialize in window coverings—mini-blinds, shades, draperies and woven woods—selling them for a nice 25% discount off retail. On draperies, you save money on the fabric and their labor charge is very reasonable. To give you a quote, they request that you take some measurements first, and if necessary then they may go to your home and measure again. Installation is not included, so your savings are reduced unless you can do the installation yourself. It's always a good idea to call ahead first, just make sure someone is home to show you the samples; and don't go during lunch, they close between 12 and 1pm. They're very nice about lending samples.

**THE YARDSTICK**
2110 S. Bascom Ave., Campbell 95008. Phone: 377-1401. Hours: M-F 9am-9pm, Sat 9am-6pm, Sun 10:30am-5pm. Purchases: BA, MC. Parking: Lot.

If you need draperies right away or you want luxury window treatments at budget prices, check the mezzanine at *The Yardstick.* They usually have about 3,000 readymades (guaranteed 2½ fullness) from their own workrooms ready for you to take home and hang. Bring your measurements and in no time at all you'll be walking out the door with your selections. The fabrics used in their draperies are suitable for windows in a cabin or at the other extreme, in a formal dining room. *The Yardstick* always has "specials" for the seamstress.

Check their ads in the San Jose "Mercury" for your dress, drapery, or upholstery needs. Pass up those high prices on notions by checking their low prices and selection of closeouts on buttons, zippers, buckles, and trims.

# Custom Draperies

**DECORATOR'S BEDSPREAD OUTLET**
(See **Linens**)

**DOMICILE**
(See **Furniture—Catalog Discounters**)

**WESTERN CONTRACT FURNISHERS**
(See **Furniture—Catalog Discounters**)

# EYE CARE

I would hope that in 1982 everyone would be acquainted with the new trade regulations enacted by the Federal Trade Commission (FTC) in June 1978. These regulations have significant impact on the prices you pay when buying eyeglasses or contact lenses. The most important features of these new regulations were:

(1) Makes unenforceable any state or professional laws prohibiting price advertising; and,

(2) Requires the prescribing doctor to give to his or her patient a copy of his or her prescription *before* dispensing glasses or contact lenses.

Previously, retail dispensers of glasses have been able to charge whatever the traffic would bear in the absence of competitive advertising. The 1978 Federal Trade Commision study on the eye care industry reported that the average wholesale cost of a pair of single vision glasses was $10, which included the lens blanks, the polishing and grinding, and the frames. Since only a handful of suppliers produce most of the lenses in the U.S. and they maintain relatively high standards, it is possible to buy almost uniformly good quality glasses regardless of price. As long as the person dispensing the glasses checks to see that your prescription is accurately filled and the frames are properly

fitted, you should be able to get high-quality, single-vision glasses for low prices.

When buying glasses today you should: (1) demand a copy of your prescription at the time of your eye exam; you'll need it to comparison shop; (2) keep your prescription as part of your medical records; (3) shop around to get several sets of prices; (4) ask if you can return the glasses if they need adjusting without paying an additional charge; (5) have the person who wrote the prescription check your new glasses when they are ready.

I have retained my listing *For Eyes* from my previous edition, not only because of their prices and reliability, but because they were in the forefront of the consumer movement that has brought about the changes in pricing for this industry.

## FOR EYES

610 Sacramento, San Francisco. Phone: 391-3030. Hours: M-Sat 10am-6pm. Purchase: Cash, check. Parking: Pay Garage, Street.

**Other Stores:** 2104 Shattuck Ave., Berkeley; 2500 Telegraph, Berkeley; 219 Town & Country Village, San Jose; Space 82, Town & Country Village, Palo Alto.

If you have a friend who just bought a new pair of glasses don't tell them about *For Eyes*, you'll only make them unhappy. This company was started several years ago on the East Coast by a group of consumer oriented opticians from Philadelphia. Since then the company has grown and now boasts its own processing lab and

38 shops operating across the country which gives them considerable volume buying power. The primary goal of *For Eyes* is providing the highest possible quality for the lowest possible price. The standard price for single vision glasses is $35 which includes frame, lenses, and tinting, even for photochromatic lenses. Glass bifocals with frames and tinting cost $46. This is not a bait and switch operation, there are over 400 frames in the selection for men, women, and children. Rimless and designer frames are available at slightly higher prices. Delivery time is normally 2-2½ weeks.

An important consideration is their guarantee. All frames are guaranteed against defects for one year. The lenses are made by the same reliable companies that are used by other dispensing offices and stores. They are guaranteed to be filled according to the Doctor's prescription. If any mistakes occur, they will be replaced free of charge. Adjustments are free at any time. The *For Eyes* concept is long overdue in the Bay Area for people on fixed incomes or tight budgets. Others, less budget minded, will feel euphoric at the prospect of buying three pairs of fashionable glasses for the price of one elsewhere.

# FABRICS

## General

### BOLTS END
29014 Redwood Rd., Castro Valley 94546. Phone: 537-1684. Hours: Tues-Sat 10am-5pm, Thurs till 8pm. Purchases: Cash or Check. Parking: Lot.

A tiny little shop absolutely crammed with fabrics, trims, buttons, linings and othe paraphernalia. The owner buys mill ends, fabrics from apparel manufacturers, or in other words, leftovers. Prices are very good, the selection is always interesting even though somewhat eclectic.

### CHEAP AND CHEERFUL FABRICS
1811 Powell Street, San Francisco 94133. Phone: 397-5722. Hours: T-Sat Noon-6pm. Purchases: MC, VISA.

*Jeanne-Marc*'s fabric store offers fabrics at wholesale and below wholesale prices. Featuring fabrics from the preceding season's collections, including everything from terry cloth to silk, quilted and pleated fabrics, cotton prints, broadcloths, and batistes, the store is only open Tuesdays through Saturdays. All textiles are first rate and many are imports from Paris or printed exclusively for *Jeanne-Marc*. Many of the fabrics match the jackets and skirts available next door at *Cheap and Cheerful, Jeanne-Marc*'s well established clothing outlet store. Included in the stock are many textiles suited for interior use. Deliveries are made every week and smart shoppers will stop in often to obtain the best buys. Notions such as threads, patterns, zippers etc. are not carried. Parking is frustrating at best in this area of North Beach.

**CARY & MOUSEFEATHERS**
(See **Apparel—Children's**)

**COMPANY STORE**
(See **Apparel—Women's Factory Outlet**)

**EMERYVILLE CLOTHING & FABRIC OUTLET**
(See **Apparel—Women's Factory Outlets**)

**EXOTIC SILKS**
252 State St., Los Altos 94022. Phone: 415-948-8611. Hours: M-Sat 9am-5:30pm. Purchases: VISA, MC. Parking: Street.

*Exotic Silks* is a wholesale business with a small retail store to clear out excess inventory. The company buyers scour the Orient in search of beautiful silks to import. These silks are used by artists, decorators, lampshade manufacturers, fashion designers, smaller yardage

shops and individual sewers. The silks available to the public are the 'leftovers' in plain or print silk crepe de chine, silk satin, raw noil silk, silk corduroy, handwoven Thai silks in vibrant colors, taffeta, pongee, and brocade silks. Yardage may be limited to a few remaining yards on a bolt or up to 40-50 yards. But when it's gone, your chances of finding a particular fabric again are nil. So buy as much as you need the first time around.

Unlike other yardage shops, *Exotic Silks* sells no patterns, threads, zippers or other notions. However, they always have several racks of silk apparel that are well priced. Silk scarves, cotton and fine linen handkerchiefs, beautifully embroidered tablecloth and napkin sets are usually available when they've found them at a good price on their buying trips. The silk yardage may be discounted 20-40% off retail prices. Catch their ads in "Vogue" pattern magazine if you would like to order sample fabrics.

**FABRIC WAREHOUSE**
2327 McKee Road, San Jose 95116. Phone: 926-3203. Hours: M-F 10am-9pm, Sat 10am-6pm, Sun 10am-5pm. Purchases: BA, MC, VISA. Parking: Free lot.

**Other Stores:** 3690 El Camino Real, Santa Clara; 898 Blossom Hill Road, San Jose; 651 W. Hamilton, Campbell.

Picture a supermarket-sized store filled with fabrics and you can understand how overwhelmed you'll feel on your first visit to these warehouse stores, located next to K-Mart. Most of these fabrics are purchased directly from Eastern mills, and all are first quality. Except for wools, their selection is very extensive in all categories.

Prices on upholstery and drapery fabrics are low enough to lure upholsterers into the store to buy fabrics for their customers; they're often 50-60% off retail. Everyday regular prices reflect savings of 20-50% off established retail prices on all their goods, greater reductions are on fabrics advertised in their special weekly promotions.

They have an interesting dual pricing policy based on full bolt purchases vs. cut to order. The full bolt lower price refers to any amount of yardage remaining on a bolt, whether it's 3 yds. or 40 yds. All notions are discounted 15-25% off manufacturer's list price and all patterns are discounted 15%.

## FACTORY OUTLET
(See **Apparel—Children's**)

## FARR WEST DESIGNS
(See **Apparel—Women's Factory Outlets**)

## GUNNE SAX OUTLET
(See **Apparel—Women's Factory Outlets**)

## HARAN'S
2853 Mission, San Francisco 94110. Phone: 647-7746. Hours: M-Sat 9:30am-6pm; Sun noon-5pm. Purchases: BA, MC. Parking: Free lot.

**Other Store:** 820 Clement, San Francisco.

*Haran's* offers all kinds of fabrics at fantastically reduced prices—some fabrics here are for sale elsewhere at twice the price. There are cottons from 69¢ a yard, acetates at $1 a yard, and drapery and upholstery fabrics at $1.98 a yard. Almost everything in the store is specially purchased from mills in other states. Good buys are plentiful here, but be alert for second-quality merchandise; check the fabric for flaws before purchasing. This store will make exchanges, but you will save time if you're careful before you buy.

## IMPORO
149 10th Street (upstairs), San Francisco 94103. Phone: 552-0132. Hours: M-Sat 9am-5:30pm. Purchases: BA, MC, check. Parking: Street.

Located between Mission and Howard, *Imporo* offers a wide selection of fabrics at bargain hunters prices. There are many synthetics and natural fibers (including wools) that make sewing your own clothes a real money saver.

## LILLI ANN FACTORY OUTLET
(See **Apparel—Women's Factory Outlets**)

## OLGA FASHIONS & FABRIC OUTLET
(See **Apparel—Women's Factory Outlets**)

## STONEMOUNTAIN & DAUGHTER

2516 Shattuck Avenue, Berkeley 94705. Phone: 845-6106. Hours: M-Sat 10am-6pm, Sun Noon-5pm. Purchases: MC, VISA. Parking: Street.

The owner of this small shop has long established connections with the apparel industry in Los Angeles. He attempts to combine quality with low price in making his purchases so that he can pass on worthwhile savings to consumers. Often I've spotted a fabric that I've I've just seen on a garment in a department store. Along with somewhat ordinary fabrics, he usually has wools, silks, cottons and rayon blends that are quite special. Bring your patterns, he doesn't sell patterns or any notions.

# Drapery and Upholstery
## Yardage and Supplies

(Also see **Furniture and Accessories—Catalog Discounters; Draperies—Ready Made**)

## ALAMEDA UPHOLSTERY SHOP

863 W. San Carlos, San Jose 95126. Phone: 295-7885. Hours: M-F 9am-5:30pm, Sat 9am-4pm. Purchases: BA, MC. Parking: Street.

Whether you need supplies for reupholstering a piece of furniture or just advice about doing it, this shop can help you. They cater to do-it-yourselfers, with some nice fringe benefits. For example, they make up a small beginners' kit that includes most of the tools needed to start reupholstering on your own, and they usually have a few books on the subject as well. Their selection of upholstery fabrics is huge, and they can order from almost any major manufacturer in the country, including Van Waters & Rogers, Waverly, S. Harris, Schumacher, and many others at savings of 25%. (Students can get another 10% discount.) Draperies, woven woods, and mini-blinds are sold for a 25% discount when the customer measures and hangs their own. They will also cut to order foam rubber that comes in 30 sizes, ¼" to 6".

## BERESSI, S. FABRIC SALES

1504 Bryant St., San Francisco 94103. Phone: 861-5001. Dates: Fall and Spring. Hours: By Announcement. Purchases: Cash, Check. Parking: Lot.

For two months each year, S. Beressi, a bedspread manufacturer popular with interior designers and local stores, opens its doors to the public and gives everyone a chance to buy fabrics, threads, polyester fiberfill and bedspreads from its upstairs warehouse. Prices on the huge assortment of "leftovers" are less than wholesale to encourage fast sales and speedy removal. Most all of the fabrics sold are first quality, discontinued patterns and colors from their regular line. These fabrics are used not only for bedspreads, but for draperies, upholstery, slipcovers, costumes, apparel, crafts and theatre set decorations. Mr. Beressi can help determine the amount of yardage required for your project and also give a lot of how-to information. Call the office for specific sale dates and times. This is one sale you don't want to miss for budget decorating needs.

## CALICO CORNERS

2700 El Camino Real, Redwood City 94061. Phone: 364-1610. Hours: M-Sat 9:30am-5:30pm, Sun Noon-5pm. Purchases: BA, MC. Parking: Free lot.

**Other Stores:** 5764 Paradise Dr., Corte Madera; 39A Almaden Plaza at 5353 Almaden Expry, San Jose; 5753 Pacheco Blvd., Pacheco.

The real bargains are not calico, actually, but beautiful imported and domestic upholstery fabrics—some of the finest upholstery fabrics, drapery and slipcover fabrics I have seen, for 50% off regular retail price. Hanging rolls neatly display beautiful fabrics whose only fault are tiny minute flaws that can easily be worked around (some weren't even visible to the unprofessional eye). Each piece is tagged with fiber content, width, price and place of manufacture. This store is an absolute pleasure to shop in, not only for its extraordinarily low prices, but also for its neat arrangement and its helpful clerks, who will refer you to a custom upholsterer, or slipcover expert. Draperies are sent out to be made by the store with the wholesale labor price being passed on to the customer. They will allow customers to borrow a bolt of yardage for home evaluation. The Pacheco store is not too far removed from the Sun Valley Shopping Center in Concord.

## FIELD'S FABRICS

1229 Park St., Alameda 94501. Phone: 865-7171. Hours: M-Sat 9:30am-5pm. Purchases: VISA, MC. Parking: Street.

This small shop offers a complete stock of beautiful home decorating fabrics at 40-60% off retail. The reason: these are seconds, discontinued patterns and mill overruns. The ladies who work here couldn't be more helpful in giving suggestions and assistance to the novice.

# FLOWERS, PLANTS, POTS

(Also see **General Merchandise—Discount Stores**)

## ARCHITECTURAL CERAMICS WEEKEND SALES
1940 Union St. (1½ blocks off Grand Ave.) Oakland 94607. Phone: 893-5314. Hours: Occasional Weekends. Purchases: Cash or Check. Parking: Street.

The pots and containers manufactured by this outfit are usually seen accommodating large plants and indoor trees in lobbys and office buildings. Their smallest container is a one gallon 8" x 7". They make low 6" x 17" pots for color spots or succulent containers, while their largest container accommodates a 15 gallon plant and is 17" x 20". As this book was going to press, the decision had been made to allow the public to have an opportunity to buy their seconds on occasional weekends. Prices will be 50-65% off retail depending on the flaws in the glaze or the size of the chip. If you're interested in these bargains which will range from $4.50-$30, be sure to call ahead to verify that they will be open.

## FANTASTICO
(See **Arts, Crafts, Hobby Supplies**)

## FLOWER TERMINAL
6th and Brannan, San Francisco. Hours: M-F 2am-11am. Purchases: Cash or check.

Several wholesale nurseries are located within this block of buildings. Retail sales of house plants are made to the public at wholesale prices. Because these businesses are basically wholesale operations, this is certainly not the place to shop with your children or to expect information on plant maintenance or other advice. The quick cash sale is appreciated but there is neither time nor personnel for retail services. You are required to pay sales tax unless you have a resale number. Only people with resale numbers are allowed to park within their lot and street parking can be a real problem! For the best service and selection I recommend shopping on Tuesdays and Thursdays. Several dealers in the complex sell dried flowers, ribbons, papers, and other craft essentials. I would not say that prices are 'wholesale' on anything, however many items are simply not sold at the retail level. From October through Xmas these dealers are crowded with shoppers anxious to get a head start on their holiday decorations.

## FUJII'S PLANT OUTLET

24949 Soto Road, Hayward 94544. Phone: 415-886-1577. Hours: Daily 9am-5pm. Purchases: MC, BA.

*The Plant Outlet* was previously a wholesale growing operation that decided to deal directly with the public. The results are gratifying for all concerned. The best buys and largest selection are in the hanging plant categories: ferns, creeping charlies, piggybacks, spider plants, etc. The uprights, palms, philodendrons, ficus trees, etc., are available in good quantity and at good prices. There are thousands of plants under the roof of this huge growing shed and I've never seen anyone leave with just one plant. At their prices you can't resist buying three or four. It's very nice too, to deal with a grower who has so many helpful employees to give advice and help you with your selection. Customers are appreciated at *The Plant Outlet!*

## MAINLY SECONDS

15715 Hesperian Blvd., San Lorenzo 94580. Phone: 481-1902. Hours: M-Sat 9am-6pm, Sun 10am-6pm. Purchases: MC, VISA. Parking: Street.

**Other Store:** 701 San Pablo Ave. (2 blocks No. Solano Ave.), Albany, 94706. Phone: 527-2493.

When warm weather rolls around and you're in a potting mood, you'll find the best buys on pots and planters at these two stores. Both are stocked with a wide array of planters and pots to suit almost any style of interior or exterior decor. True to their name, much of the merchandise is classified as seconds, with small flaws or irregularities that will not deter the bargain hunter. I've brightened up my patio with several of their terra cotta hen-shaped pots and strawberry planters at 30-40% discounts. The ceramic pots suitable for small trees made by Architectural Ceramics are always 50% off. Handthrown stoneware pots are 40-50% off: I spotted one for $7.99 that sold elsewhere for $15. Unrelated to their other merchandise, they display tables laden with ceramic bathroom accessories like toothbrush holders, tissue holders and soap dishes at approximately 70% off. These must be checked carefully for flaws. Closeouts of terra cotta gourmet cookware are 50% off and great for microwave cooking. Of course all these pots are surrounded by plants, dried flowers, silk flowers and macrame holders to provide a complete selection. Everything is discounted!

## PAYLESS DRUG STORES GARDEN CENTERS

2130 Contra Costa Blvd., Pleasant Hill 94523. Phone: 685-2450. Hours: M-F 9:30am-9pm, Sat 9am-8pm, Sun 9am-7pm. Purchases: Cash, check, BA, MC. Parking: Free lot.

**Other Stores:** Castro Valley, Dublin, Fremont, Hayward, Oakland, San Mateo, San Pablo, San Rafael, Santa Rosa, Vallejo.

For garden plants it's hard to find better prices than the ones at *Payless Drug Store's Garden Centers.* Their secret is volume buying and quick turnover. Each store does its own buying to suit the special climatic and soil conditions of its area. Since this is a self-service store, you won't get the attention you might get at a nursery.

Prices are as much as 50% below those of independent nurseries during their seasonal sales. Usually garden department sales are held every three weeks throughout the year; these are advertised in local papers. During spring and fall, the peak gardening seasons, sales occur weekly. Even without the sales, prices are 25-35% less than you'll find almost anywhere else.

*Payless* will accept exchanges on plants that do not thrive or aren't satisfactory if you have your sales slip (otherwise at the discretion of the garden center manager).

## "SECONDS ONLY" POTTERY OUTLET

1793 Lafayette St., Santa Clara 95050. Phone: 408-984-0467. Hours: Mon-Sat 9am-5pm. Purchases: VISA, MC. Parking: Street.

You'll find some of the bargains out in the yard and some inside the two story yellow building at the back of the lot. They distribute pottery containers of all types (from basic red clay to fancy glazed) and sell discontinued styles plus pottery seconds for 20% above wholesale. They buy inventories from other manufacturers when they go out of business to produce an ever-changing selection. Badly damaged pots are priced very low—they need to be, since some seem barely usable.

## SUNOL NURSERIES

1000 Calaveras Rd. (at Hwy. 680), Sunol 94586. Phone: 862-2286. Hours: Daily 8am-4:30pm. Purchases: BA, MC. Parking: Free lot.

Take a ride out to the country, not only for fun but for the money you can save here. *Sunol Nurseries* is a wholesale nursery open to the public. Bud Martin, the owner, and his men are congenial and willing to help and will give you detailed landscaping instructions. Take your landscaping plans with you to make it easier when you get there, and pick up a catalog when you are there—it describes and illustrates most of the plants and shrubs they sell, with some planting instruction. No catalogs will be sent by mail. There is a very helpful price guide with the retail price listed next to the wholesale price. You can get further discounts, if, or when, you buy in lots of 5, 10, or 25 plants. "Sunset" garden books are 20% less, too.

# FOOD AND DRINK

(Also see **General Merchandise—Discount Stores,—Liquidators**)

## Bakery Thrift Shops

There is a large assortment of bakery goods available in San Francisco and the rest of the Bay Area at low, low prices if you're willing to make the trip to one of the outlets (not a long trip, because there are bakery thrift shops turning up all over the place). The *Orowheat*, *Langendorf*, *Parisian*, and *Kilpatrick* baking companies have thrift stores throughout the Bay Area where you can buy either day-old bread at about 50% off regular retail prices or freshly-baked (surplus) goods for about 20% off. Save on the purchase of cakes, cookies, donuts, and sweet rolls, too. Buy a lot at one time—you can freeze whatever you don't use right away.

## Groceries

**ALUM ROCK CHEESE CO.**
215 E. Alma Ave., San Jose 95110. Phone: 408-293-9400. Hours: Sat only 9am-3pm. Purchases: Cash or Check. Parking: Lot.

Saturdays are bargain days at this cheese company. Drive around to the back of the building to find their retail store. Ricotta, mozzarella, cheddar, Swiss, American and processed cheeses are sold for considerably less than at your neighborhood deli. There's no minimum purchase required. If you're planning a pizza party, take the easy way out. Buy their thick or thin prepared pizza crusts, sauce, diced blended cheeses and meats that will keep your efforts to a minimum.

**BETTER BUYS**
(See **General Merchandise**)

**CALIFORNIA CHEESE CO.**
1451 Sunny Ct., San Jose 95116. Phone: 288-5151. Hours: M-S 8:30am-5pm. Purchases: Cash or Check. Parking: Lot.

Don't go on an empty stomach or you'll be tormented by the aroma of fresh cheeses, deli meats and pizza products. Although they have a wide variety of cheeses, their speciality is mozzarella and ricotta which is made in their own factory. Their prices on all products are discounted about 50¢ a pound from supermarket prices.

At the time of printing their mozzarella was $2.05 a pound and 5 pound blocks were $1.90 a pound. Very nice if you're buying for a large party, a church supper or a hungry bunch! They're at the end of a dead end street, but it's easier to call for directions if you're not familiar with the area.

## CANDY OUTLET

209 Utah, South San Francisco 94080. Phone: 871-1800. Hours: M-F 8am-4:30pm. Purchases: Cash or Check. Parking: Street.

You may rue the day you set foot in this store especially when you step on your scale. This is the Bay Area distribution center for *Blum's* candies. Theoretically, everything that comes in should go out with mathematical precision. Of course, reality is quite different. All the candies and *Blum's* products that are leftover are sold for 25% off minimum and daily specials may go for 40-50% off. All the candies are sold in packages, boxes, bags or clever promotional containers. In the selection you'll choose from mints, fudge, peanut brittle, mixed creams, nuts and chews, also ice cream toppings, cookies and fruit cakes. You won't leave empty-handed!

## CANNED GOODS

1717 Harrison (14th St., entrance), San Francisco 94103. Phone: 552-9680. Hours: M-F 9am-7pm, Sat 8am-6pm. Purchases: Cash, Check, Food Stamps. Parking: Lot.

**Other Stores:** Berkeley, Redwood City, San Jose, Sacramento, Stockton.

These are the quiet guys in town. They don't advertise for two reasons: (1) the items they stock change in quantity and variety from day to day, and (2) not advertising helps to lower their overhead and prices. *Canned Foods* specializes in buying carload shipments straight from packers and canners. They also buy overstocks, label-change goods, odd lots and some cannery dents. But they buy wholesome food and stand behind their products 100% with a money back guarantee. To save money, they do not carry a full line of groceries but whatever you buy is usually priced below the competitions' regular prices. A recent shopping trip at *Canned Foods* resulted in a basket of goods totaling $31.12. Shopping for the same items in a major grocery store would have yielded a total of $52.79. Your success at *Canned Foods* depends on your ability to spot super values, so it's important to know the food prices of items you consistently buy. Don't shop *Canned Foods* with a prepared list, shop instead with an eye towards exceptional values that you can stock up on and by-pass the marginal ones you can easily buy at local stores. Some of the labels that are unfamiliar are from Eastern companies, or have been repackaged to protect the identity of the regular manufacturer. Best buys often include seasonal items like halloween candy, summer drink mixes, or Xmas labeled items.

## CASH AND CARRY WAREHOUSE

2915 Kerner Blvd., San Rafael 94901. Phone: 457-1040. Hours: M-F 8am-4pm, Sat 8am-1pm. Purchases: Cash & check. Parking: Lot.

**Other Store:** 3440 Vincent Rd., Pleasant Hill, 932-1414.

If you're cooking for a crowd, the Girl Scouts, your church, or just planning a big party, the *Cash and Carry Warehouse* may have some products that will not only save you money, but make your preparations easier. Paper products like plates, cups, doilies and gift boxes may be purchased by the dozen or by the case at considerable savings. I was most intrigued by their food products like 5 pound General Foods Cake mixes (a restaurant staple) at $4.84; their 4 pound jars of artichoke hearts at $5.70; restaurant size cans of tomato sauce, nuts, tuna, Bisquick and pancake mixes which make quantity cooking a snap. They will special order for you if they don't have what you need in stock and also take phone orders that will be ready when you arrive. For a warehouse their merchandise is neatly arranged and the whole store is immaculate. You can find this place easily by taking any Francisco Blvd. offramp from U.S. 101.

## CIMINO FOODS INC.

95 Phelan Ave., Unit 1, San Jose 95112. Phone: 408-275-9553. Hours: M-F 8am-5pm, Most Sat 9am-Noon. Purchases: Cash or Check. Parking: Lot.

*Cimino* is very similar to other nut and dried fruit listings in this section except that they do their own roasting. If you're a peanut freak, you can buy them unroasted, or roasted and salted in 1 lb. or 5 lb. boxes at super prices. Call for prices. Also, check their prices on dried fruits and gift packs. *Cimino* is behind the *A-1 Linen Company*. Don't go to one without stopping at the other.

## CITADEL'S CANNERY WAREHOUSE

405 East Taylor (between 9th & 10th), San Jose 95112. Phone: 275-0410. Hours: M-Sat 9:30am-6pm, Sun 11am-5pm. Purchases: Cash, check. Parking: Lot.

The selection of dented cans and odd lots for sale here covers the whole warehouse floor. They charge 25¢ extra for cutting cases, but the buys are still good enough to make your trip here worthwhile. Prices on canned goods average usually at least 30% less than retail. Both institutional and regular sizes are available, but not every size in every item. There are many nationally known brands for sale, along with *Citadel's* own brand. The quality of all items is guaranteed. You should shop here early in the morning on a weekday, since the afternoons and Saturdays are fairly busy. Save money by shopping with friends and splitting cases.

## CO-OP SUPERMARKETS
### (Consumers Cooperative of Berkeley Inc.)

1414 University Ave., Berkeley 94702. Phone: 526-0440. Hours: M-F 9:30am-8pm, Sat 9am-8pm, Sun 10am-7pm. Purchase: Cash, check. Parking: Free lot.

**Other Stores:** Berkeley, Corte Madera, El Cerrito, Oakland, Walnut Creek.

If you can't face grocery shopping with any enthusiasm, you probably haven't discovered the *Co-op Supermarkets*. You'll be delighted by all their little extras, the paperback book exchange, home economists who can answer questions and give advice, and the community and swap-shop bulletin boards.

The *Co-op* is owned by the more than 100,000 member families. Together they own the business; they're buying from their own organization. The best bargain is having a voice in the policy and operation of the business, which is a real education. You can shop in the market even if you are not a *Co-op* member; if you want to be a member-owner after investigating the store and other services, then join. Shares are $5 each; every member has a vote in the organization.

Not only are the grocery prices competitive with other stores', but you'll also have these added features when shopping at the Co-op: bargain priced *Co-op* label products (detergent, paper goods, canned goods, pastas), bulk grains and cereals, kosher foods, Oriental products, El Molino flours and cereals, and other hard-to-find imported foods. There are informative newsletters, consumer education displays, suggestion boxes, a library of *Co-op* literature, and other *Co-op* sponsored activities. The most popular *Co-op* services include the credit union, health plan, legal services, Camp Sierra, and travel service.

## COUNTRY CHEESE

2101 San Pablo Ave., Berkeley 94710. Phone: 841-0752. Hours: M-Sat 10am-6pm. Purchases: Cash or Check. Parking: Street.

Domestic and imported cheeses, meat products, dried fruits, nuts and seeds, grains, spices by the ounce, and health food items at wonderful prices keep Berkeley residents happy. If you're in the East Bay and haven't checked them out, you don't know what you're missing! Inquire about their discounts for co-ops and volume orders.

## FOOD BARN

3232 Foothill Blvd. (at Fruitvale), Oakland 94601. Hours: M-Sat 9am-7pm, Sun 10am-7pm. Purchases: Cash, Check, Food Stamps. Parking: Lot.

The *Food Barn* is *Safeway's* answer to all the other no-frills stores that have cropped up in the last few years. Gone are the baggers, assistance to your car, free grocery bags (they charge if you don't bring your own) and lenient check cashing privileges. Instead, overhead is carefully controlled so that all the products sold at the *Food Barn* can be discounted 10-30%. The overall selection is not as extensive as their full service stores, but you can usually buy most items on your grocery list.

## H & J PRODUCTS
2547 San Carlos Avenue, Castro Valley 94546. Phone: 415-582-1806. Hours: M-F 9am-5pm. Occasional Saturday. Purchases: Cash or Check. Parking: Street.

I'm not about to make any claims about food supplements, vitamins or minerals. For those of you who regularly use these products you might be interested in checking the prices at the *H & J Products* Factory Outlet. This company manufacturers food supplements, i.e. Vitamin c-1000mg, Super Stress Formula B-Complex with Vitamin C, Bee Pollen, Pure Spirulina, A-D Chewable, and various Hi Protein tablets and powders, plus a full page of other products that are pure, safe, and fresh, but may have a crooked label, label change, or they are just surplus products. These are discounted 40-50% but a few are discounted a modest 20%.

   *H & J* sells their products to Bay Area and nationwide wholesale distributors who in turn sell to local retail nutrition stores. Their products are sold under their own label and they also private label products for special accounts. Finally, *H & J* sells DMSO. If you have been wary of buying this product in some of the unconventional retail outlets that advertise this product, you'll probably feel more confident buying here. If you would like a complete discount price list, send a self-addressed stamped envelope to the address above. They will ship anywhere in any amount, but of course you pay the shipping.

## HOOPERS CHOCOLATES AND GIFTS
4632 Telegraph Ave., Oakland 94609. Phone: 654-3373. Hours: M-Sat 9:30am-6pm. Purchases: BA, MC. Parking: Street.

Just because you don't see their seconds (*Hoopers Bloopers*), don't think they're not here. Just ask and they'll sell you whatever they have on hand in their stock room. Regularly priced at $4.50, the seconds in chews and creams are just $2.75 a pound. Candy seconds at *Hoopers* may be irregularly shaped or lacking in gloss, or that little squiggle on top may be messy instead of artistic. One thing for sure, they still taste good. You have to buy a 50¢ minimum, but that's not hard as you contemplate rum, maple, almond, raspberry, or chocolate creams, or how about walnut, caramel, coffee, or almond nugget chews? Deeee-licious!

## INTERNATIONAL CHEESE
2191 Morrill Ave. (at Landress), San Jose 95131. Phone: 408-262-8026. Hours: M-F 10am-9pm, Sat 10am-6pm, Sun 11am-6pm. Purchases: Cash or Check. Parking: Lot.

Right on the border of Milpitas, this company can provide local residents a resource for pasta products, cheeses from around the world and luncheon meats. They deal with Co-ops in the area and extend their wholesale prices to the general public. The hitch is that you have to buy in larger bulk quantities. For instance, many cheeses come in 5 pound bricks and pastas come in 5 pound boxes. They will have your order ready for pick up or delivery if you call in advance.

## JANA'S SUPER BUYS
22224 Redwood Road, Castro Valley 94546. Phone: 582-6770. Hours: Daily 10am-6pm. Purchases: Food Stamps, Cash or Check. Parking: Lot.

The owners of this store will sell anything from A-Z if they can get a good buy on it. Primarily they're selling grocery items and food products. Prices on meat and cheese are super! Institutional size cans, salvage canned goods, promotional items and just plain regular grocery items are all discounted. The constant arrival of such a disparate collection of products defies any attempt at immaculate displays, however, their loyal customers don't complain.

## NORTHSIDE WALNUT SHELLING CO.
590 North 5th St., San Jose 95112. Phone: 408-294-0336. Hours: M-F 8am-5pm, Sat 8am-Noon. Purchases: Cash or check only.

Sweets and snacks filled with dried fruits and nuts are not only tasty and sometimes nutritious, they are also expensive. To trim those costs, consider the good buys on walnuts, pecans, pistachios, almonds as well as dried apricots, peaches, pears, prunes and raisins that are sold at this processing plant. The walnuts from the Patterson and Modesto area are shelled and processed for several name brand food companies right here. You may purchase fresh nuts and dried fruits in quantity from their office. They have sample packages on display to give you an idea of quantities and size of the nut meat in each package. When you order, fresh shelled nuts are pulled from their back warehouse. Walnuts are sold in 5 pound boxes for $10.00 and 25 pound boxes for $43.95. Refrigerated or frozen they will keep for several months. There is no shipping so your best bet is to take orders from several friends, split the gas and make one big haul.

## OLD WORLD CHEESE COMPANY
107 Monument Plaza, Pleasant Hill 94523. Phone: 798-9107. Hours: Daily 9am-5pm. Purchases: Cash, check, food stamps. Parking: Street.

**Other Store:** 932 El Camino Real, Sunnyvale.

Rather barnlike in appearance, the customers seem to appreciate the savings more than the decor. This is where I stock up on cheeses and other goodies for my pantry. For cheese priced low in bulk 5-10# packages, I simply cut them into one pound blocks and freeze. Cheese will keep up to three months in the freezer. Mozzarella at $2.09/pound is quite a savings from the typical supermarkets' $2.79/pound. Bulk pastas, cases of canned goods and other bulk grocery items are bargain priced. One item that I've found a lifesaver is their fresh pizza crusts, spread with sauce and cheese—they're ready for the oven.

## SUGARIPE FARMS
2070 South Seventh St., San Jose 95150. Phone: 408-280-2349. Hours: M-F 8:30am-4:30pm, Sat-Xmas season only. Purchases: Cash or Check. Parking: Lot.

To buy nuts and dried fruits, you don't have to go all the way to San Jose to take advantage of the bargains at this packer's warehouse store. You can do it over the phone. They'll ship anywhere as long as you pay the freight. If you do go into the store you'll find their own *Sugaripe* brand prunes, dried apricots, dried peaches, dried pears, dried apples, walnuts in their traditional shell (or, walnuts already shelled); also discover other fine products such as prune juice, an assortment of canned apricots, canned tomato items, raisins, dates, almonds, cashews, filberts and brazil nuts. These are all sold for lower than supermarket prices. Walnuts by the pound-$1.85, 10 pounds-$9.95; apricots (fancy) $3.29 per pound or broken slabs for $2.78 per pound. Everything is absolutely fresh! For gifts at holiday times inquire about their holiday gift packs, pre-made or to your specifications.

# Produce

### FARMERS MARKET ARCADE
100 Alemany Blvd., San Francisco 94110. Phone: 826-9821. Hours: M-F 9am-5pm, Sat 8am-5pm. Purchases: Cash only. Parking: Free lot.

There is something about open-air markets and fresh produce that appeals to everyone. *The Farmers Market,* where smaller farmers come to sell their produce direct to you, is a very enjoyable place to shop. The prices are reasonable, and you can count on freshness. This market place has been here a long time; many people have been customers for years. The thirty or so stalls are arranged side by side, with a small overhanging roof in case of rain. I suggest checking out the produce at each stand and noting prices before deciding just what to buy. Many of the vendors are real characters. (I noticed that some of the sellers are quite willing to let you sample before you buy, but ominous signs above other stalls read "NO TASTING.") Shop early because it gets quite crowded after 11am.

### GOLDEN GATE PRODUCE TERMINAL
Produce Ave., South San Francisco. Hours: M-F 1:30am-10am.

Just look for the long row of buildings and then try to find a parking place. Although they will do business with co-ops, you'll not find the service of your friendly neighborhood grocery store.

### OAKLAND PRODUCE MART
Dealers located at 2nd & Franklin (near Jack London Square), Oakland. Hours: M-F 1:30am-approx. 11am. Purchases: Cash, check. Parking: Street.

The *Oakland Produce Mart* handles 90% of the produce sold by independent retailers in the East Bay. The 15 wholesalers buy and sell from a cavernous open stall divided by high wooden walls and floor-to-ceiling wire mesh. They start work about 1:30am, trading peaks early in the morning, and they begin to close at 11am. For housewives seeking escape from high retail food costs, this source is about the best way I know to save money on vegetables, fruit, beans, rice, even peanuts. All the produce is sold by the crate, dozen, or sack.

Co-op shoppers are welcome, as well as individuals willing to buy in bulk quantities. The sellers at the *Produce Mart* prefer selling to the public during the middle of the week. On Mondays, Fridays, and days before and after holidays, they're just too busy.

This is one of the few businesses left that operates by supply and demand. Prices vary according to the quality and kind of food, time of day, and how well the sales are going. You can usually count on saving at least 25-50%.

Starting a co-op is not difficult and it behooves every bargain hunter to consider the effort and try to round up friends and neighbors to share in the benefits of co-op shopping.

My co-op has 12 member families. Every two weeks, two members take our grocery list and "do the shopping." We prefer getting there early in the morning around 6:30am). We can usually make our selections, have our wagon loaded, and be back home by 7:30am, just in time to get everybody off to school. I don't mind the early hours because my turn comes only once every three months. Occasionally I'll buy a crate of asparagus or favorite fruit for myself and put it all in my freezer. How nice to have asparagus for months instead of weeks!

**SAN FRANCISCO PRODUCE TERMINAL**
2000 block of Jerrold Ave., San Francisco. Hours: 1:30am-9:30am.

This large complex is overwhelming with its high loading docks and vast selection of produce. When I went to shop I felt very insignificant moving around between huge trucks and busy, busy men.

# Produce "Down on the Farm"

If you're really feeling the pinch of high food costs, try saving money by going to the source—the grower—and eliminating all those middleman expenses in between. Many farmers and ranchers seasonally set up fruit stands on or near their farms and sell to the public. You benefit in two ways: first, you'll save money; second, you'll be buying really fresh, farm-ripened flavorful produce. It's well worth the drive into the country, especially if you buy in quantity or if you have a talent for home canning. Some farmers invite people to pick their own for even greater savings.

Many farms do not advertise, but the word is spread by satisfied customers who return year after year during the harvest season. The San Jose "Mercury" and San Jose "News" have a classified section entitled "Good Things to Eat," with listings of local growers.

Following is a list of Growers' Associations who print brochures complete with maps pinpointing the growers who sell to the public, the foods they harvest and harvest times. Send a *self-addressed stamped envelope* to the addresses below to get a copy, then plan your summer excursions.

*Contra Costa County:*
**HARVEST TIME**
P.O. Box O
Brentwood, Ca 94513

*El Dorado County:*
**APPLE HILL GROWERS**
P.O. Box 494
Camino, Ca 95709

*Sonoma County:*
**SONOMA COUNTY FARM TRAILS**
P.O. Box 6043
Santa Rosa, Ca 95406

*Yolo and Solano Counties:*
**YOLANO HARVEST TRAILS**
P.O. Box 484
Winters, Ca 95694

# FURNITURE AND ACCESSORIES

## General

**A.C. GRAPHICS**
79 Belvedere Street #12 (1 block East of Francisco Blvd. East.) San Rafael 94901. Phone: 456-0363. Hours: M-F 9am-5pm, Sat 9am-noon. Purchase: Cash, check. Parking: Lot.

Seconds on stretched handscreened printed cotton graphics are 50% off the wholesale price. These fine graphics are frequently seen on walls in lobbies and business offices around the Bay. You can buy one or combine two or more to fill a wide expanse of bare wall. Photographs of fruits and vegetables are mounted on masonite and protected with a clear lacquer finish. Available in 16" x 20" and 30" x 40", they're reduced 75% as seconds. They also sell 2nds and 3rds of fabric for do-it-yourselfers at prices that are hard to beat anywhere. Metal picture frames, cut to size are sold at wholesale prices to the public. Many quilt makers find *A.C. Graphic's* quality fabrics and prices easy on the wallet. *A.C.* has a space in an industrial complex so be sure to look for door #12 down the side of the building.

## A.S.I.D. DESIGNERS SALE

101 Henry Adams St. (formerly Kansas), (The Galleria), San Francisco 94103. Phone: (For sale dates and information) 989-5363. Hours: 10am-4pm. Purchases: BA, MC. Parking: Pay lots.

For the past several years the *ASID* (*American Society of Interior Designers*) has sponsored two sales a year to benefit their educational fund. There is a certain mystique regarding this showplace because unless you are a designer, a decorator or working with one it is unlikely that you will have access to the treasures within. These beautiful facilities are the resource centers for designers. The showrooms inside are the repository for some of the finest furnishings in home decorating. Many lines are not displayed through retail furniture stores which makes the prospect of seeing them first hand and having the chance to buy the showroom samples and rejects particularly appealing.

Members of *ASID* staff the sale and receive a percentage of the profits for their fund. They also charge $1.00 for admission. If you are interested in buying living room, dining room and bedroom furniture, decorative accessories, lamps and lighting fixtures, carpets, outdoor furnishings, antiques and exotic and unusual one-of-a-kind items, consider trekking into the City for the big event. It's advisable to bring carpet, paint, and fabric samples of existing furnishings that figure in your decorating scheme. The designers staffing the sale are very willing to help you with your selections so it's to your benefit to come prepared. Because the showrooms are attempting to clear out the old to make way for the new, prices are reduced 25-60%. Delivery arrangements can be made for you. Watch for announcements in local newspapers for these semi-annual sales. 1982-83 dates are scheduled as follows: November 20-21st, 1982; June 11-12, 1983; November 19-20th, 1983.

## ABBEY RENTS . . . AND SELLS

1314 Post St., San Francisco 94109. Phone: 673-5050. Hours: M-F 8am-5pm. Purchases: BA, MC. Parking: Street.

**Other Stores:** Hayward, Oakland, Redwood City, Santa Clara, San Mateo.

We all think of *Abbey Rents* as the best-known renter of all kinds of furniture and equipment. However, are you aware that they have a new name, *"Abbey Rents . . . and Sells,"* and that the same merchandise is also for sale at any one of the stores in the Bay Area? Periodically, certain goods are judged obsolete and put on special sale at each office-warehouse. You can buy furniture, party paraphernalia (in San Francisco store only), sickroom equipment, and reducing gear. The condition of these items ranges from slightly to very used, with prices corresponding. Most are reduced about 40-60% from their original price at the discretion of each individual manager. Occasionally sales are announced in the local papers, but it's best to call and inquire at the store nearest you.

## ANGELES FURNITURE CLEARANCE & DISCOUNT CENTER

4701 Coliseum Way, Oakland 95601. Phone: 532-3511. Hours: Wed-Sun 10am-6pm. Purchases: MC, VISA. Parking: Street.

*Angeles* has an out-of-the-way location in the East Bay right next to the Nimitz Freeway, not far from the Coliseum Complex. Their ads state that they buy closeouts and current lines of furniture from major manufacturers at substantial discounts. They are then able to sell these furnishings at great discounts to the public from their no-frills warehouse store. The selection and quality of furnishings runs the gamut from budget to best with brands like Lane, Broyhill, Bernhardt, Burlington, Basset, Thomasville, American of Martinsville, Hibriten and Mt. Airy in living, dining, bedroom and occasional furniture. They usually have a good selection of upholstered furniture, i.e. chairs, sofas, sleeper sofas and love seat combinations. This is a good place to pick up a wall unit or cocktail table. The selection is changing all the time so one visit is just the beginning. To find what you want you may stop by several times and then VOILA! Delivery is provided at an additional charge.

## BREUNERS CLEARANCE CENTER

1600 Duane Ave., Santa Clara. Phone: 408-727-7365. Hours: M-Sat 10am-6pm. Purchases: BA, MC, Store Charge. Parking: Lot.

**Other Stores:** 100 Admiral Callaghan Lane (off Fwy 80), Vallejo. 3254 Pierce St., Richmond.

A large selection of left-overs, floor samples, discontinued, cancelled orders, slightly damaged or distressed furniture pieces from *Breuners* retail stores, are offered here at outlet prices, 30-50% off. There are great values in furniture, carpet remnants, dinettes, bedroom sets, mattresses, and a few accessory items. Each item is tagged with the original price and the as-is clearance price. Delivery is extra and varies according to the size of the item and delivery distance. You may go around in circles trying to find this outlet which is located right next to Fwy. 101, off the San Tomas Expressway. At Vallejo and Richmond (Albany area) stores the clearance centers are located within the retail stores.

## BULLOCKS FURNITURE CLEARANCE CENTER

600 East Hamilton Ave., Campbell 95008. Phone: 408-446-8248. Hours: WThF Noon-9pm, Sat 10:30am-6pm, Sun Noon-5pm. Purchases: Cash, Check or Bullocks charge. Parking: Lot.

*Bullocks Clearance Center* is much like all the others, that is, you'll find discontinued, one-of-a-kind, and a small percentage of damaged goods. Prices are reduced from 20-50% on their linens, housewares, furniture, area rugs, bedding, and home accessories. Prices get lower as merchandise stays on the floor. Delivery is $15 a piece with a miximum charge of $45. All sales final.

## BUSVAN

900 Battery St., San Francisco 94111. Phone: 981-1405. Hours: F-Sat 9:30am-6pm, Sun Noon-6pm. Purchases: BA, MC. Parking: Pay lot, off street.

**Other Stores:** 244 Clement, San Francisco.

If you are on a low budget, or trying to furnish a vacation home at bargain prices, *Busvan* offers real possibilities. Almost anything can be purchased from their huge three-story warehouse: furniture, appliances, rugs, pianos, antiques, paintings, books, bric-a-brac and office furniture. The basement features used furniture that has seen better days, but the prices are rock bottom. The main floor is filled with furniture from Art Deco through traditional mahogany and walnut pieces. The selection is always changing; it pays to stop by often.

The top floor features new budget-priced and moderate-priced furniture at substantial savings over retail prices. Especially good values are the large number of floor samples and factory seconds that *Busvan* offers. If you can live with a few imperfections, you can save a lot. All sales are final. A 20% deposit will hold merchandise for 30 days. Bring your own station wagon or van; *Busvan* will pad your furniture and tie it on your vehicle for free. The minimum delivery charge is $23.50.

## CALIFORNIA FURNITURE RENTAL AND SALES

3021 Kenneth Street, Santa Clara 95050. Phone: 415-961-0110, 408-722-RENT. Hours: M-F 9:30am-6pm, Sat 10am-6pm. Purchases: MC, BA.

**Other Stores:** 351 Foster City Blvd., Foster City; 1501 W. Campbell Ave., Campbell.

If you don't have the time to scout the garage sales, this is the place to go for budget-priced home furnishings. This furniture rental company always has a good selection of used home and office furniture. Some pieces, well—you know they've been used—but they're still usable, and sofas for $50-$150 are good values. Then there are many pieces that were on display in apartment or condominium models. They look like new but truly can't be sold as new furniture or for new prices. You'll save 20-40%. The styles go right down the middle, conventional or traditional—the type that appeals to the majority of people. You can also pick up tables, chairs, lamps, pictures, mattresses, bedroom and dining sets, and accessories. Check their prices on the new furniture too: I saw some good buys. Delivery is free on purchases over $300 in the Bay Area.

## COTTAGE TABLES

101 Brannan, San Francisco 94107. Phone: 957-1760. Hours: Tues-Sat 9am-6pm. Purchases: VISA, MC. Parking: Lot.

Tony Cowan, the owner of *Cottage Tables*, is a craftsman of the old school. His trademark is the pine table, suitable for kitchen, dining or office environments, that is completely hand made from solid wood using dowel and glue construction. There are no nails, screws or staples in his designs. His tables are then given a hand-rubbed Varathane finish resulting in a soft sheen that is deceptively durable. The quality and timelessness of design of all of his tables provide the consumer with a 100 year table that can withstand the rigors of family use, and will no doubt be handed down from this generation to the next. When buying tables from his shop, you can see construction in progress, finished products waiting for delivery, and stacks of wood waiting to be used. In addition to his basic 3' by 5' pine table that sells for $300 (the same table in oak is $375), he will take orders for tables to suit your dimensions, add turned legs, drawers, etc., and offer a choice of pine, oak, ash, Koa or walnut. Delivery is usually made within a month's time. If you need chairs of classic design to go with your tables he sells a line of compatible chairs for a 20% discount off retail prices at other stores. This is an opportunity to get a superbly made table to suit your size requirements at a price that is at least half of what comparable tables sell for in designer showrooms.

## DESIGNERS EXCHANGE
340 Kansas Street, San Francisco 94103. Phone: 552-4022. Hours: M-Fri 10am-5pm. Purchases: MC, VISA. Parking: Street.

The furnishings on the floor at *Designers Exchange* are typical of what you would have seen at the *W.J. Sloanes* stores before they went out of business. These pieces are placed for sale on consignment from showrooms at the *Galleria, Showplace, Furniture Mart* and occasionally they represent returns or cancelled orders from interior designers. In fact, *Designer's Exchange* functions as a clearinghouse for showrooms and businesses located in the West from the Canadian to the Mexican border. Prices are appropriately reduced to bring you about a 40% savings off of original retail. Keep in mind that these are the Cadillac lines of the industry so even discounted they're not inexpensive. Area rugs, pictures, accessories, lamps, chairs, sofa beds, rattan, tables and cabinet pieces are well represented in their selection. If you want to take your chances you can wait and watch a piece to see if the price will drop as it stays on the floor. Delivery is extra, so haul it yourself if you can. When time permits, the sales staff at *Designers Exchange* will take customers to the wholesale showrooms to select furnishings they may not have on their showroom floor. They'll let you buy at showroom cost, and charge you a 10% buyers fee. Because they deal with so many designers, they can also refer you to one who will work with you on a mutually satisfactory basis.

## DESIGNER'S RESOURCE CENTER
1359 Park Street, Alameda 94501. Phone: 523-3322. Hours: Tues-Fri Noon-5pm, Thurs & Fri 7pm-9pm, Sat 10am-5pm. Purchases: VISA, MC. Parking: Street.

If you need to buy your home furnishings at discount prices to afford the quality you desire, yet you lack the confidence or knowledge to make your own selections, the *Designer's Resource Center* (formerly *Home Zone*) offers a winning solution. Staffed by independent designers, the customer will receive assistance and will be able to make selections from an array of catalogues and samples, and will also be able to buy at discount prices. With professional design assistance customers can order furniture, carpet, wallpapers, fabrics, lamps, pictures, accessories, area rugs, office furniture, window coverings and beds and bedding. Prices are discounted 30% on most furnishings with the exception of wallpaper which will be discounted 25%. Prices do not include freight or delivery.

Professional services are not free, but for an hourly fee you can elect to receive an escorted tour of wholesale furniture showrooms in San Francisco, or you can receive individual assistance in your home or office. With the rash of furniture store closings in the Bay Area, it's becoming more difficult for consumers to survey furnishing styles or choices in the marketplace as a basis for decision making. If you don't need the professional assistance you will not be charged if all you want to do is place your order. With this concept, overhead must be carefully controlled. Therefore all sales are final, no refunds or exchanges are allowed, and credit cards are accepted only on purchases of $50 or more. Payment in full must accompany orders up to $300 and an 80% deposit is required on orders exceeding $300. While these policies are not liberal, they are fairly standard for discount operations.

## EMPORIUM CAPWELL
## HOME CLEARANCE CENTER

1789 Hillsdale Ave., San Jose 95129. Phone: 408-265-1111. Hours: M-F 10am-9pm, Sat 10am-6pm, Sun Noon 5pm. Purchases: Cash, check, Store Charge. Parking: Lot.

The really sharp consumer will watch the San Jose "Mercury" ads for the frequent 4-day specials when the bargains become 'super buys'. With 28,000 sq. ft. of floor space you'll have a good selection of furniture for every room in the house, plus area rugs, accessories and household linens. The merchandise is sent to the clearance center from all the stores in Northern California. These are floor samples, some slightly damaged, some discontinued, etc. You can be sure of getting more than your dollars' worth, with discounts of 30-60% off retail all the time. Delivery costs extra. This is one of the largest clearance centers in the Bay Area.

## FOSS ANNEX

1326 E. 12th St., Oakland 94601. Phone: 534-4133. Hours: M-F 9:30am-5pm. Purchases: Cash, check. Parking: Street.

*The Foss Annex* is located right next to the *Foss Factory*, a company that has been in business for 60 years making some of the finest lampshades you can buy. Their customers are usually interior decorators (shopping for their clients), hotels, restaurants, and prestige home furnishing stores. They've been entrusted with the job of restoring and replacing shades for places as famous as the Hearst Castle.

Occasionally something goes wrong in the factory; an imperfection in fabric, finishing, construction, or patterns becomes evident on the final inspection. These "misfits" are sent to the annex, where less fickle people like you or me will delight at marked-down prices. Since all Foss shades are handmade, even outlet prices may seem high until you consider the level of craftsmanship and original pricing. You can spend from $6 to $50. Be sure to bring your lamp in with you (you wouldn't buy a hat without trying it on). On floor lamps just bring in the measurements of the reflector bowl. Pick up a simple basic shade, then jazz it up with some of their trims.

## GRANTREE
3530 Stevens Creek Blvd., San Jose 95117. Phone: 408-248-3344. Hours: M-F 10am-9pm, Sat 10am-6pm, Sun 11am-5pm. Purchases: VISA, MC. Parking: Free lot.

**Other Stores:** 771 Jackson St., Hayward, 881-7744; 3274 Sonoma Blvd., Vallejo, 707-554-2502.

*GranTree* has nine stores in the Bay Area that specialize in providing rental furniture for home or office situations. At three of these showrooms, rental furniture that has been 'retired' from their rental stock is marked down for sale. Many pieces of furniture have a well-used appearance, while others are still quite new looking. Prices are usually about half of what they would have cost if purchased new and prices are related to the condition of the piece. Rental furniture is not what it used to be. Although there is a selection of what I call 'budget motel modern', there is also more traditional, more expensive, and better quality furnishings that will impress even the snootiest shopper. Often you can find good buys on the overstocks of commercial firm mattresses: a double mattress and box spring might be sold for as little as $79. The desks for offices usually sell for $100-$300. There are no returns, so choose carefully.

## KING STREET FURNITURE FAIRE
128 King Street, San Francisco 94107. Phone: 495-5907. Hours: M-Sat 10:30am-5pm. Purchases: Cash, Check. Parking: Street.

Have you ever wondered what happens to the furniture at manufacturers' and decorators' showrooms like the *Furniture Mart* or *Showcase* when its purpose has been served? A lot of it ends up here. This large warehouse store is full of one-of-a-kind, fine quality furnishings—the same furniture you see in those beautiful home furnishings magazine spreads. Because most pieces are unique and high-priced to begin with, the 30-50% savings may still reflect what some would consider a hefty price. There are sofas, chairs, area rugs, wall units, some lamps, graphics, and on the day I stopped in, a preponderance of butcher block tables and bentwood chairs. This is not a typical department store selection of furniture—far from it—and that's precisely what I liked about it. Here's your chance to pick up a really unique piece of furniture. With these price reductions, of course, delivery is extra and all sales are final.

## LAMPSHADE OUTLET
22-E Commercial Blvd., Novato 94947. Phone: 883-1175. Hours: Tues-Sat 10am-4:30pm (Call ahead). Purchases: Cash or Check. Parking: Lot.

This distributor sells lampshades to the public from their warehouse at 20% off retail. Come prepared with your lamp, but not your old lampshade. In their selection you'll find drums, empires, cylinders, clip-ons, bridge and floor shades in a wide variety of sizes, fabrics and colors. Some shades are plain or casual, some have trims. They have washable, silk and pleated shades as well. Prices range from $3-$50 on most of their shades with a few better shades near $100. They also repair lamps with very reasonable charges for the basic rewire, new socket and harp repairs. You can find their warehouse by locating the industrial park just north of Hamilton Air Force Base in the Ignacio area, also near the Marin County SPCA.

## LAWRENCE CONTRACT FURNISHERS
(See **Carpeting**)

## MACY'S FURNITURE CLEARANCE PLACE
5160 Stevens Creek Blvd., San Jose 95129. Phone: 248-6343. Hours: M-F 10am-9pm, Sat 9:30am-6pm, Sun Noon-5pm. Purchases: Cash, check, Macy's charge. Parking: Lot.

**Other Store:** 567 Floresta Blvd., San Leandro.

*Macy's Furniture Clearance Place* is where you'll find furniture and appliances for 20-40% off. Some pieces are purchased just for *Clearance Place* (budget lines never found in *Macy's* regular stores); others are buyers' mistakes, distressed or damaged goods, department store overstocks, and discontinued models or lines. You can shop for almost any room in your home for furnishings, appliances, and entertainment needs. Delivery is extra and you'll want to look your selection over carefully, since all sales are final. You can use your *Macy's* charge account to arrange special terms.

Their linen department, which occupies a space at the back of the store, is where I have found good buys on sheets, towels, comforters, bedspreads, bath rugs etc. When all these discontinued lines, broken lots and leftovers arrive here from the 16 other stores they are priced below cost. By this time *Macy's* wants them sold and out of their warehouses where space is always in demand. Ann Klein, Halston, Vera, Calvin Klein, Martex, Wamsutta linens are among the fine quality brands sold at these rock bottom, last chance prices. Imagine: a designer king sized sheet for $8.00! Often the case during the frequent special sales advertised in the San Jose "Mercury."

Each clearance center now has a large department of family clothing that is sent from their retail stores. While prices are drastically marked down, it's obvious that these fashions have been on racks for a long time.

## NATIONAL SOFA BED AND MATTRESS CO.
2328 Telegraph Ave., Oakland 94612. Phone: 444-2112. Hours: M-Sat 9am-6pm. Purchases: BA, MC. Parking: Street, free lot.

You'll find good values in furniture and appliances at *National*. To start with, here is a great way to get a good-quality Simmons mattress at savings up to 50% off. There are usually many slightly irregular factory seconds or mismatched sets to choose from. The defects or flaws are carefully explained to you when you are making a selection. They also have first-quality mattresses, as well as an extensive selection of sofa beds and recliners.

Savings on nationally advertised name-brand recliners and sofa beds are 25% off. I recognized some truly worthwhile savings on this good-quality name-brand furniture. Each piece has two prices, the lowest representing the special values offered by this company. If you have shopped around you will recognize the savings available. Most sales will include free delivery.

*National* has a complete G.E. appliance department, all with gratifying discount prices. Finally, they are an excellent resource for carpeting from name brand manufacturers.

## NIGEL'S
1450 Franklin Street, San Francisco 94109. Phone: 776-5490. Hours: M-F 10am-5:30pm, Sat 10am-4pm. Purchases: BA, MC, VISA. Parking: Validated, Sutter Place Garage.

It's rather hard to comparison shop imported oriental furniture but I feel *Nigel's* offers far better values, dollar for dollar, than stores selling comparable quality furniture in the Chinatown and downtown areas that cater to the tourist trade. The showroom has a beautiful selection of dining, living, and bedroom furniture, as well as occasional pieces in a choice of natural or dark rosewood. All sofas and chairs are offered in a choice of fabrics. I was particularly impressed that the backs of all cabinet pieces are finished and need not be pressed up against the wall. I also found the owners to be very knowledgeable and helpful!

## PACIFIC FURNITURE RENTAL
600 50th Ave., Oakland 94601. Phone: 533-3700. Hours: M-F 9:30am-6pm, Sat 9:30am-5:30pm. Purchases: MC, VISA. Parking: Lot.

You can't complain about the prices on the used rental furniture for sale in the back room. Club chairs for $69.95, sofas for $129, and loveseat combinations in herculon plaids for $359, roll-away beds for $59.95, $99 for a kitchen table with four chairs and on and on. Some furnishings look a little worse for the wear. Most is utilitarian and very much in keeping with the conventional image of rental furniture.

## RONEY'S FURNITURE

14000 Washington Ave., San Leandro 94578. Phone: 352-1175. Hours: M-Sat 10am-6pm. Purchases: BA, MC, VISA. Parking: Lot.

Many of my friends will be distressed to see this listing because they've considered *Roney's* "their special place" for years. They will not welcome competition from new buyers over the amazing assortment of freight-damaged merchandise that *Roney* collects direct from local railroad and trucking companies. Although *Roney's* has a little of everything at super bargain prices, I'm most intrigued by his furniture selection. The selection includes low-priced budget lines to topnotch companies. I've seen Ethan Allen pieces on his floor as well as Henredon and Drexel. Damaged pieces are often expertly repaired to like-new conditions or left as is and priced accordingly. These prestige pieces are snatched up pretty fast, which is why people become *Roney* regulars, stopping in often to see what's new. I've often been amused to see a stack of tires next to a fancy dining room hutch—but that's why *Roney's* is such fun. It's really impossible to list the different kinds of merchandise sold here, but it's worth a visit. Delivery is extra and you can save even more than the 30-60% off by carting it home yourself.

## SAUSALITO DESIGN CLEARANCE CENTER

1301 Folsom Street (corner 9th St.), San Francisco 94103. Phone: 431-2225. Hours: Sat 10am-6pm, Sun Noon-6pm. Purchases: MC, VISA. Parking: Street.

*Sausalito Designs* has eight stores in the Bay Area that specialize in contemporary home and office furnishings. Their clearance center is located in their Folsom Street warehouse store and is only open weekends. Prices are generally 50% or more off their regular retail prices. The merchandise encompasses a variety of discontinued floor samples, one-of-a-kind items, manufacturers' closeouts and slightly damaged as-is merchandise. All sales are final and delivery is provided at an additional charge. I was impressed with the prices on their sofas, chairs, sleepers, occasional tables, lamps, desks and file cabinets. You'll definitely want to 'scout' the clearance center from time to time.

## SEARS FURNITURE OUTLET

1936 West Ave.—140th St., San Leandro 94577. Phone: 357-6622. Hours: T-Sat 9am-4:30pm. Purchases: Cash, check, store charge. Parking: Lot.

**Other Store:** Sacramento.

*Sears'* warehouse in San Leandro has a showroom which has (slightly) freight-damaged and returned furniture for sale at reduced prices. The customer returns have been reconditioned, and all bedding has been sterilized. There is usually a selection of more than 50 large appliances and televisions (your best buys here), and a smaller group of furniture, upholstered pieces, and mattresses. There are also accessory items, such as tables, also building supplies (doors, heaters, central air conditioners, floor covering, and fencing). The *Sears* warranty applies to all appliances purchased. You must pay for delivery—so, if you can, bring a truck.

## SOFA BEDS LTD.
7190 Regional Street, Dublin 94566. Phone: 828-2401. Hours: M-F 10am-9pm, Sat 10am-6pm, Sun Noon-5pm. Purchases: MC, VISA. Parking: Lot.

There's no fancy merchandising evident here, instead their aim is to provide as extensive a selection as possible in the space allowed. Their basic concept is to make a profit through volume sales rather than high mark-ups. Therefore, you can expect to save 25-40% on sofa-beds from approximately twelve major manufacturers. The best buys are on sofabed and loveseat combinations and sectional sleeper combinations. They concentrate on offering a wide selection in fabrics and styles on medium priced pieces that become terrific bargains when the discount is applied. The average price is somewhere around $450, with many good buys for far less and a smaller selection of higher end goods often acquired through special purchases from the *Furniture Mart Showrooms*. Some pieces are just right in the anonymity of the back bedroom, others formal enough for the living room, and most are perfect for the casual living or heavy use in a family room. For a really custom selection they will special order and extend a dis-

count that may not be as great as in stock merchandise, but is still worthwhile. Delivery charges are minimal.

## TRADEWAY STORES WAREHOUSE
(See **Carpets/Floorcoverings**)

# Baby Furniture New & Used

## BABYLANDIA
6340 Mission St., Daly City 94014. Phone: 992-1750. Hours: M-S 10am-6pm. Purchases: MC, VISA. Parking: Street.

*Babylandia* just keeps getting better. Originally only used baby furniture, equipment and clothing were sold, and they still are. But now you can pick up new clothing for infants and children in infant sizes through size 12 for 20% off. (These are samples.) The new furniture is also discounted to be very competitive with similar operations. Many people have bought used furniture from them and then turned around at a later date and sold it back to *Babylandia*. If you're looking for a particular item, call ahead to check availability.

## BABY FURNITURE UNLIMITED
518 Tamalpais Drive (Madera Park Shopping Center), Corte Madera 94925. Phone: 924-3764. Hours: M-Sat 10am-5pm, Sun Noon-4pm. Purchases: Cash or check.

**Other Store:** 1029 First St., Novato, 892-2644.

There is hardly room to navigate around the crowded floor which is jammed with 'quality' reusable baby furniture and equipment. Starting with very basic needs, i.e. cribs, play pens, high chairs, strollers etc., they also have some unusual items like wicker bassinets, baby carriers, and snuggle pouches. You don't have to be 'truly needy' to appreciate the racks of clothing for infants, children, and the expectant mom. Most of the clothing is used, but in very good condition. Keep in mind that while they're primarily interested in selling goods, in order to do this they are buying all the time: so if you're not interested in buying, maybe you've got something to sell. The Corte Madera store is tucked discreetly at the back of the shopping center, just keep looking and you'll find it.

## CRIBS AND BIBS
118 El Portal Center, San Pablo 94806. Phone: 237-4927. Hours: M-Sat 9:30am-5pm. Purchases: MC, VISA. Parking: Lot.

Sensible parents realize that 'little ones' do not need everything brand new, and that quality reusable furniture can take the sting out of providing for the new addition. This store is trying to maintain an inventory of cribs, playpens, strollers etc., but to supplement this, they also sell new baby furniture at a nice discount. They've added a clothing department with 'like new' merchandise (they're very picky) for infants-21 and maternity clothing in all sizes. They will take your name and let you know when new (old) merchandise arrives.

## FACTORY OUTLET (NEW KID IN TOWN)
344 139th Ave., San Leandro 94578. Phone: 352-1778. Hours: M-F 8am-4pm. Purchases: MC, VISA. Parking: Street.

For absolutely charming baby and shower gifts you can't top the selection of infant accessories and carriers manufactured in this out-of-the-way factory off Washington Ave. Using extra heavy cotton duck and 100% cotton calico prints the baby carriers with or without hoods, matching diaper bags, infant seat covers, bib sets, and zip totes are discounted 30-60%. The discount price varies according to the classification. They may be discontinued fabrics, slightly irregular, or overruns. Sample pieces are on display in the very small reception room and then merchandise is pulled from the back when you place your order. They will send catalogs on request and it's possible to order by mail, however, you'll pay shipping.

## LOU'S BABY FURNITURE
221 Willow Ave., (½ block off Meekland) Hayward 94541. Phone: 581-6082. Hours: TWFS 9:30am-5:30pm, Th 9:30am-9pm. Purchases: BA, MC, VISA.

This is a most unconventional store. Years ago when this family wanted to get started in business they didn't rent a store downtown; instead they cleared out their garage and put up a sign. Their garage is now a small warehouse located behind the family home. Low overhead, no frills, and no advertising accounts for the low,

low prices. All the major brands of fine-quality furniture are available—everything for babies' needs except clothing and toys. Simmons, Lullaby, Strolee, Peterson, Childcraft and Hedstrom are among the brands represented in cribs, play pens, high chairs, dressers, infant seats, etc. All those hard-to-find repair parts will keep your furniture going through several children. They also have good values on used furniture. They accept trade-ins and lay-aways and also rent furniture.

# Unfinished Furniture

## DECOR
3677 Stevens Creek Blvd., Santa Clara. Phone: 984-8188. Hours: M-F 9:30am-9pm, Sat 9:30am-6pm, Sun Noon-5pm. Purchases: BA, MC, FN. Parking: Lot.

**Other Stores:** 1889 W. San Carlos St., San Jose; 910 El Monte, Mt. View.

*Decor* has a tremendous selection of new unfinished furniture waiting for some loving hands to apply the finishing touches. Unfinished furniture stores are very competitive as far as prices go, but I think *Decor* has an edge because they are high-volume dealers and can get by with a smaller mark-up. Their newspaper ads in Peninsula and San Jose areas always feature some intriguing bargains.

The assortment of furniture is unbelievable; you could furnish an entire house. I especially like the selection of cubes and modules, great for storage walls or displays. Maple, birch, oak, hemlock, ramin, mahogany, redwood, poplar, beech, pine, and even pressed board are there for you to choose from. Of course, harder woods do cost more, but there is a wide range of quality and price in their selection. All the finishing materials are here too—oil, stain, antiquing kits, etc. For the novice there's expert advice (no charge for this). There is a small delivery charge. Be smart and bring your van!

## NEW ERA UNFINISHED FURNITURE
4920 Telegraph Ave., Oakland. Phone: 653-3003. Hours: M, Th 9:30am-8:30pm; T, W, Sat 9:30-5:30pm; Sun 11am-5pm. Purchases: BA, MC, VISA. Parking: Street.

*New Era* is one of the best ones in the East Bay for unfinished furniture. Not only is their selection unusual, but their prices are very good. I particularly liked the particle board cubes that are great for making storage walls in bedrooms or family rooms. *New Era* seems to be a "human" place where if there is anything you don't like about what you've bought, they'll fix it or take it back—pleasantly. They also deliver free on purchases over $40 in the East Bay.

# Warehouse Sales

*Capwell's, The Emporium, Macy's* and *Liberty House* all have major warehouse sales 2-3 times a year. The reason is obvious. Space is a problem in their warehouses just as it is in your closet at home. These sales are well advertised in all major Bay Area newspapers, usually accompanied with maps to lead you directly to these sites, far removed from the retail stores, most often located in some obscure industrial area. At these sales the major emphasis is on clearing out the hard lines of merchandise, i.e. furniture, appliances, and boxsprings, etc. However, accessories, remnant rugs, linens, and housewares are usually sold too.

If you want first crack at the sale merchandise, you'd better bounce out of bed early on those week-end mornings. There are so many one-of-a-kind items, priced so low, that you can't afford to dally. All sales are final. Usually delivery is extra, so if you want to save even more, borrow a pick-up from a friend and forget the delivery charge.

# Catalog Discounters

When it comes to buying new furniture for your home or office, the catalog discounters offer the best alternative to high retail prices. The businesses I have listed are all similar in that they take a lower mark-up, elimi-nate costly services, and usually don't advertise. Since their businesses are maintained on referrals and repu-tation alone, it is significant that they can be so suc-cessful without advertising. (You wouldn't send a friend to a place you'd been dissatisfied with.) Some of these places have no furnishings at all on their showroom floors; some have quite a lot. Most of their sales are from manufacturers' catalogs. Buying furniture this way will usually enable you to save from 20-40%. You'll pay for freight and delivery one way or another, whether they quote just one price or a breakdown on the costs. Most do not have credit plans other than Mastercharge or VISA.

## BARNAL FURNITURE CO.

111 Minna Street, San Francisco 94105. Hours: M-F 9:30am-5:30pm, Sat 10am-3pm. Purchases: Check, BA. Parking: Difficult.

This small furniture store is tucked away in an alley type street between Mission and Howard. They contend that there are 30% discounts on bedroom, dining room, living room, draperies, lamps etc.; 25% savings on mattresses, Hide-a-Way Beds. Carpets are *their* cost plus $1.00 a yard. Appliances, TV's, stereos, etc., are cost plus 8%. Most merchandise is special ordered because their showroom is very limited in selection.

## CONTRACT DESIGN CENTER

1985 San Ramon Valley Blvd., San Ramon 94583. Phone: 838-8330 or 838-1772. Hours: M-F 9am-5pm, Sat 9am-4pm. Purchases: MC, VISA. Parking: Lot.

Southern Alameda County and Contra Costa residents can buy all their furniture closer to home now at discount prices. Except for the prices, service approximates that of other retail stores. Their showroom is notable for the many fine quality furniture groupings in the moderate to higher price ranges. Furniture is discounted 20-30% which *does not* include freight and delivery. Wallpaper from any book is 25% off, wood shutters are 30% off, and upholstery and drapery fabrics are 20% off. Other areas covered are vinyl flooring, window coverings, lamps, patio furniture and mattresses. The carpet selection is very extensive with the most prestigious lines represented. Appropriately, their prices are very low! Naturally, if they don't have just what your heart desires on their showroom floor you can refer to, and order from their many catalogues representing some of the most highly regarded and well known manufacturers. All furnishings in the store are tagged with the retail price and the discount price is provided by the sales personnel. Phone quotes will be given, how nice.

## DEOVLET & SONS

1660 Pine Street, San Francisco 94109. Phone: 775-8014. Hours: M 8am-9pm, T-Sat 8am-6pm. Purchases: BA, MC. Parking: Validated parking, Union 76 Station at Pine & Franklin.

This store has been around for a long time and for good reason. The children of their original customers are returning to get the same good values and prices that their parents received 20 years ago. *Deovlet* has three floors of furniture. They appear to be energy conscious; you have to have someone turn on the lights of the second and third floor if you expect to get a good look at the bedroom, dining, breakfast and living room furnishings. They have very moderately priced goods in upholstered lines, better quality in case goods (bedroom and dining) and many major lines of appliances. Their carpet selection is somewhat limited but their prices are right on what they carry. Don't be shattered by those retail prices . . . they're just for show. You can count on a 25-30% discount when it comes to writing out the check.

## DOMICILE

911 Sir Francis Drake Blvd., Kentfield 94904. Phone: 454-7881. M-Sat 10am-4:30pm. Purchases: BA, MC. VISA. Parking: Lot.

Furniture, wallpaper, carpeting, vinyl and hardwood flooring, drapery and upholstery fabrics, custom bedspreads, accessories, window shades and blinds, are sold for 20-40% discounts at *Domicile*. The racks of samples and shelves of catalogs can be unnerving at first glance. The furniture selection is small but choice. Most customers special order with a 50% deposit, balance due on delivery. Delivery and freight are extra.

I've noticed that they are very gracious about lending samples and they're equally helpful in assisting with selections. *Inneroffice* at the same address in their downstairs showroom provides service to professionals, doctors, etc. in their office furnishing needs, selling at 30-40% off retail. Professional lay-out and design is available on a fee basis.

## DUNNIGAN FURNITURE CO.

943 Columbus Ave., San Francisco 94133. Phone: 673-7990. Hours: M-F 9am-4:30pm, Sat and eves by appointment. Purchases: BA, VISA. Parking: Street.

The name is slightly misleading, since there is no furniture on display, only a large selection of catalogs of name-brand furniture, appliances, TV's, carpets, and draperies. You will save 25-30% on most orders, including freight and delivery charges. Since every item is a special order, there are no returns or exchanges. Bob Dunnigan, a businessman of long experience, gives personal, reliable service and will stand behind his merchandise. Business is on a cash basis, although VISA is accepted on orders over $150. Long-term credit can be arranged through a nearby bank. A deposit is required with your order.

## EASTERN FURNITURE CO. OF CALIF. INC.

1231 Comstock Street, Santa Clara 95050. Phone: 248-3772. Hours: M, T, Th 9:30am-9pm. W, F, Sat 9:30am-5:30pm. Purchases: MC, BA. Parking: Lot.

Upon entering this store which is right off the Central Expressway you'll be greeted by a receptionist. She will provide you with a salesman who will familiarize you with the showroom. There is a good selection of home furnishings including sofas, chairs, bedroom, formal dining, tables, mattresses, and even grandfather clocks. (No carpets or draperies sold here.) All are in the moderately priced lines. Don't be taken back by the price tags, which may not reflect the bargain prices you expect; you'll pay about 30% less. The styles are mostly traditional and you can choose from the floor selection or from their catalogs. This isn't the place to shop for those sleek contemporary styles. They ask you to be discreet about their prices. It's unfortunate that stores often have their lines jeopardized by the unthinking customer who quotes their prices to other retail stores. Let's not ruin a good thing!

I've been told that to shop here you need a membership card or referral. Check with them to see if your company is on their list, or call them to inquire about your shopping privileges.

## FRENCH BROS.

1850 Market Street, San Francisco 94102. Phone: 621-6627. Hours: M 9:30am-9:00 pm, TWTHF 9:30am-6pm, Sat 9:30am-4pm. Purchases: Cash, check. Parking: Street and Lot.

If it weren't for the sign right at the edge of the parking lot you might never find this furniture store. When you reach the door and see the stairs leading to the showroom, you marvel at the success of such an unconventional location. *French Bros.* has been in business in San Francisco for 25 years. They are an excellent resource for appliances, home furnishings and carpeting. Their showroom has a modest selection of upholstered goods in a moderate price range, and then you have their catalog resources to further extend the selection. I found all their salespeople to be friendly, helpful and knowledgeable. They can special order many lines of furnishings with a deposit and the balance on delivery.

## GALLERY WEST

1501 Bryant St. (3rd Floor), San Francisco 94103. Phone: 861-6812. Hours: Tues-Sat 9am-5pm. Credit cards accepted. Financing available. Parking: Private lot.

*Gallery West* has a large showroom with many traditional groupings of furniture. Combined with their gracious service and considerable expertise you're shopping excursion should result in complete satisfaction. Like others they compliment their showroom selection with many catalog resources and samples from leading manufacturers of sofas, chairs, bedroom and dining room furnishings, occasional tables, lamps, accessories, draperies, and window coverings, carpeting, vinyl and hardwood flooring, appliances and TV's. In short, they provide one-stop shopping. Their prices usually reflect a discount of 25-30% off the prices of conventional retail stores, and their appliances are sold for 'their' cost, plus 10%. Delivery is extra.

Most lines of furniture in their selection fall into the mid-to-higher priced ranges associated with better quality. Before delivery, each order is uncrated and carefully inspected. They offer a complete design service at no extra cost when combined with major purchases. *Gallery West* works closely with many employee groups providing cards of introduction. Check with your employee credit union, personnel office or employees club to see if arrangements have been made for your group and, if not, suggest they be made.

## HOMEWORKS

370—Suite C, Park Blvd., Moraga 94556 (Rheem Shopping Center). Phone: 376-7750. Hours: Tues-Sat 10am-4:30pm. Purchases: BA, MC, VISA. Parking: Street.

This store in Moraga provides convenient shopping for Contra Costa shoppers. The store is small, more like a decorator's studio, but the resources for home furnishings are extensive. You can order carpeting, vinyl and hardwood flooring, drapery and upholstery fabrics, shutters, wallpapers, furniture and accessories from their samples and catalogs. Savings range from 20-40% off retail prices, depending on the price they can get. Delivery and freight are extra. They request a 50% deposit with the order and the remainder on delivery. The store is located at the back of the building next to a children's shop.

## HOUSE OF KARLSON

351 9th St., San Francisco 94103. Phone: 863-3640. Hours: M-Sat 9am-5pm. Purchases: Cash or Check. Parking: Free at 445 9th St.

This store offers good savings on your home furnishing needs—sofas, chairs, bedroom and dining room furniture, TV's, and accessory items. They carry a large inventory of special purchases on rolls of carpet that were overstocked by leading manufacturers. Savings are impressive. Because they are located in a low-rent district, they are able to pass on substantial savings to their customers. 'Preferred customers' are extended 20-30% off on their purchases. (I'm not really sure how they determine whether you will be extended preferred customer privileges, though I was told that members of many business firms or large companies qualify. Be sure to inquire to see if you do, too.)

The *House of Karlson* is a full service store. Most brands in the medium to upper quality price range are carried or can be special ordered for you. Their showroom has furniture beautifully displayed in room-type settings.

## HOUSE OF VALUES

2565 So. El. Camino Real, San Mateo. Phone: 349-3414. Hours: M-Sat 9:30am-5:30pm, Evenings M & F 7pm-9pm. Purchases: BA, MC. Parking: Street.

It seems like *House of Values* has swallowed up several stores on this block. Just when I think I've seen every-thing I'm directed out the door and down the street to their next showroom. Many people reported on their outstanding selection and savings offered. I have to agree after comparison shopping their merchandise. Although they sell no carpeting or draperies, their in-store selection of fine quality dining room, bedroom, and living room furniture is quite extensive. You can save 30% and also have immediate delivery of your preference. They will also custom order furniture if they don't have the pieces you want.

## HOUSE OF LOUIE
(See **Appliances**)

## LAWRENCE CONTRACT FURNISHERS
(See **Carpets and Floorcoverings**)

## MASTERMART

2919 El Camino Real, San Mateo 94403. Phone: 345-5271 or 341-3246. Hours: M-S 9am-6pm, evenings by appt. Purchases: VISA, MC. Parking: Street.

Their cost plus 10% is the inducement for many customers who've done business with this small store. They quote one price which includes all services, freight and delivery. Basically a custom catalog operation, I'd suggest that you shop around first because they have only a few pieces of furniture to show. They also sell appliances and carpets, mini blinds, shutters and wood shades.

Once you've bought your new furniture, talk to them

about buying your old stuff. They own a used furniture store and would be willing to add your furnishings to their selection.

## MILLBRAE FURNITURE COMPANY
1781 El Camino Real, Millbrae 94030. Phone: 761-2444, 344-6782, 589-6455. Hours: T, Th 10am-6pm, W, F, 10am-9pm, Sat 9am-5pm. Purchases: BA, MC. Parking: Street.

Three floors of furniture, appliances, carpets, draperies, TV's and stereo equipment make this a one stop resource for consumers. In their back room there are cabinets full of manufacturers' catalogues that provide additional resources for their customers. On most items the savings run about 30% off prevailing retail prices; however, appliances are 10% over cost. Like most discounters they don't advertise but do a steady business based on referrals.

## MONROE SCHNEIDER ASSOCIATES
(See **Carpets and Floor Coverings**)

## DAVID MORRIS CO.
253 So. Van Ness Ave., San Francisco 94103. Phone: 771-1376, 771-1377, 771-1378. Hours: M-Sat 9am-5:30pm. Purchases: MC. Parking: Street.

This small company is little more than "a hole in the wall," but it offers big savings on furniture, appliances and especially carpeting. Scotty Morris is a real whiz at locating some of those hard-to-find franchise lines and items. They sell genuine Oriental rugs from Mainland China. By importing directly, they are able to offer savings of approximately 40% below downtown retail prices. You'll save 30% on almost all purchases, including freight and delivery. Everyone here is congenial. For those making large purchases, decorator assistance is available. A deposit is requested at the time the order is placed with the balance on delivery. Their prices are guaranteed to be the lowest obtainable anywhere; or they will refund the difference on any item that can be bought for less elsewhere thirty days from date of purchase.

## NOREIGA FURNITURE
1455 Taraval (at 25th), San Francisco 94116. Phone: 564-4110. Hours: M, T, W, F 10am-5:30pm; Th 1pm-9pm; Sat 10am-5pm. Purchases: BA, VISA. Parking: Street.

*Noriega Furniture* is highly appealing for two things in particular: their beautiful showroom and their personable decorator consultants. Their specialty is expensive, high-quality furniture; you can order from their manufacturers' catalogs everything you could conceivably need to decorate your home—furniture, carpets, drapes, wallpaper, and beautiful accessories—at savings of at least 20% and as much as 30%. *Noriega Furniture* stresses quality and in doing so everything is inspected and serviced in their shop prior to delivery into your home. Appliances are available at a cost plus 10% basis. They ask that you stop by the showroom to get an idea of what you want, though their decorators will go to most Bay Area communities with samples. You deposit 25-30% of the total when you order, and pay the rest on delivery (delivery is included in the price). All sales are final—no returns. They can arrange financing for you too.

## PIONEER HOME SUPPLY
667 Mission St. (4th floor), San Francisco 94105. Phone: 543-1234, 781-2374. Hours: M-F 9:30am-5:30pm, Sat 10:30am-2pm. Purchases: Cash, check. Parking: Street or pay lot.

Informality is the order of the day—there are always two phone calls on hold and at least three people waiting to place their order—but no one seems to mind because the savings are worth waiting for.

The owners (they must have a last name but they're Sam and Lucille to everyone) have been in business for over 20 years on the strength of their reputation and referrals that pass from one satisfied customer to another. They have never advertised, and you'd have to be psychic to discover them on your own.

You can buy almost anything in home furnishings from their floor samples or catalog resources: sofas, chairs, bedroom and dining room, sofabeds, carpeting, also mattresses, appliances (only top-quality lines are carried in freezers, washers and garbage disposals, etc.), microwave ovens, TV's, vacuum cleaners and VTR's.

The price they quote includes freight and delivery, and reflects savings from 20-40% below retail depending on what is purchased. (Appliances are sold for the lowest mark-up that I've found so far.) You can order most merchandise with a deposit and the balance due on arrival if you're an established customer.

## PLAZA FURNITURE & APPLIANCE CO.
647 El Camino Real, South San Francisco 94080. Phones: 583-7050, 761-0866. Hours: M, T, Th, S 9am-6pm; W, F 9am-9pm. Purchases: VISA, MC. Parking: Street, lot.

You know after visiting this store that the entire staff has been in the business for a long, long time. Their experience shows as you discuss the merits of one piece of furniture over another, and which is the best value for the money you have to spend. I was particularly impressed with the selection of bedroom furniture for adults and children, although other types of furnishings are also well represented. The selection on display represents many moderate and higher-priced manufacturers. On the price comparisons I made, I would estimate you'll save 25% on almost all of your purchases except appliances. Here's what you can buy: sofas, chairs, tables, appliances, TV's, stereos, lamps, carpeting, and draperies. On many furnishings and appliances you get quick delivery if they have your choice on hand in their warehouse nearby. Of course, other selections ordered from their catalogs will take longer.

## WESTERN CONTRACT FURNISHERS

4400 Broadway, Oakland 94611. Phone: 652-3400. Hours: M-F 9am-5:30pm, Sat 10am-5pm. Purchases: BA, MC. Parking: Private lot.

**Other Stores:** 555 DeHaro, San Francisco, 861-3838; 175 Stockton, San Jose, 408-275-9600; 1508 Howe St., Sacramento, 916-927-2942; Carmel Valley, 408-624-0971.

*WCF* showrooms are simply beautiful. The furnishings displayed are the best and will appeal to people with discriminating taste and those who appreciate the best quality in home furnishings. However, if your budget is modest (starting out in your first home) you can still avail yourself of their facilities and good service.

Here is just a partial list of the types of merchandise you can order from approximately 2,500 catalogs they keep in their files: patio furniture, living, dining, bedroom, breakfast furnishings; mattresses; carpets and Oriental rugs; wallpapers; bedspreads; accessories; antique reproductions; upholstery and drapery fabrics. The list is endless. Regardless of the style—contemporary, traditional, Early American—their catalogs will provide the source and even after freight and delivery charges you'll still save approximately 30%. You have to pay in full when you place an order. You can use their bank financing plan, BA or MC. Of course, these options will cost you a little more.

To enable their salesmen to give you the best service, call in advance for an appointment, especially on Saturdays. There's no pressure here—something I like very much. Be sure to get on the mailing list for their semi-annual sales!

## JOHN R. WIRTH CO.

1049 Terra Bella, Mountain View 94043. Phone: 967-1212, 408-736-5828. Hours: Tues-Sat Noon-6pm, Thurs & Fri 7pm-9pm. Purchases: Cash or Check. Parking: Lot.

For years you could not get into *John Wirth's* showroom to do business unless you had a personal referral. That's why they were never listed in previous editions. Referred customers, it was thought, would understand that home furnishings must be paid for in full when ordered and also that credit card plans and credit cards were not accepted. South Bay and Peninsula residents who want to do business with *John Wirth's* have only to explain that they've read the "rules" in this book and there will be no hassle with referrals.

Serious buyers will want to check their showroom selection of mid-to-higher priced lines of furniture. The 1st floor showroom is well stocked with living room, dining room, bedroom, and patio furniture and accessories. Look for the special reductions on furnishings that have been marked to clear at less than wholesale prices. Upstairs you can spend hours pouring over wallpaper books, fabric swatches for draperies or upholstery, and an almost overwhelming selection of carpet, vinyl and hardwood flooring samples. They can handle any window covering or treatment, including shutters. If there's anything else you want in home furnishings, and it's not in their showroom, you can go to their catalog resource files for additional choices. Their sales staff is experienced and helpful, but not pushy. They'll even provide a cup of coffee while you plot and scheme how to spend your money. The prices on furnishings (including freight and delivery) are discounted from 20% on a small percentage of merchandise to a more likely 35% on the rest. They also pass on extra savings to customers when they participate in manufacturers authorized sales. You get their discount plus the manufacturer's discount. They do not give phone quotes. Take note of their atypical hours. Directions: Heading South on 101, take the Stierlin offramp West. Terra Bella is the first street on the left, go 1½ blocks.

**HARRY YOUNG & CO.**
Call for new address. Phone: 781-7010. Hours: M, W, Th, F 10am-6pm, Tues 10am-9pm, Sat 10am-5pm. Purchases: BA, MC. Parking: Street.

For years, *Harry Young* has been doing business with many members of Bay Area credit unions, but all customers are welcome. The atmosphere is relaxed, and like most discounters this store always seems to have more furniture than space to display it in. On most major brands of moderately priced furniture, you can save 25-30%. You can refer to one of their many catalogs for your purchases if the brand is not displayed in the store. Appliances are sold for cost plus 10% and on draperies and bedspreads you can save approximately 30%. Check here for TV's, stereos, vacuum cleaners, and carpeting. A deposit must be placed with your order and the balance on delivery. If you're on their mailing list you'll keep up with their biannual sales. Plan on waiting 8-12 weeks for items made in the East and Midwest.

# Office Furniture

(Also see **Furniture and Accessories—Catalog Discounters**)

**ARVEY PAPER CO.**
(See **Paper Goods, Stationery**)

**THE DESK DEPOT**
310 W. Evelyn, Mountain View 94041. Phone: 969-3100. Hours: M-S 9am-6pm. Purchases: BA, MC, VISA. Parking: Lot.

This place specializes in used office furniture. The selection is always changing depending on their sources. On the day I visited there was a large selection of metal desks (what I call California State modern) that an earthquake wouldn't dent. Prices were around $100, very reasonable for something almost indestructible, if somewhat plain in appearance. You can also buy chairs, coat trees, tab card files, chalk boards, school desks, wastebaskets, etc. They have some new office furniture at 20-40% off list prices.

## LAIRD'S DISCOUNT WAREHOUSE
(See **Paper Goods, Stationery**)

## REPO DEPO
1669 Bayshore Blvd., Burlingame 94010. Phone: 692-5000. Hours: M-F 9am-6pm, Th 9am-9pm, Sat 9am-6pm, Sun 12am-5pm. Purchases: BA, MC. Parking: Free lot.

**Other Store:** 1523 Parkmoor, San Jose, 408-294-3600.

*Repo Depo* specializes in repossessed office equipment of all kinds. They have bits and pieces of almost everything in stationery supplies, too. The many prizes in office equipment range from electronic calculators to safes, from typewriters in excellent condition to expansive walnut desks with matching chairs. The back room contains many slightly damaged pieces of furniture at 30-40% less than regular retail.

Much of their used merchandise is priced very well, although some items seemed a little high. Generally, however, you can be sure to save money here on most general office equipment and supplies. New office furnishings are 30% off retail. *Repo Depo* is specializing in telephone answering systems with all the appropriate interconnected accessories. They also have repossessed accounting systems, bookkeeping machines, word processing systems and other exotic electronic devices.

## RUCKER FULLER SOUTH—
## USED OFFICE FURNITURE
601 Brannan St., San Francisco 94107. Phone: 495-6895. Hours: M-F 8am-5pm, Sat 10am-2:30pm. Purchases: BA, MC. Parking: Lot.

This is the clearance warehouse for *Rucker Fuller*, a firm that deals in only the best brands of office furniture. Their biggest customers are large companies willing to pay the price for quality and durability. Samples and manufacturers' closeouts are sent to this warehouse from the main store. Here there is also a large selection of good-quality used furniture received as trade-ins. The savings on the samples and closeouts may range from 40% off retail to below cost. The used furniture is priced accordingly to condition and original price; you can expect to save from 40-60% off the original cost. All the defects or signs of wear are carefully pointed out to you by the manager who has had years of experience in this business.

# GENERAL MERCHANDISE

## Catalog Discounters

The catalog discounter can make shopping a super bargain finding time for you. Most of the catalog companies carry a representative sampling of merchandise and a few special items that you won't see in the others. Prices can vary, too; comparative shopping pays off in dollars if you take the time to check out all the catalogs before you buy. All catalog sales operations have the same basic policies: returns are accepted within a certain period of time; there are no layaways; every article is guaranteed as described in the catalog. Prices quoted in the catalog are subject to change, but are basically rock-bottom low. Some places require that you have their special shopping pass, claiming that they are wholesale only (sometimes the pass is available for the asking, or you may be able to get one where you work.)

**BEST PRODUCTS**
550 W. Hamilton Ave., Campbell 95008. Phone: 408-374-6630. Hours: M-F 10am-9pm, Sat 10am-6pm, Sun Noon-5pm. Purchases: Cash, check. Parking: Lot.

**Other Stores:** Citrus Heights, Colma, Mountain View, Newark, Pleasant Hill, Pleasanton, Sacramento, San Jose, So. San Francisco, Stockton.

*Best Products* claims to be the biggest consumer catalog company in the country. They have 74 showrooms throughout the U.S. with 10 stores in the Bay Area and more coming. Their 480-page catalog is the largest in the Bay Area; the prices are as good as the rest and better on some items. Sales are limited to cash and checks (keeps overhead down). All merchandise has the full manufacturer's warranty and all the best national brands are carried. 94% of the merchandise in the catalog is on display and available immediately at their stores. It pays to look for their Best special tags (limited time sales) and Clearance tags (discontinued catalog selections) when you're in the showroom.

It's to your advantage to obtain a *Best Products* catalog for $1 to become a preferred customer and be eligible for special sale opportunities. This catalog is a very good source for jewelry, sterling silver (30-50% off traditional store prices), and toys.

## CONSUMERS DISTRIBUTING

731 Market St. (at O'Farrell), San Francisco 94103. Phone: 777-2555. Hours: M-F 10am-7pm, Sat 10am-6pm, Sun Noon-5pm. Purchases: BA, MC. Parking: Lot. (at most locations).

**Other Stores:** Antioch, Campbell, Capitola, Colma, Concord, Dublin, Fairfield, Fremont, Hayward, Larkspur, Millbrae, Mountain View, Oakland, Pleasant Hill, Redwood City, Salinas, San Bruno, San Francisco, San Jose, San Mateo, San Pablo, San Rafael, Santa Clara, Sunnyvale, Terra Linda, Vallejo, Walnut Creek.

You don't have to wait for a sale to get a break! For really great savings, stop at one of the 28 *Consumer Distributing* catalog showrooms, which carry a complete stock of almost 5,000 first-quality name-brand items, including brands like Samsonite, Eastman Kodak, Spalding, Revere, and General Electric. The firm prepares its own catalogs of merchandise twice a year, and tries to hold the prices listed throughout the lives of the catalogs. After browsing in the catalog, the customer fills out an order blank and hands it to a clerk, then receives the merchandise on the spot.

*CD* will accept for exchange or refund merchandise returned in the condition in which you would like to buy it (that is, unused, complete, and in the original carton). In the event of any merchandise defect, the makers will honor their guarantees and warranties.

## SERVICE MERCHANDISE

2680 Union Ave., San Jose 95124. Phone: 408-371-3011. Hours: M-F 10am-9pm, Sat 10am-6pm, Sun Noon-6pm. Purchases: MC, VISA. Parking: Lot.

**Other Stores:** 39055 Cedar Blvd. (Mowry Plaza), Newark; 5553 Almaden Expressway (Almaden Plaza), San Jose.

The newest discount catalog store in the Bay Area, *Service Merchandise* is similar in operation to *Best Products* or *Consumer Distributing*. Same type of catalog, store layout, and coded prices.

## UNITY BUYING SERVICE

3491 Mission Oaks Blvd., Camarillo 93010. Phone: 805-484-2761 or 213-889-7121. Purchases: Check, money order. Hours: Mail order only.

To obtain this company's 484-page catalog you must first become a member of their buying service, which will cost you $6. Write to the address above for membership information. With the catalog discounters so readily available, you may wonder if the *Unity* catalog is necessary. I couldn't resist the urge to find out. Their catalog is much like those of all the other discounters; however, I was intrigued by the many items it has that the others don't, like garage door openers, heaters, tractors, and a wider selection of tools, all at very good prices. Ordering from *Unity* is more complicated than from the other discounters, because there is more involved: freight, service charges, tax, and insurance. But on many comparisons I made with merchandise from local catalogs, I found there were worthwhile savings on many, many items that ranges from 7-12% less, including all the extras. One large purchase would justify the $6 membership fee. With so many members (600,000) they have a lot of buying muscle; hence the great prices.

# Discount Stores

(Also see **Part II: Damaged Freight Outlets**)

You don't always have to drive miles out of your way to go bargain hunting. Throughout the Bay Area discount stores like *Payless, K-Mart, Gemco, Long's Drugs, Pay & Save, Value Giant,* and *Maximart* do a respectable job at pricing their merchandise lower than the full service retail stores. If you're in the habit of comparison shopping, and you can recognize a genuine sale price, you can do very well just by taking notice of the ads from these discount stores. Then, snap up those loss leaders they use as a lure to get you into the store. If you can resist buying non-sale merchandise at these times, you truly come out ahead. Books (hardcover and paperback), records, stationery supplies, paper goods, food products, plants, and small appliances are some of the best buys at these nearby, convenient discount stores. Don't overlook them!

**BETTER BUYS**
4615 Clayton Road, Concord 94521. Phone: 671-0828. Hours: M-Sat 10am-6pm, Sun Noon-5pm. Purchases: VISA, MC. Parking: Free lot.

**Other Store:** 15 Boyd Rd., Pleasant Hill, 932-6566.

You can really get hooked on this store which acquires merchandise through liquidations, factory overruns, bankruptcies, manufacturer's overstocks, freight salvage and closeouts. While they have a huge selection of merchandise, they may have only one or two of some items in stock. You don't go shopping here with a list; you peruse the selection and buy whatever is available that day at a good price, and then buy as much as you can. I really stocked up on cans of hearts of palm at 79¢ each; they had become an expensive treat at the regular price of $1.79. They tend to carry most types of merchandise that you find in grocery or drug stores, primary sources of their liquidated stock. Be sure to get on their mailing list for notice of special shipments. They do very little advertising, and who wants to miss out on these prices that are 30-70% off retail!

**COST PLUS IMPORTERS**
2552 Taylor St., San Francisco 94133. Phone: 673-8400. Hours: Daily 10am-6pm. Purchases: BA, MC. Parking: Good luck!

**Other Stores:** Hillsborough, Mountain View, Oakland, San Jose, Walnut Creek.

*Cost Plus* is the largest and probably the best-known importer in the Bay Area. Their largest store, near Fisherman's Wharf, has almost become a San Francisco landmark. All that, and it is still probably the best place in the entire Bay Area to save money on all kinds of imported goods! This main store is so large that it is now housed in three adjacent buildings. The main store (the one that started it all) contains a complete dish and glassware department, and sections for clothes, baskets, toys, cookware, and papergoods. Furniture, objects d'art, and a nursery are in the other buildings. Some people have practically furnished their whole home from *Cost Plus*. There are few amenities here. Sometimes it's so crowded and so difficult to find a parking place that it's exasperating. But the atmosphere and the bargains usually pay you back for the inconveniences.

## PIC 'N' SAVE
75 Weller Lane (Between Abel & Main) Milpitas 95035. Phone: 408-262-9967. Hours: M-Sat 9am-9pm, Sun 10am-7pm. Purchases: Cash or check.

**Other Store:** 510 Redwood St., Vallejo, 707-552-9214.

It isn't elegant or trendy and it doesn't even do much advertising, but this Southern California-based chain has shown it knows a few things about retailing. Unlike many retailers, who buy merchandise in normal distribution channels and then display it amid glossy promotions and carpeted coziness, *Pic 'n' Save* is strictly bargain-basement. It buys carloads full of so-called "close-out" merchandise and sells it at deeply discounted prices (40-70%) from pipe racks and cluttered shelves in austere, warehouse-like stores. Goods include such diverse items as candles, jewelry, linens, toys, books, housewares, giftwares and clothing. This is definitely not for snobs or the elitist, unless they're bargain hunters at heart. Much of their merchandise may not appeal to you when you shop, but when you find your particular "I can't wait to tell everyone" bargain, the whole outing is worthwhile. Once hooked, you'll be a regular customer!

## U-SAVE DISCOUNT OUTLET
75 Phelan, Bldg. No. 1, San Jose 95112. Phone: 408-295-5266. Hours: M 11am-4pm, Tues-F 10am-5pm, Sat 10am-4pm. Purchases: MC, VISA. Parking: Lot.

For people travelling through this area of San Jose it's worthwhile stopping by *U-Save* to see what the owners have scrounged from the marketplace. There is usually an eclectic selction of household goods, kitchen items, linens, some clothing, stationery, party supplies and other miscellaneous categories. These include discontinued lines, promotional goods and closeouts that the owners buy when the price is right. Discounts range from 20-50% off. Note: This is right around the corner from the *A-1 Linen Co.*

## THE WAREHOUSE
15 Dodie Street, San Rafael 94901. Phone: 456-5090. Hours: M-Sat 10am-5:30pm, Sun Noon-4pm. Purchases: Cash or check. Parking: Lot.

If you're going to be visiting the post office or Marin Surplus in San Rafael, go just a little bit further and size up the bargains at this small store which specializes in liquidated merchandise, close-outs and overruns. It has the atmosphere of a variety store and with the same types of merchandise, but the prices are much lower. This store falls in the category of "you name it, and we might have it" type. This can include stationery, toys, paper goods, hardware, pet foods, giftwares and at times, luggage, clothing and even athletic shoes. With markdowns of 40-70% it's worthwhile stopping when you find yourself in this part of town.

**THE WHOLE EARTH ACCESS STORE**
2990 7th St. (corner of Ashby & 7th), Berkeley 94710. Phone: 845-3000. Hours: M-Sat 9am-5:30pm, Sun 11am-5pm. Purchases: BA, MC. Parking: Lot.

This is the contemporary version of the general store. Their merchandise will appeal to people who are energy conscious and quality minded. In kitchen equipment, they carry the best brands in food mixers, grain mills, food processors, coffee grinders, espresso makers, electric dough makers, and a complete selection of cookware. These Kitchen Aid, Hamilton Beach, Krups, Foley and other brands are discounted according to the margin they have to work with. Discounts will range from 15-30% on all their merchandise. Their Henckel's cutlery is 25% off and their price on Kitchen Aid mixers was about the lowest around. Power and hand tools, wood burning stoves, tillers, windmills, even cameras, binoculars, Swiss Army knives and durable clothing fill the store. A comprehensive selection of books relating to the home, energy conservation, food preparation, cultivation and nutrition will provide hours of intriguing browsing. If you're tired of planned obsolescence, you owe it to yourself to check out the carefully selected quality merchandise that I've briefly described.

# Liquidators

(Also see **Part II, Damaged Freight Outlets**)

**CONSUMER'S DISTRIBUTING CLEARANCE CENTER**
1828 Norfolk (Parkside Plaza), San Mateo 94403. Phone: 345-8467. Hours: M-Sat 10am-6pm. Purchases: BA, MC. Parking: Private lot.

You can't be as big as *Consumers Distributing* and not have some "problem" merchandise. Damaged, defective, discontinued, overstocked and returned items all end up here at the clearance center next to regional headquarters. Their repair department rights the wrongs, and then the items are placed on display shelves to be sold. The savings here just boggle the mind, 25-35% off the catalog discount price! You can expect to find anything here that is featured in their catalog. The selection changes all the time. All sales are final.

## MONTGOMERY WARD DISTRIBUTION CENTER

3000 Alvarado St., San Leandro 94577. Phone: 357-7800. Hours: M-F 10am-9pm, Sat 10am-6pm, Sun 11am-5pm. Purchases: Cash, check, store charge. Parking: Free lot.

**Other Stores:** Richmond, Oakland.

This huge clearance center is where all catalog returns and discontinued, freight-damaged, and overstocked merchandise is sent. You can find just about anything that might be sold in their catalog from ankle socks to tractors. There are racks and bins of clothing and shoes, furniture, linens, carpets, home-improvement items, garden tools and equipment, TV's, appliances, etc. There is a 30-day guarantee on appliances or home entertainment items that are labeled "as-is" or freight-damaged. There is a delivery charge on this merchandise. Credit terms can also be arranged. Savings at the clearance center range from 10-50%.

*Ward's* has another store in Richmond at 211 Cutting Blvd., (just furniture and appliances). Their newest clearance center is located at the old *Montgomery Ward Store* at 2825 East 14th St., Oakland. It covers the whole first floor of this huge building and features a larger fashion selection than the San Leandro store, with some retail store returns in furniture and appliances plus a complete paint department.

# GIFTWARES

(Also see **General Merchandise—Catalog Discounters; Dinnerware and Accessories; Jewelry and Diamonds**)

**BLUEGATE CANDLE FACTORY OUTLET**
(See **Arts, Crafts, Hobby Supplies**)

**THE CANDLE SHOP**
(See **Arts, Crafts, Hobby Supplies**)

**CLASSY GLASS**
1310 A Fulton Ave., Sacramento 95825. Phone: 916-971-1118. Hours: M-F 10am-5:30pm, Sat 10am-5pm. Purchases: VISA, MC. Parking: Lot.

While this store is a little far afield for Bay Area shoppers, there are so few local stores that discount fine giftwares I felt I should give you the option to decide if a visit is warranted because only a few local stores discount fine glassware. Basically, *Classy Glass* scours the various wholesale trade shows and pounces on every opportunity to acquire samples, promotional merchandise and closeouts. They have also developed some very good connections with many well known manufacturers so that they buy their seconds and discontinued merchandise. All of these 'goodies' are discounted 10-60% in their store. They stock Arabia dinnerware and glassware plus sell most of the line for 42% off retail. Mikasa dinnerware is approximately 15% off; Toscany, Colony and J.G. Durand stemware are sold for discounts which are related to their own purchase price. You can buy lovely gifts in brass and copper. The owners will even ship merchandise if you give them merchandise that you're interested in. If you plan to visit, *Classy Glass* is in the Northeast section of Sacramento between Arden Way and Hurley Avenue.

## COST PLUS IMPORTERS
(See **General Merchandise**)

## CRESALIA JEWELERS
(See **Jewelry and Diamonds**)

## DANSK II
(See **Dinnerware and Accessories**)

## EDAR MANUFACTURING CO.
Hunter's Point Naval Shipyard, Bldg. 351 (4th floor), San Francisco, 94124. Phone: 822-2066 or 822-1199. Hours: Wednesday Only, 10am-3pm, or by appointment. Purchases: Cash or Check. Parking: Lot.

The Edar line is sold through fine stores and status catalogs. It is also sold at the factory located at Hunter's Point Naval shipyard. Their unique line of gifts are functional and attractive with distinctive covers using charming and sophisticated fabrics. Albums, telephone books, diaries, recipe files, gift enclosures, memo pads, legal pads, binders, clipboards, desk sets, paperback book covers, journals in parchment and portfolios provide many options for gift occasions. For travelers, their line of cosmetic cases and related accessories, are wonderful! When a fabric is discontinued or there is a product overrun prices are reduced 50-65% off original retail, important because at retail prices are somewhat expensive. If you must have something from the current line of merchandise you'll end up paying full retail.

Don't let the offbeat location deter you from a visit. From Fwy 101 North or South take the Army St. off-ramp, go East to the first stoplight and turn right on Evans. Follow Evans until it changes names to Isley and leads you right into the main gate. At the gate, you must stop and get a pass and directions to Edar which is only three minutes away. It's worth a trip!

## GALLERY ART GLASS—FACTORY OUTLET
4070 Halleck St., Emeryville 94662. Phone: 655-9200. Hours: M-F 1pm-4pm. Purchases: VISA, MC. Parking: Street.

Don't try to find this place without calling for directions. Halleck is not on the maps, but I can try to get you there. From Fwy. 80 in Emeryville, take the Powell St. offramp East, turn right on Hollis, right on Park, left on Halleck. Pray for a parking place. In the small front office of *Gallery Art Glass* the seconds, prototypes, and discontinued designs are sold from their line of stained glass wind chimes, sun catchers, ovals for window decoration, cache boxes and whatever else they may be producing. These stained glass decorative accessories are not inexpensive at retail because they are all hand made and hand leaded by one person. Your savings may range from 20%, but more likely 50% off retail. Price range at retail for most of their products is from $15-$80. They do not sell any raw materials, just finished products.

## GIFT EXCHANGE
3526 Geary Blvd., San Francisco 94118. Phone: 752-1208. Hours: T-Sat 10am-5pm. Purchases: Cash, check, trading stamps. Parking: Street.

This is one of America's unique stores—here's how it works. Take your unwanted but new and undamaged gift to the *Gift Exchange,* where they will determine the gift's current value based on their files of about 150,000 gift and houseware items. You may then select other items of equal value from their store display for a service charge of 20%.

For example, if your gift is worth $10, you select $10 worth of other items, and they charge you a service charge of $2. You may select items of higher value for the same service charge plus the difference. You may also use your credit at a later date; they will issue a credit slip.

The store includes an inventory of housewares, accessories, appliances, toys, paintings, leather goods, chinaware, silverware, toiletries, baby items, linens, and other items. The service charge and sales tax must be paid in cash or by check; they accept trading stamps.

If you have no gifts to exchange you still have a reason to shop here, since you'll receive 20% discount on any item in the store.

## HEATH CERAMICS AND STONEWARE
(See **Dinnerware and Accessories**)

## LUNDBERG STUDIOS
131 Marine View, Davenport 95017. Phone: 408-423-2532. Hours: M-Sat 10am-3:30pm. Purchases: MC, VISA. Parking: Street.

Davenport is little more than a wide spot in the road ten miles north of Santa Cruz on Hwy. 1. Jim Lundberg is the recognized leader in Tiffany art glass reproductions. His pieces sell in fine galleries and world renowned stores. At any one time there are usually 150 seconds in the studio which are discounted 50-75%. A Lundberg paper weight retails for about $85, a Tiffany lamp in the thousands! These seconds in lamps, paper weights, vases, crystal and glass perfumes, as well as tiles may have minor flaws, an off color, a pattern that was not pleasing to the artist, minute bubbles, or they may be simply discontinued. In exchange for the low seconds price you may have to forego *Lundberg's* prestigious signature on the piece. If you are a collector of art glass the trip to Davenport is worth your while.

**MARJORIE LUMM'S WINEGLASSES**
(See **Dinnerware and Accessories**)

**MASLACH ART GLASS
STUDIO & SECONDS STORE**
(See **Dinnerware and Accessories**)

**NOUROT GLASS STUDIO**
675 East H Street, Benecia 94510. Phone: 745-1463. Hours: Special sales 3 times a year. Purchases: Cash or check. Parking: Street.

If you would like to own a museum-quality piece of art glass that is individually crafted in the ancient tradition, be sure to get on the *Nourot* mailing list. Approximately three times a year, they have a sale for pieces that have slight imperfections, that may be experimental designs or are last year's works. Demonstrations of the hand-blown glassmaking are given during their sales and open houses. Their prices at retail are steep, but the quality of their designs is impeccable, and the sale prices that are reduced 50% make them more affordable. Works by the *Nourot Glass Studio* are included in the collection of the Corning Museum of Glass. Pieces from the studio are also shown in museum shops and contemporary art galleries across the country as well as in Europe and the Orient.

**PLASTIC PRODUCTIONS**
1270 Oddstad Drive (off Veteran's Blvd.), Redwood City 94063. Phone: 361-1133. Hours: M-F 9am-11am, 12:30pm-3pm. Purchases: Cash or check. Parking: Street or Lot.

Grainware, an expensive giftware line made from clear lucite, includes salad bowls, serving bowls, trays, buffet servers in many types and styles, and other bath and kitchen accessories. It is sold at *Plastic Productions* in a small clearance room next to the main office. Prices are reduced at least 50% on salesman's samples, discontinued styles and seconds of current products. This small outlet falls in the feast or famine category. One visit may prove very disappointing because the selection is so limited both in quantity and variety, while the next visit will provide more temptations than you can deal with. This company is located in an industrial park just across the street from the Redwood City Kaiser Hospital. Remember: they close for lunch!

**RODIN'S NEST SAMPLES 'N' SECONDS**
140 East Napa Street, Sonoma 95476. Phone: 707-996-4169. Hours: M-Sat 10am-5:30pm, Sun 11am-5:30pm. Purchases: MC, VISA. Parking: Street.

Going to the wine country? Then stop off at this delightful little shop that sells kitchenwares, giftwares, gourmet cooking accessories, small kitchen appliances, and kitchen linens for 30-60% off retail. You can save money because these are seconds, closeouts, or discontinued items and samples from gift shows.

## THE SECOND LOOK

510 Broadway, Seaside 93955. Phone: 408-899-4442. Hours: M-Sat 11am-5pm, Sun Noon-5pm. Purchases: VISA, MC.

Turn your next trip to the Monterey Peninsula area into a bargain hunting expedition by stopping in at this outlet for *Couroc* products. This line which is sold in better gift shops and department stores is unique for its hand inlaid designs which give each piece its own character. *Couroc* products include trays, glasses, and cheese boards. Even as seconds, the quality is good and the prices are ½ off first quality retail prices.

## R. STRONG SECONDS STUDIO

1235 4th St. (at Gilman), Berkeley 94710. Phone: 525-3150. Hours: M-F 9am-4pm. Purchases: MC, VISA. Parking: Street.

*R. Strong* is associated with a distinctive line of hand blown art glass and sculptured glass. In the seconds studio the vases, goblets, paper weights, perfume bottles are sold at wholesale. They may have slight flaws, may be somewhat irregular in conformation or size or may have been rejected from the regular line for esthetic reasons. Prices in the outlet range from $15-$150. I was particularly tempted by the large ornamental plates which are not only functional but would be lovely on display. When you go to the studio, ring the bell and wait a few minutes until someone opens the door.

## THRIFTY GOURMET

312 Town & Country Village, Mill Valley 94941. Phone: 388-COOK. Hours: M-F 10am-6pm, Sat 10am-5pm, Sun Noon-5pm. Purchases: MC, VISA. Parking: Free lot.

**Other Store:** 1862 El Centro, Napa, 707-257-2665.

The selection of fine quality gourmet cookware at *Thrifty Gourmet* is simply fantastic! The prices are 'rockbottom' because the owner has some terrific connections with many manufacturers and she also buys samples and closeouts from trade shows. Her locations, which are removed from the mainstream of Bay Area retail business, are ideal for those manufacturers who need to dispose 'discreetly' of their seconds, samples, closeouts, and overstocks.

Always prevalent in her selection is a large quantity of white ceramic platters, casseroles and soup toureens from a well-known manufacturer that are always discounted 50% whether perfects or seconds. In addition, you'll find copper cookware kitchen accessories discounted 40%, stainless steel pots and pans, wine coolers, picnic baskets, gadgets, coffee mugs, cookie jars, Cappucino makers, salt and pepper sets, knives, plastics and other gems all at 20-70% off. Obviously, the owner is buying 'right' to pass on such hefty discounts. The *Thrifty Gourmet* is a wonderful shop for weddings, anniversaries and birthday gifts. They don't gift wrap or have gift boxes for many items, a minor detail.

# Handbags

## GRIFFCO HANDBAG CO.
373 4th St. (Mezzanine), Oakland 94607. Phone: 444-3800. Hours: M-F 9am-5pm, Sat 9am-4:30pm. Purchases: Cash, check. Parking: Street.

For casual, genuine soft leather handbags, you'll never find a better buy than right here at the *Griffco Factory Store.* All the handbags are well made. Many are lined. You'll have 15-20 styles to choose from in several different colors. Most all the handbags are factory overruns and sell for approximately half the retail price. Factory prices range from $9.50-$29.00. The 2nds are priced even lower. To utilize all the scrap leather accumulated in the sewing room downstairs they've filled a showcase with coin purses, wallets, credit card holders, portfolios, and many other little leather accessories at good bargain prices. Another aspect of their business involves ladies and infants sandals made to fit. This outlet is off Broadway in the vicinity of Jack London Square.

# Jewelry and Diamonds

(Also see **General Merchandise**)

## AZEVEDO JEWELERS & GEMOLOGISTS, INC.
210 Post St. (3rd floor), San Francisco 94108. Phone: 781-0063. Hours: M-F 9:30am-5:30pm, Sat Dec. only. Purchases: VISA, AE, MC. Parking: Pay lots.

For substantial savings and a beautiful selection of diamonds, colored stones, gold jewelry and watches, this is a place well worth seeking out. *Azevedo Jewelers* has been in the same third floor location for more than 45 years. Their success is owed to low overhead, careful and selective buying, and referrals from satisfied customers. Appraisals are done by graduate gemologists. This is one of six A.G.S. stores in San Francisco.

## CRESALIA JEWELERS
278 Post St. (next to Gump's), San Francisco 94108. Phone: 781-7371. Hours: M-F 10am-5:30pm, Sat 10am-5pm. Purchases: AE, MC, VISA. Parking: Union Square Garage.

This store has been located on the second floor at 278 Post Street since 1912. It is evident that this is a very fine jewelry store when you alight from the elevator and enter the immaculate, luxuriously carpeted showroom full of gleaming displays of silver and showcases of fine jewels. There are no toasters or waffle irons, just the finest in jewelry and watches. You will also find a nice selection of silverware and dinner accessories here. The showroom will surely have just what you want right there on display.

Savings obtained here are substantial, with prices below the usual retail at other fine jewelry stores. (Because jewelry pricing is very complicated and varies from firm to firm, no hard-and-fast percentage can be quoted.)

In addition to sales, *Cresalia* has a complete gemological laboratory, managed by graduate gemologists from the Gemological Institute of America to help you in the choice of any diamond or gem, and to grade and appraise any jewelry you may already have.

### NIEDERHOLZER JEWELERS

140 Geary (4th floor), San Francisco 94108. Phone: 421-7871. Hours: M-F 9am-5:30pm, Sat 10am-2pm. Purchases: VISA, MC, and terms. Parking: Street, pay lots.

For many years this has been a resource where 'people who know' go for better quality jewelry at lower prices. The showroom on the 4th floor is just a block off Union Square. There are substantial savings on prestige brand watches, sterling silver flatware, hollow ware, personal gold and silver accessories, jewelry, diamond rings and rings or precious stones. The salespeople here are interested in customer satisfaction which means attentive service and fine quality merchandise.

### THE SMALL THINGS COMPANY

760 Market Street, Ste. 217 (Phelan Bldg.), San Francisco 94102. Phone: 397-0110. Hours: By appointment. M-F 10am-4pm, Sat Noon-5pm. Purchases: VISA, MC. Parking: Downtown lots.

The owner of this small company offers very special services and values. Her success is related to her 'connections'. Over the years she has canvassed the Bay Area as well as the markets in New York, Florida and Los Angeles to find out 'who has what' in the line of fine jewelry, and 'who' performs quality service for the best price. Her talent lies in finding maximum value for the best price, often 30-50% below prevailing retail. If you are interested in a special gift, whether it's pearls, lapis, jade, diamonds, precious gem stones, gold or silver, the owner will probably have it in stock or she will find it for you. Her files of catalogs, her inventory, her connections and her expertise all result in customer satisfaction.

If you need a watch repaired, pearls restrung, jewelry repaired or remodeled, custom design or appraisals, it can be done. The owner watches the retail marketplace carefully so that when you describe a particular piece of fine jewelry, she can then go to her sources and buy it for you, passing along a worthwhile savings because her overhead and markup is much lower.

This business is not confined to the 'affluent'. You can purchase gift items that start at $15 and end only when your money does. A selection of small items, appropriate as gifts for business associates or members of the wedding are always available.

This business is conducted from a small office in the Phelan Building where the wholesale jewelry market is located in San Francisco. I recommend calling for an appointment and discussing your jewelry needs so that a selection of merchandise can be obtained for your perusal.

## ZWILLINGER & CO.

760 Market St. (at Grant Ave.), San Francisco 94102. Phone: 392-4086. Hours: M-F 9am-5:00pm, Sat 9:00am-3pm. Purchases: VISA, MC. Parking: Downtown garages.

To find this 60 year old jewelry company first look for the Phelan Building on Market Street, the make your way up to the 8th floor to Suite 800. You'll feel like you're entering a bank vault as you pass through their security doors. You'll feel more comfortable if you wear your Sunday best while in the presence of such beautiful jewelry.

For those great occasions in life—engagements, anniversaries, and graduation—where the remembrance you desire should be very special, a fine piece of jewelry can be purchased here at a considerable savings. Their prices on 14-carat gold jewelry were very impressive as well as their prices for watches and diamond rings. They have extended hours at Christmas.

# LIGHTING

I have to concede defeat in locating a super discount for lighting fixtures. I'm sure that everyone shares my disappointment because even the plainest fixture can cost an arm and a leg. In my research I found that most retailers offer a 30% discount off the manufacturer's list price. Since everyone seems to be doing this, some will whisper it in your ear as if they're the only ones, others will be much more straightforward. You have to assume that the prevailing retail price for this merchandise is the 30% discount price. Occasionally, you can persuade them to give you an extra 10% off if you are in the process of remodeling and working with a contractor. They all seem to have good sales in January, other sale times vary with the retailer. Pity the poor consumer who is working with a decorator who charges the full manufacturer's list price . . . that really hurts!

# LINENS

(Also see **Furniture—Catalog Discounters**)

**A-1 LINEN COMPANY**
1660 Monterey Hwy., San Jose 95112. Phone: 408-995-5544. Hours: T-F 9am-5pm, Sat 10am-3pm. Purchases: Cash or Check. Parking: Lot.

The *A-1 Linen Company* that sells commercial and institutional linens also sells name brand towels, sheets, bath rugs, pillows, comforters and kitchen linens to the public at 30-50% discounts. What is most unusual is that these linens are not old 'leftovers', but the same colors and styles that you're seeing currently in better stores. For instance, a very luxurious towel that retails for $23 is sold for $14.50. There are several brands and price ranges, all discounted far more than the 'tiny' savings offered on white sale prices by major stores. The irregulars, a smaller part of the selection, are discounted even more. Regular and waterbed sheets are sold. Some patterns have been around for a while, although others are as current as your latest department store ad. The sheets are sold in packaged sets. Both standard and electric blankets are well represented. Everythng is beautifully arranged. You can discuss the possibility of special orders and, if they can, they'll try to order for you. Finally, you can always opt for the institutional linens, which are cheaper. For instance, a dozen basic white towels like the ones you see in hotels and hospitals sell for approximately $28 per dozen. The discounts off retail prices are attributed to what the owner defines as 'good connections'.

## BULLOCKS FURNITURE CLEARANCE CENTER
(See **Furniture and Accessories**)

## CAPWELL'S BUDGET STORE
(See **Family Clothing**)

## DECORATOR'S BEDSPREAD OUTLET
5757 Pacheco Blvd. (½ mile north of New York Fabrics), Pacheco 94553. Phone: 689-3435. Hours: M-Sat 9.30am 5.30pm, Th & F eve till 8:30, Sun Noon-5pm. Purchases: BA, MC, VISA. Parking: Lot.

**Other Store:** 1580 Howe Ave., Sacramento.

It's so nice to find a store owner who is able and willing to operate a business with a lower overhead, take a smaller mark-up, and pass on savings to consumers. It helps to have good connections, too. The selection of bedspreads, goose down comforters, dacron filled comforters, decorator pillows and dust ruffles has the depth and variety to suit the taste and requirements of just about everyone.

Savings on regular, first quality merchandise (the same merchandise you see in better stores) is approximately 25% below prevailing retail. On custom orders you can save 15%. The best buys are on special purchase items—overcuts, cancellations, or discontinued merchandise from manufacturers—that result in savings of 40-70%. The price range in their selection is very accommodating. There are budget priced goods for lean budgets, and higher prices for fine quality custom-type spreads. The goods are neatly displayed and there are several "mock beds," useful for seeing your spread in a home situation. They also have a reasonable trial purchase policy, which allows you to take the merchandise home on approval. Customers who bring in their own measurements will be pleased with the hefty discounts on ready-made and custom-made draperies.

## EMPORIUM/CAPWELL
## FURNITURE CLEARANCE CENTER
(See **Furniture and Accessories**)

## HOUSE OF BEDSPREADS
417 Town & Country Village (Stevens Creek Blvd. & Winchester), San Jose. Phone: 244-2148. Hours: M-S 10am-5:30pm, Th till 9pm. Purchases: BA, MC. Parking: Lot.

With 1,500 spreads neatly displayed on hangers, choosing just one might seem like an overwhelming task. Bring your carpet samples, paint colors, fabric swatches and pillow cushions to make the job of finding the "right" spread a little easier. These spreads are from

11 different companies, plus their own company in Los Angeles. If you can't find something in their vast selection you're really picky. The discounts vary from 20-60% below retail . . . that will take the sting out of decorating your bedroom. They will even special order matching draperies, dust ruffles or pillow shams.

## LINEN FACTORY OUTLET
2200-D Zanker Road, San Jose 95131. Phone: 408-263-8300. Hours: M-F 8am-4pm, Sat 10am-4pm. Purchases: MC, VISA. Parking: Lot.

**Other Store:** 2190 Meridan Park Blvd., Concord.

No, you're not in the wrong neighborhood—not if you're looking for bargains. True, this industrial park is an unlikely area for a factory outlet but this apron and linen outlet is a surprise in many ways. The merchandise is beautifully displayed and neatly organized. All the delightful kitchen and gourmet aprons are displayed on racks. The oven mitts, pot holders, kitchen towels, tablecloths, placemats and napkins are arranged neatly on shelves and tables. Everything made by this manufacturer is from good quality cotton and polyester blends that wash beautifully and are permanent press.

I did all my Xmas shopping for the women in my family here one year, I took real pleasure in buying the "little luxuries" they're too practical to buy for themselves. Samples, imperfects and discontinued lines are sent to the outlet from the factory next door. Savings range from 40-70% off.

Be sure to check the new store in Concord . . . you'll love the new damask and lace tablecloths and napkins they've added to their line.

## MACY'S FURNITURE CLEARANCE PLACE
(See **Furniture and Accessories**)

## MARSHALL'S
(See **Apparel—Family**)

## MONTGOMERY WARD CLEARANCE CENTER
(See **General Merchandise—Liquidators**)

## SATIN BED LINEN OUTLET
3650 Standish Ave., Santa Rosa 95401. Phone: 707-585-0991. Hours: Tues-Fri 10am-4pm. Purchases: MC, VISA. Parking: Lot.

The ultimate luxury for some people is to sleep on satin sheets surrounded by satin comforters, pillow shams and dust ruffles. Of course, for most, the reality fades to fantasy when considering the price to create such a look. If the price is your obstacle, then this factory outlet in Santa Rosa is your salvation. Everything sold at this outlet is a 'second' priced at 50-60% off retail. Each item is marked with one of the ten classifications of a second. It may have a tear, a stain or dirt, a stitching irregularity, a scratch or run, poor fill, a burn, an irregular size, a discontinued color or fabric.

One wall of the outlet is covered with comforters hanging from rods. These can be unfolded and inspected prior to purchase. The packaged goods must be bought 'as is' without inspection. The linens are made in polyester satin, nylon tricot, or novelty satins which look and feel elegant. Fabrics are sold by the scrap or by the yard. Be forewarned that it may not be possible to get a complete matching set of linens at any one visit. If you're trying to match sets, you can buy what's available, and then call from time to time to see if the rest have come into the outlet. The best time to shop this facility is during the fall months when production at the factory is at its peak and, therefore, more seconds are created.

Directions: Going North on Hwy. 101, take Todd Ave. exit, then take overpass west on Todd to Standish Ave. Turn right and go approximately 2 blocks.

## TOWEL PLUS

1774 B Piner Road, Santa Rosa 95401. Phone: 707-525-9800. Hours: M-Sat 10am-5pm. Purchases: BA, MC. Parking: Lot.

For residents in Northern Marin and Sonoma Counties that have reason to do business in Santa Rosa, a stop by this small store may be justified. However, if you're going to spend more than a few dollars on gas, it may not be worth the trip. *Towels Plus* specializes in bath and kitchen linens. All of their merchandise is discounted, some just a piddling 10%, and others as much as 50% off.

One side of the store is stocked with irregulars (your best buys) of bath towels and bathroom rugs. These towels and rugs have Grade A flaws, which means a pattern may be off, the stitching is missing, or the binding is crooked. All these linens are from name brand manufacturers. While bed sheets are not carried, the Vellux blankets are always 20% off. Call first if you want a specific color or size. Empire wool blankets are always 30% off. Colors, sizes, and patterns are limited to stock on hand. When possible, the owner will try to special order and pass on a price savings. First quality goods are rarely discounted more than 20%. Local residents should watch their newspaper ads for frequent specials.

## WHEREHOUSE FOR BEDSPREADS, INC.

729 E. Francisco Blvd., San Rafael 94901. Phone: 454-3949. Hours: M-F 10am-6pm, Sat 10am-5pm. Purchases: MC, VISA. Parking: Street.

Other Store: 535 El Camino Real, Menlo Park, 322-6224; 22436 Foothill Blvd., Hayward, 581-6240.

I'm amazed that any store that offers such a huge selection of bed and bath linens can manage to keep it all looking as neat and well organized as they do in this store. Their ability to offer 25-35% discounts is due to the fact that they buy directly from the manufacturer instead of the factory representatives. Their selection includes many styles of spreads, comforters, canopy sets, monogrammed towels, satin sheets, throw pillows, floor pillows etc. Just about everything in linens is sold except blankets. The prices of the bedspreads range from $25.00-$200.00. If you can't find anything in their vast selection you can custom order a spread or comforter from their manufacturers' sample books and get a respectable discount.

# LUGGAGE

(Also see **General Merchandise**)

**AAA LUGGAGE REPAIR DEPOT**
585 Howard Street (Near 2nd), San Francisco 94105. Phone: 781-5007. Hours: M-F 8am-5pm. Purchases: BA, MC. Parking: Street, pay lot.

You'll wonder where you are when you walk in the door because all the luggage, attache cases, trunks, totes, portfolios and wallets are in the back room. *AAA* is the authorized repair station for most national brands of luggage. Their speciality is trunks made from vulcanized fiber over plywood that is very strong and sold at great prices.

    *AAA* is not a retailer, but specializes in airline repairs and replacement. Their back room has therefore become a clearance center for samples and department store returns, plus some factory special clearances. All deficiencies have been taken care of. Savings range from 20-50% off. You may not be able to buy six matching pieces of luggage from their shelves, but if one or two are your "bag" you should have no trouble. Their attache cases range from the very inexpensive to the deluxe quality, and if special features are required, their shop is equipped to install, or revise, or make from scratch.

## FACTORY OUTLET (GO/LIGHTLY)
344 139th Ave. (off Washington Ave.), San Leandro 94578. Phone: 352-1778. Hours: M-F 8am-4pm. Purchases: MC, VISA. Parking: Street.

If you would like some colorful travel accessories like garment bags, suit carriers, duffle style totes, backpacks and sport totes then you should give this outlet a visit. These accessories are made from tough 100% nylon parapack cloth or quilted nylon taffeta. Discounts range from 20-50% on overruns, seconds, and discontinued styles or colors.

## HARBAND'S LUGGAGE
517 Mission Street, San Francisco 94105. Phone: 986-2751. Hours: M-F 9am-5pm. Purchases: MA, BC, VISA. Parking: Street, lot.

The extensive selection of portfolios and attache cases makes this a very good gift shopping resource for the executive man or woman. Fine quality leather is their speciality, although vinyls and hard cases are also available. Lark, Skyway, Ventura, Samsonite, Bayley Bags, Atlantic and Halliburton are some of their lines but there are many more. Best of all you receive a 20% discount on all their merchandise. I was particularly pleased with their selection of better wallets, passport

cases and travel accessories. Please note: they are closed on Saturdays.

## LUGGAGE CLEARANCE CENTER
780 Coleman Ave., San Jose 95110. Phone: 408-294-4779. Hours: M-F 10am-6pm, Sat 10am-5pm, Sun Noon-5pm. Purchases: MC, VISA. Parking: Street.

**Other Stores:** 2737 El Camino Real, Redwood City; 955 Contra Costa Blvd., Pleasant Hill; 2221 Shattuck Ave., Berkeley.

Many people driving to the San Jose Airport spot the sign out in front of the Luggage Clearance Center and wish they'd known about it sooner. This is where luggage from Taylor's and Burke's luggage stores in the Bay Area is sent when it is discontinued. These luggage pieces are all first line merchandise from manufacturers like American Tourister, Skyway, Samsonite, Lark, Amelia Earhardt and others. There are no seconds. Their savings which range from 40-65% are also attributed to special purchases directly from the manufacturers' warehouses. They have a good selection of travel accessories, attache cases, purses and wallets at discount prices. They will make exchanges and even give refunds with a receipt and that's almost unheard of in a clearance center!

# Musical Instruments

## CURRLIN'S MUSIC CENTER

448 So. Winchester Blvd., San Jose 95128. Phone: 408-241-2051. Hours: M & F 9:30am-6:30pm, TWTh 9:30am-8pm, Sat 9:30am-5pm. Purchases: MC, VISA. Parking: Lot.

Parents are usually thrilled when their children express interest in learning how to play a band instrument then they find out how much it costs. If money becomes an obstacle to your budding musician, consider the different options at *Currlin's.* Along with low rate monthly rentals, they have one of the largest stocks of used instruments available for sale (generally 50-60% off of the current new price). For those wishing to buy new instruments, their discounts range from 10-40% off, including hard to find instruments. Another angle is their consignment department. They will sell those old unwanted horns, guitars, or whatever on consignment. They take 20-25% to handle charge card fees, salesman's commission and profit. The folks at this store are very helpful in getting you started within your budget and will even price quotes over the phone.

## GUITAR CENTER

928 Van Ness Street, San Francisco 94109. Phone: 441-4020. Hours: M-F 10am-9pm, Sat 10am-6pm, Sun Noon-6pm. Purchases: VISA, MC. Parking: Street.

**Other Store:** 96 North Second Street, San Jose.

At *Guitar Center* their motto is "Don't go on stage without us". From all reports this is 'the' source for the Rock N Roll crowd. With seven stores nationwide they operate on a volume basis which enables them to offer prices to the consumer that the competition just can't beat. Prices are negotiable, so sharpen your horse trading skills. Watch their ads for heavily discounted promotions that are the stuff dreams are made of. For professional quality musical equipment, P.A. equipment, keyboard equipment and accessories, you have a chance to buy maximum value for the money you have to spend whether you're a rank amateur or a big money professional. They will take your old equipment in trade, offer lay-a-ways, haggle, do anything to make that sale.

# PAPER GOODS AND STATIONERY

(Also see **General Merchandise—Discount Stores, Liquidators**)

## ARVEY PAPER CO.
2275 Alameda St., San Francisco 94103. Phone: 863-3664. Hours: M-F 8am-5pm, Sat 9am-2pm. Purchases: Cash, check. Parking: Street.

Other Stores: 229 Castro St., Oakland 94607; 1381 No. 10th St., San Jose 95112; 1101 Richards Blvd., Sacramento 95814; 1445 Veterans Blvd., Redwood City 94063.

*Arvey* is a large distributor of paper goods and office supplies; their showroom has almost any type of office equipment or stationery you could think of. The display room is neat and well organized, and the salespeople very helpful. Delivery is available for a small additional charge. Special weekly sale brochures announce super buys to mailing-list customers.

You will save a minimum of 15-50% on all stationery goods, though I noticed substantially greater savings on some items. On office equipment, such as file cabinets and desks, you can save 15-40%. Janitorial supplies, such as tissues, mops, and paper towels, sell for 10-20% off. Printing supplies are a large proportion of their business; you will certainly save here. Returns and exchanges are gladly made if the sales receipt is presented.

## CASH AND CARRY WAREHOUSE
(See **Food and Drink**)

## LAIRD'S DISCOUNT WAREHOUSE
*727 Kennedy St., Oakland 94606. Phone: 534-8320 Ext. 268. Hours: M-F 9am-6pm, Sat 10am-4pm. Purchases: MC, VISA. Parking: Lot.

*Laird's* has everything for the office from stationery to office furniture. At their warehouse store you can get good buys on overstocked merchandise, discontinued office supplies and damaged goods which are sent over from their distribution warehouse. I spotted many items that were selling below cost. The inventory is somewhat eratic. On one visit you may find tables stacked with office stationery and desk accessories but no typewriter ribbons, or a wide selection of damaged file drawers, while on another visit, they're all sold out. When I stopped in my visit wasn't wasted. I picked up Bic pens for 9 cents each, canary pads at 41 cents each, and file folders for $5.29/100. If you run through office supplies like I do, get on their mailing list for sale bulletins that

will let you know what they're getting rid of CHEAP. You can negotiate the prices on office desks, credenzas, file drawers and other big items. Anything is possible!
*Laird's should be relocated in the address above after August 1, 1982.

# SHOES

I have tried to include those shoe stores with the best quality shoes at the lowest prices. Since you will be saving 20-60% off retail prices, you should be prepared to forgo some of the creature comforts of a regular shoe store. Many stores are self-service, and you may have to dig into a pile to find what you want. To try on your discoveries, you may have to perch on a hard wooden bench or even lean against a wall. Since the stock consists mostly of factory closeouts, samples, cancellations, and seconds, there is a limited selection of sizes, colors, and styles.

### ATHLETIC SHOE FACTORY STORES
320 Walnut (Peninsula Boardwalk), Redwood City 94063. Phone: 932-9056. Hours: M-F 9:30am-9pm, Sat 10am-6pm, Sun Noon-5pm. Purchases: BA, MC, VISA.

**Other Stores:** Alameda, Citrus Heights, Colma, Concord, Campbell, Los Gatos, Modesto, Mountain View, Napa, Newark, Palo Alto, Petaluma, Oakland, Sacramento, Redwood City, Rancho Cordova, San Jose, San Francisco, San Lorenzo, San Mateo, San Rafael, Santa Cruz, Sunnyvale, Walnut Creek.

If anyone in your family is engaged in running, tennis, basketball, soccer or racketball, or just prefers the comfort of athletic shoes, they'll find a terrific selection and good prices at this chain of stores. About a third of the inventory is new, first quality and regularly priced. The remaining two-thirds is where you'll find bargains or promotionally priced shoes. On the seconds (which refer to cosmetic flaws only) you can save from 30-60%. If you look carefully you may note a smudge of glue on the canvas or suede, the stitching may be crooked or overstitched for correction, or you may be hard pressed to find the flaw. In addition to seconds they also have discontinued styles or colors. Anyone following the shoe scene can't help but notice that shoe styles and colors are more abundant and seem to change faster than the car models each year. Of course, this is all contrived to keep the fashion-minded jogging back into stores to get the "latest." They have a good size range for men, women and children and everyone in the family can readily help themselves. These stores are geared to self service. After you've selected your new shoes, you can check the discounts on active sportswear. Warm-up suits, jogging shorts, shirts and socks and many other accessories all geared to the jock are available.

## BROWN BROS. ALAMEDA SHOE WAREHOUSE
848 Lincoln Ave. (at 9th St.), Alameda 94501. Phone: 865-3700. Hours: M-Sat 9:30am-6pm. Purchases: Cash or Check. Parking: Street.

Brown Bros. has been in business for over 45 years with little fanfare or advertising. Their new store is just three blocks off Webster and is an improvement over their old store on East 14th Street in Oakland, but it's still not fancy. Their shoes are all first quality, purchased in volume lots or in special make-up orders from manufacturers like Freeman, Walk-Over, Stacy Adams, International and Florsheim, and sold under the Brown Bros. label. Shoe sizes in boys range from 2½ to 6, with men's sizes in 6-14 to EEE widths. Their athletic shoes by Nike and Converse are sold for solid discount prices. They have the lowest prices on Santa Rosa boots that I've been able to find, which is why so many hardworking fella's go miles out of their way to do business with them. Whether you're building houses or presenting a case before the judge, you'll find a good shoe, at a reasonable price. Usually 25-40% off retail. Exchanges and refunds allowed.

## CLOTHES RACK
(See **Apparel—Women's, Chain Store**)

## CASBAH II
751 Bridgeway, Sausalito. Phone: 332-2018. Hours: M-Sun 10:30am-7pm. Purchases: MC, VISA. Parking: Lot.

The Casbah I store in Sausalito is known for fine quality high fashion shoes. To handle the end-of-season, broken size lots, odds-n-ends, they have opened Casbah II which is a few doors away and upstairs. At Casbah II you also find special purchases, manufacturers' overstocks, plus all the *Casbah I* rejects. Sizes for women are 5-10. The selection includes casual styles like espadrilles, moccasins, sandals, also casual and dress heels, boots, but no jogging shoes. Some styles are very current and still sold in other stores at higher prices while others have passed their season by a few months. I've had very good luck here, and I make a point to visit the store when I'm going through Sausalito.

## FACTORY OUTLET
(See **Apparel—Active Sportswear**)

## FRY'S WAREHOUSE SPORTS
(See **Sporting Goods**)

## KUSHIN'S HAYWARD SALE CENTER
22443 Foothill Blvd., Hayward 94541. Phone: 537-2411. Hours: M-Sat 10am-6pm, Thurs & Fri eve. till 8pm. Purchases: VISA, MC. Parking: Pay lot.

**Other Store:** 39166 Paseo Padre, Fremont, 793-8079.

One of *Kushin's* regular shoe stores has been converted into an outlet for all the shoes that didn't sell at their other stores. Moreover, they buy factory samples, cancellations, and special factory make-up orders from name brand manufacturers that they private label and sell for considerably less than the branded merchandise. Familiar *Kushin's* labels are Red Cross, Joyce, Cobbie, Sabicca, Bear Traps, Famolare, and Freeman and Hush Puppies for men. Discounts on all these shoes may range from 30-75% depending on how dated the styles may be or the manner in which they were purchased by the store. There are usually about 5,000 pairs of shoes on racks for convenient self service and many more in the back room that can be brought out by the sales personnel.

## KUTLER BROS.
(See **Apparel—Men's**)

## MARSHALL'S
(See **Apparel-Family**)

## MONTGOMERY WARD'S CLEARANCE CENTER
(See **General Mdse., Liquidators**)

## ON A SHOESTRING
1207 Bridgeway, Sausalito 94965. Phone: 332-1684. Hours: M-Sat 10am-6pm, Sun Noon-5pm. Closed: Tuesdays. Purchases: MC, AE, BA. Parking: Lot.

**Other Stores:** 1615 Bridgeway, Sausalito; 360 West Portal, San Francisco.

The motto here is "Nothing but the very best for the best price." By keeping in close touch with Los Angeles jobbers, and buying in-season closeouts and cancellations, the owners are able to offer 20-60% savings on their selection of better brands. You won't find any cheap imitation leathers. Some of the brands you'll consistently spot are Ferragamo, Evans, Julienelli,

Pappagalo, Panalijo, Amalfi, Andrew Geller, Famolare, Cobbie, Geoffrey Beene, Beene Bag and many others in women's sizes with widths that range from AAAA-D. Men's brands are Famolare, Yves St. Laurent, Pierre Cardin, Bally, San Remo, Padrino, etc. in mostly medium widths. Their stock changes frequently. You won't always find all shoes in a complete size or color range. Their new Marin store is right across the street from Zacks.

## THE ORTHO-VENT DIVISION INC.
115 Brand Road, Salen, Virginia 24156. Phone: 703-389-8121. Mail Order Only. Purchases: BA, MC, AE.

For several years I've been receiving unsolicited catalogs from this company which I quickly relegated to the circular file. I would have continued forever if it hadn't been for the recommendation I received from a man who's been wearing these shoes for years. His recommendation has real credibility for me because he owns a very nice men's clothing store, and certainly knows more about the industry and value than most. In the latest catalog I surveyed, all the shoes were made with leather uppers, leather insoles, many with leather linings, and all with their long wearing "Extra Life" sole (man-made). The size range covered in many of their shoe styles goes from 6-13 and widths of B-EEE. All of their shoes are made with the Goodyear Welt or Littleway processes which are the strongest shoe constructions and always found in quality shoes.

Each catalog (new ones are issued several times a year) has a selection that provides choices for casual, work, formal or dress occasions. They have dress and casual boots, Chukka and storm boots, brogue's and wingtips, cordovans, slip-ons and moccasins, etc. all look-alikes of popular current and classic styles at 20-35% off. If you have reservations about ordering shoes by mail, you're not alone. I did. So I ordered and returned shoes to verify that their 30-day, no risk, home trial offer measured up. Sure enough, I received a full refund including postage, just like they promised. If you're not getting their catalogs, write and have your name put on their mailing list.

## PATTI QUINN'S
(See **Apparel—Women's, Chain Stores**)

## DONNA PILLER'S
12 Clement Street, San Francisco 94118. Phone: 752-9106. Hours: M-Sat 11am-6pm. Purchases: MC, VISA. Parking: Street.

Leave your sensitivity outside the door, plan to spend a lot of time, and wear comfortable shoes. This small boutique which is actually associated with *Jerry Piller's* in Los Angeles (a favorite with bargain hunters in that area) made its debut in the Bay Area in 1977. Since then it has attracted a dedicated following of women who are searching for clothes with high-fashion appeal and clothes noted for fine quality. The Piller family buys sale apparel from the finest boutiques around the country, plus samples from better manufacturers, and call themselves a 'sale' store, not a discount store. You'll find a lot of designer clothes, last year's, maybe, but classic high-fashion holds up well. Before going upstairs to their shoe department, they'll take your purse for 'safekeeping,' and then you're free to browse through boxes of designer shoes. I find going through boxes a bit tedious; others find it exciting. The shoes which range in sizes 4-10 in narrow and medium widths, sport some very prestigious labels. Charles Jourdan, Mignani, Maud Frizon, Walter Steiger, Campione, and are sold for 50% off the original retail prices. You won't find many shoes for under $50 even at the reduced price because many of these shoes are priced from $100-$400 at retail. This is just the place for the 'shoe freak.'

## SAMPLE SHOE SHOP
202 Clement, San Francisco 94118. Phone: 386-4582. Hours: M-Sat 10am-6pm. Sun Noon-5pm. Purchases: MC, VISA. Parking: Street.

For good shoe buys this small store offers some real possibilities for those who can stop in now and then. Discounts from 15-50% prevail on ladies' shoes in sizes 4-10, with a bonus selection for those who wear sample sizes 6 and 6½. Each shoe is marked with the size range available in that particular style. There are always many different styles available.

## THE SANDAL FACTORY
2560 El Camino Real, Redwood City 94063. Phone: 363-0505. Hours: M-F 10am-6pm, Sat 10am-4pm. Purchases: MC, VISA. Parking: Street.

At the *Sandal Factory* all products in their factory store are sold at the current wholesale price plus 10%. This represents about a 40% savings to the customer on their Paw Print (similar to Birkenstock) sandals, men's and women's wallets and many other small leather goods. All of their products are made of leather produced and tanned in the USA. Their comfortable sandals come in women's sizes from 5-10, and men's sizes from 6-12.

## SHOE CITY, U.S.A.
1910 El Camino, Mountain View 94040. Phone: 969-8393. Hours: M-Sat 9:30am-6pm, T & Th till 9pm. Purchases: BA, MC. Parking: Lot.

It pays to have good connections! The owner of this shoe store buys cancelled orders and overruns directly from manufacturers as well as from several jobbers. Manufacturers continually have to deal with the problem of cancellations from their regular accounts. If it weren't for stores like this they would suffer real losses. The big winner is you the shopper who can take advantage of this situation to save 33-80% off high retail prices. The shoes are all first quality, current season. The selection for men and women is very good, although it helps if you're flexible. You won't always find a complete size or color range in the shoes you select. Some of their impressive labels are Famolare, Garolino, Joyce, Nina, Oscar de la Renta, Latina's, Cobbies and Life Stride. For men, Nunn Bush, Bostonian and Pierre Cardin predominate their selection. Sizes for women range from 4-12, AAA-W; for men, 6-15, A-EEE. This is basically a self-service operation; however, the salespeople are helpful without being pushy. Be on the lookout for their last chance bargain specials. After 60 days in stock, they get ruthless and slash prices to as low as $3.00. It's hard to spend more than $25.00; you'll probably spend less than that on their shoes that range in price from $20-$60 at retail. If you're gas conscious, get a fix on their location and check-in when you're in the area.

## SHOE FAIR

2049 Junipero Serra Blvd., Daly City 94014. Phone: 755-0556. Hours: M-F 9am-9pm, Sat 9am-6pm, Sun 11am-5pm. Purchases: BA, MC, VISA. Parking: Free lot.

**Other Stores:** Campbell, Cupertino, Pleasant Hill, San Carlos, San Jose, San Mateo, South San Francisco, San Lorenzo.

*Shoe Fair*, the "House of Famous Brands," is a large, complete family shoe store. They have a large selection of sizes in casual, sporty, and dressy shoes. The styles vary from very conservative to wild and wonderful; brands range from obscure imported labels to well-known names like Joyce, Sbicca, Jarman, Frye, Puma, and Converse. On occasion, higher-quality imported shoes are available. One of the better selections of cancellation shoes is available here. Everything is discounted.

## THE SHOE HOUSE

5132 Broadway, Oakland 94611. Phone: 658-5347. Hours: M-Sat 9:30am-6pm. Purchases: BA, MC, VISA. Parking: Lot.

**New Store:** Orchard Shopping Center, Dublin.

You won't get salon shoe service here, but you won't expect the 'extras' when you consider the prices. Ladies' shoes are their specialty (no men's or children's). Sizes range from 4-12, widths AAAA-C. Some of my favorite brands were displayed on their racks: DeLiso Debs, BareTraps, Charm-Step, Famolare, 9 West, Cherokee, Impo, and Street Cars were just a few. The styles cover the entire fashion scene: clunkers to dainty, sophisticated dressy heels. The buyers travel to the out-of-state manufacturers and buy their odd lots and make-up orders. They also carry some inexpensive imports. You can save 30-60% on the same shoes you see downtown. New shoes arrive weekly, so stop in often. They also mark shoes down continually to keep the inventory moving.

## SHOE LAND

1691 Willow Pass Road, Concord 94520. Phone: 685-1751. Hours: MTWS 10am-6pm, ThF 10am-9pm, Sun Noon-5pm. Purchases: MC, VISA. Parking: Lot.

*Shoe Land* is the clearance outlet for *Herold's* shoe stores. For this reason, many of the ladies' shoes in particular seem way past season and are not particularly current in fashion. In the men's selection, you're more conscious of good values because their styles are not as subject to extremes in trends. The savings are approximately 30% off the original prices, but they have frequent sales with reductions up to 60% off. This is a good resource for anyone who is looking for comfort and value, rather than the "latest look." The size range for both men and women is standard, but limited in selection in each particular style.

## SHOE MART
1014 W. El Camino Real, Sunnyvale 94087. Phone: 738-9836. Hours: M-F 9am-9pm, Sat & Sun 10am-6pm. Purchases: BA, MC. Parking: Free lot.

**Other Stores:** Millbrae, San Carlos.

A complete shoe store for the entire family, this shoe mart offers nationally known and advertised brands of good-quality shoes for men, women, and children. Making large purchases of overstocks allows this store to sell shoes at considerably lower than retail prices. The styles are up-to-date and selection of both size and style is excellent. Outstanding values are standard on work boots for men, sandals for women, and play shoes for children.

## SHOE RACK (LIBERTY HOUSE)
1501 Broadway, Oakland 94612. Phone: 891-2186. Hours: MThF 10am-8pm; TWSat 10am-6pm. Purchases: VISA, MC, Store Charge. Parking: Downtown lots.

This shoe clearance center for all the *Liberty House* department stores always look a bit hectic. As the shoe season evolves from fall to winter to spring to summer, all unsold men's and women's shoes are pulled from the other stores and sent to the *Shoe Rack* in the basement of the Oakland store. Here they're immediately marked down 50%. There are frequent additional advertised mark-downs like 2 for 1, 1¢ sales, $5 off, etc. Here's your chance to get last season's shoes that were $10-$75 for $5-$31. All sales in this department are final. After buying your shoes you'll want to stop in the basement clothing clearance section, where you'll find some good values on passed over, leftover, and last season's clothing.

## SHOE WORLD
880 El Portal Center, San Pablo 94806. Phone: 236-8121. Hours: M-F 9:30am-9pm, Sat 9:30am-6pm, Sun 11am-5pm. Purchases: BA, MC, VISA.

Excellent values in shoes for the whole family. There are many fine quality name brands available in prices from $5-$20, which represents savings from 25-75%. The shoes are purchased from volume lots, short lots, make-up orders, and manufacturer's overstocks—

complicated buying techniques that result in low, low prices. Hard-to-find sizes are available as well as a complete selection of styles to suit every taste. Some of the ladies' shoes are not necessarily the latest style, but if you've a mind of your own and wear what you like regardless of what Madison Avenue dictates, you can really find some fine-quality classic styles. On current styles the discount is 10-20%. Many shoes are sold under their private label but are actually from quality makers such as Red Cross and Cobbie. I was especially pleased to find some of those expensive name-brand children's shoes (Jumping Jacks) that are factory irregulars and first quality at great discounts available here. This is also a clearance center for Carlins quality shoe chain.

## SLICK CHICK SHOE AND SHIRT SHOP

3100 D Danville Blvd., Alamo 04507. Phone: 838-2658. Hours: M-F 10am-5:30pm, Sat 10am-5pm.

**Other Store:** 1012 School St., Moraga, 376-5951.

Although this store sells clothing I am far more intrigued by their shoe selection. Their discount prices are available because they buy from jobbers throughout the country, closeouts directly from manufacturers and they buy some at regular wholesale prices and take a smaller markup. Sizes range from 5-10 in narrow and medium widths for women. Prices are reduced up to 50% off retail.

## THE SQUASH BLOSSOM

Valley Fair Shopping Center, Steven's Creek Blvd. & Winchester, San Jose 95128. Phone: 408-243-3613. Hours: M-F 10am-9pm, Sat 10am-6pm, Sun Noon-5pm. Purchases: VISA, MC.

To qualify as a bargain store I try to determine that prices are at least 20% off prevailing retail. Occasionally I make an exception when a few discounts are available for a given type of merchandise. Such is the case for *Squash Blossom*, a store specializing in Western Boots. I have not found another store that offers discounts on as wide a selection in boots, both in style and size. Everyday, boots are discounted from 12-20% or greater when selected styles are featured in their San Jose "Mercury" ads for special sales. Though modest, a 15% discount on a $500 pair of boots can add up to a tidy $75 savings.

Acme, Dan Post, Durango, Morgan, Miller, Capezio, Nocona, Texas, Hondo, Larry Mahan, Justin, Handmade and T.O. Stanley are some of their brands. Prices range from $40 for synthetic leathers all the way up to $1800 for exotic handmade, fine leather boots. Men's sizes range from 6-16 in A-EEE and ladies from 3½ to 10 in A-C. With approximately 1900 styles to choose from, combined with their fitting assistance, finding the right boot, fit and price should not elude anyone. The store is located in the lower level of the shopping mall.

## STANDARD SHOE MART
300 El Camino Real, Millbrae 94030. Phone: 697-4014. Hours: M-Sat 9:30am-6pm. Purchases: BA, MC. Parking: Free lot.

*Standard Shoe Mart* is a liquidator; they have shoes for the entire family at 30% and more off regular retail. Many styles, sizes, and brands are here in incredibly large numbers. The place is roomy and comfortable. There are salespeople ready to help you when you need it (but not before), which makes this one of the very nicest shoe discount stores to shop in.

## A STEP FORWARD
3281 Lakeshore Ave., Oakland 94610. Phone: 835-4300. Hours: M-Wed 10am-6pm, Thur & Fri 10am-7pm, Sat 10am-6pm. Purchases: VISA, MC. Parking: Street.

The owner of this shoe store has very good connections with a prestigious manufacturer of ladies shoes. The store serves in part as a clearinghouse for end-of-season, overruns, and slow moving merchandise at 15-50% off. In addition to the racks of clearance shoes, there is a choice selection of in-season shoes that are discounted less in sizes 5-10. For instance: shoes that retail for $70-$125 are sold for $59-$99. The boots at $115-$275 are $79-$225. The shoes and boots are beautifully made as the price would indicate. I try to stop by from time to time to keep up with new shipments.

## WHOLE EARTH ACCESS STORE
(See **General Merchandise**)

# SPORTING GOODS

(See **General Merchandise—all headings**)

### ALPINE HOUSE SECONDS
1028 Sir Francis Drake Blvd., Kentfield 94904. Phone: 454-8548. Hours: M-Sat 10am-6pm. Purchases: MC, VISA. Parking: Lot.

*Alpine House* says they're "First in Seconds." Well, that's almost true, with some exceptions. They have seconds and then they have old stock from their regular store, and factory close-outs from various manufacturers they do business with. These backpacking skiing and camping goods are discounted from 15-50% They have an inviting selection of apparel for the whole family: vests, rain-wear, parkas, knickers, down jackets, wool shirts and sweaters. Best of all, these are quality lines well-known to recreation minded consumers. Unlike their main store, they offer no exchanges or refunds at the seconds outlet.

### CS ENTERPRISES
350 East San Carlos Ave., San Carlos 94070. Phone: 595-1060. Hours: M-F 8am-4pm, Most Saturdays 10am-2pm. Purchases: Cash or check. Parking: Lot.

If you have a pilot, motorcycle enthusiast or frequent traveler in your midst, send them down to *CS Enterprises*. For the biker, the Cordura Moto-X pants (sizes 22-42), Enduro Street Jackets (XS, S, M, L, XL), moped saddle bags, tank bags, seatcovers, tank covers, soft saddle bags and neck shields at 30-60% off will surely meet their requirements for quality and price. This manufacturer produces a line of travel gear from virtually indestructible Cordura in sport bags for students, skiers and a neat selection of travel luggage and garment bags. Pilots can meet their needs too with chart bags, tool bags, map pockets and log book holders. All of these exotic items are overruns, occasional irregulars, discontinued colors or styles. *CS* is a little hard to find so I suggest calling for directions to get to their back alley location!

### EURO SPORT
462 Bryant St., San Francisco 94107. Phone: 982-0498. Hours: Announced. Purchases: MC, VISA. Parking: Street and lot.

Skiing enthusiasts will want to watch *Euro Sport's* ads in the "Chronicle", "Examiner", and "Oakland Tribune" that announce their sales which occur about six times every year. *Euro Sport* is associated with Swiss Ski Sports and Swiss Ski Chalet, serving as a clearinghouse for all merchandise that is left over from the previous season, or represents special purchases of closeouts from well-known manufacturers. Often merchandise from one year to the next doesn't change that much, a new color or a small modification in style replaces the old. Their warehouse on Bryant Street is close to the Bay Bridge with ample parking on Sundays, the day of their sales. Everything is organized for self-service but they have enough salespeople to help the novice at selecting skis, poles, bindings, boots, etc. For the beginner, wary of a major investment, their preassembled packages of skiing equipment represent a very good buy. Savings generally range from 20-50% off the original prices. Some of their best values are found on ski-wear for men, women, juniors and children. Bib pants, parkas, vests, ski sweaters and windshirts can be purchased, although lines for the dressing rooms may discourage the impatient.

## FRY'S WAREHOUSE SPORTS

352 East Grand Ave., South San Francisco 94080. Phone: 583-5034. Hours: M-F 9:30am-6pm, Sat 10am-4pm. Purchases: MC, VISA. Parking: Street.

If you play golf or tennis, you will be interested in the values and selection at *Fry's. Fry's* carries better Pro Shop lines of shoes, clothing and equipment, offers discount prices because of their volume purchasing power plus their ability to buy special make-up orders from top manufacturers.

In the clothing categories they carry Izod shirts and jackets, Adidas warm-up suits and shoes, Pierre Cardin, Haggar, Lilly Dache and Munsingwear lines. In equipment you can buy all the little accessories plus the basics from brands like Wilson, Lynx, Power Bilt, Dunlop, Spalding, Hogan, Bag Boy, MacGregor, Rossignol, Etonic and Foot-joy. These are not seconds or closeouts. While a discount operation, they do provide free club fitting with their golfswing computer, tennis stringing, and will take telephone orders using a credit card. In fact, I think it's a good idea to call ahead for availability if you're some distance away. Better yet, the next time you have to pick someone up from the San Francisco airport, go early and stop by their store which is just North of the Airport. Check their ads in the sporting sections of the "Chronicle" and "Examiner" if you want to keep on top of their 'extra specials'.

## MERCHANDISERS INC.
(See **Men's Clothing**)

## THE NORTH FACE FACTORY OUTLET

1238 5th St. (off Gilman), Berkeley 94710. Phone: 526-3530. Hours: M-Sat 10am-6pm, Thurs Eve till 8pm, Sun 11am-4pm. Purchases: VISA, MC. Parking: Street.

**Other Store:** 605 Cambridge, Menlo Park, 327-4865.

All you Sierra Club types and fresh air fans take note: *The North Face* manufactures functional outdoor equipment. Their aim is to provide versatile gear for comfortable and efficient wilderness travel in all climates, conditions, and places.

Their factory outlet features four categories of bargain merchandise with savings of 20% on all their seconds. These include clothing (parkas, hoods, vests for men, women and children), backpacks, sleeping bags, accessories, and even tents. They have hiking boots in limited sizes; these are mostly old styles. Wool shirts and sweaters, discontinued men's and women's shorts and turtlenecks are available in varying supply and are discounted from 30-50%. All the seconds are functional and have only cosmetic flaws such as a run or snag in the fabric, off color or patch. You can also save on used ski touring equipment.

## R.E.I. CO-OP
1338 San Pablo, Berkeley 94702. Phone: 527-4140. Hours: MT 10am-6:30pm, WThF 10am-9pm, Sat 9:30am-6pm. Purchases: BA, MC. Parking: Lot.

If you're involved in any activity or sport that requires special equipment or clothing, *R.E.I.* offers their customers and *Co-op* members good prices and a complete selection. For $5.00 you can join their *Co-op* which entitles you to a dividend at the end of the year based on your purchases. All the people I know in Scouting, back-packing, skiing, rafting, golfing, tennis, et al., check *R.E.I.* prices first. On my comparisons with other sports equipment company catalogs, *R.E.I.* came out ahead in both price and quality. In all equipment lines they offer several qualities and price ranges. It's up to you to determine what your investment should be depending upon your involvement in your sport and the use you hope to get out of your purchases.

## SECONDS BEST MOUNTAINEERING
2042 4th St., San Rafael 94901. Phone: 457-5544. Hours: M-Sat 10am-5:30pm, Sun 12pm-5pm. Purchases: BA, MC. Parking: Lot.

This store is just crammed with goodies for the mountaineer. You can save 20% on name brands like Snowlion, Class 5, Campy and Wilderness Experience. These seconds may have a stain, uneven stitching, or small snags, basically cosmetic flaws which do not impair the usefulness of the assortment of down bags, polarguard bags, parkas, packs, ponchos, tents, or rain gear. They've added a selection of closeouts and overruns at 15-25% off retail in travel luggage and wilderness apparel. All sales are final. Watch for their ads in the "Classified Gazette."

## SIERRA DESIGNS
2039 4th St. (at Addison), Berkeley 94710. Phone: 548-5588. Hours: MTh 10am-8pm, TWF 10am-6pm, Sat 10am-5pm. Purchases: VISA, MC.

**Other Store:** 217 Alma, Palo Alto, 325-3231.

*Sierra Designs* makes mistakes too! You can find their seconds in a corner at each of their two Bay Area stores. Everything is reduced 20-40%, such as down sleeping bags, jackets, tents, or occasionally, packs and other related backpacking, cross-country skiing and mountaineering equipment. Overstocked or discontinued 'Firsts' are marked down 10-15%. Each year, in the spring and fall, *Sierra Designs* has their super sales. If you get on their mailing list you won't miss out. Men's sizes XS-XL, women's 6-14.

## SKI CONTROL WAREHOUSE OUTLET
3351 Vincent Road, Pleasant Hill 94523. Phone: 945-0144. Hours: Daily 11am-6pm. Purchases: MC, VISA. Parking: Lot.

*Ski Control*, a national manufacturer of snow ski equipment and sporting goods accessories has recently opened several stores and one warehouse in the East Bay. *Ski Control* products are nationally advertised and are very well known throughout the sports world. The novice skier is usually overwhelmed with the prices and selection of ski merchandise at many ski retail shops. At *Ski Control's Warehouse Outlet* (behind their corporate offices) the merchandise has been carefully selected to provide all the essentials at a minimal price. The more sophisticated, expensive equipment and apparel, geared for the advanced skier, is available at their four other stores. Beginning and intermediate skiers can buy boots, bindings, skis, and poles, with a one year guarantee, in new or used packages or individually. They'll be assured of receiving appropriate and adequate equipment for their level. The *Ski Control* Size-Ma-Graph assures you that your equipment is suitable for your height and weight.

The discounts of 30-50% off name brand merchandise are possible because of their buying techniques and their ability to deal directly with manufacturers in obtaining closeouts at below wholesale prices. With your $1.00 membership fee you are entitled to other services which include travel, lift ticket reservations, equipment rentals, ski repair and tune-ups as well as snow and road condition reports from their Hotline.

Additional services and programs that *Ski Control* members may take advantage of are: a monthly newsletter, ski rental reservations, full service and repair department, a lay-away program as well as a full spring and summer program that includes water and racquet sports, camping, jogging and a complete selection of general sporting goods at excellent savings either from their inventory or their unique catalog program.

## SONOMA OUTFITTERS
600 Mendocino Ave., Santa Rosa 95401. Phone: 707-528-1920. Hours: M-Sat 10am-5:30pm, Sun Noon-5pm. Purchases: VISA, MC.

To take the bite off the expense of getting dressed and equipped for your backpacking or camping adventure, check the selection and prices here. The owners buy seconds, closeouts and special purchases from many well known manufacturers. Discounts range from a minimal 10% up to 50% off retail. Some name brands that I spotted in their selection are Kelty, Jan-Sport, Wilderness Experience, Lowe (for packs and camera gear) and Vuarnet (sunglasses). Weekend pilots might want to peruse the selection of flight suits and leather bomber jackets at 20% off. Travellers might also consider the closeouts on soft luggage from local manufacturers.

## SPORTS EXCHANGE

2121 Staunton Ct. (off El Camino and Oxford), Palo Alto 94306. Phone: 857-0771. Hours: M-Sat 10am-6pm, Th 10am-9pm.

A first-of-its-kind recycled, sporting equipment outlet where people can buy, sell, trade, or repair *used* bicycles, skis, tennis rackets, golf clubs, balls, camping gear, etc. Customers bring in their used sports equipment and receive cash for it, or they may place it on consignment (they receive 60% of the selling price) or they may trade it on other merchandise in the store. If goods are in need of repair, they are reconditioned by the *Sports Exchange* before being placed on display. Periodic team equipment exchanges, such as Soccer Shoe Swaps, backpacking and ski swaps, are also conducted.

So that you can test the merchandise there is a tennis rebound court, artificial turf golf putting area, bicycle 'test driving' accommodation and fully-equipped repair shop. This is a great place to outfit your children at budget prices! *Sports Exchange* also has three winter stores in Tahoe. Check them out!

# STEREO, HI-FI COMPONENTS

(Also see **General Merchandise—all headings**)

## General

### HALTEK ELECTRONICS

1062 Linda Vista Ave., Mountain View 94043. Phone: 969-0510. Hours: T-Sat 9am-5:30pm. Purchases: BA, MC.

*Haltek* carries all those esoteric electronic components, i.e. TV tubes, batteries, transistors at 40-50% off. To keep on top of the market involved in ecology and energy saving products, they're selling parts for solar panels, motors for wind power generators, etc.

### HOUSE OF LOUIE
(See **Appliances**)

### MACY'S FURNITURE CLEARANCE PLACE
(See **Furniture and Accessories**)

## PJ'S APPLIANCE
(See **Appliances**)

## PACIFIC STEREO
2702 No. Main St., Walnut Creek 94596. Phone: 933-9900. Hours: M-F 9am-9pm, Sat 10am-6pm, Sun Noon-6pm. Purchases: BA, MC. Parking: Street.

**Other Stores:** Concord, Hayward, Larkspur, Mountain View, Sacramento, San Francisco, San Jose, Santa Clara, San Mateo, San Rafael, Colma.

When it comes to purchasing stereo systems and equipment most people tend to overlook the obvious. *Pacific Stereo* splashes big ads throughout Bay Area newspapers with such frequency that many people assume that all their advertising will result in higher prices. Yet, because they are the biggest volume dealer in California (approx. 60 stores), it is possible for them to offer tremendous values on most of their merchandise. You can often wheel and deal and walk out with an entire system at 10% above cost. A lot depends on your assertiveness.

The mark-up on stereo equipment is about 25-30% above wholesale. There is a higher mark-up on their own store brands, a smaller mark-up on some of the finer quality, more expensive lines. The larger mark-ups are on loud speakers, turntables, and accessories. You have the best chance for negotiating a special deal when you are buying a whole system. On their prominently advertised 'loss leader' items (that sends competitors into a spin) prices are firm. Don't expect to dicker on these low prices.

For the novice, a few suggestions: never put yourself at the mercy of a hi-fi salesman. Determine your budget *first,* then check the rating in Consumer Reports and Consumer Guide. Use them as a general guide. *Pacific Stereo* offers a good warranty and very important, a reliable service department.

## QUEMENT
1000 S. Bascom Ave., San Jose 95128. Phone: 998-5900. Hours: M-Sat 9am-6pm. Purchases: MC, VISA. Parking: Free lot.

*Quement* is a complete stereo sound center located in a huge warehouse-like building, with 40,000 square feet of electronic parts, components, tubes, accessories, video recorders, projection TV's, antennas, and ham gear. They have most well-known brand names, including Dual, Marantz, Sony, Pioneer, Technics and Panasonic. The prices here are "wholesale to all"—all who make the trip to *Quement.* Since they have been in business since 1933 and do a tremendous volume (they even sell to other commercial and industrial outfits in the southern Peninsula area), they can offer low low prices to you stereo and ham operator bugs. They also have a complete service department to help you with any problems.

## RECYCLED STEREO

2797 Shattuck Ave., Berkeley 94705. Phone: 843-2381. Hours: M-F 10am-9pm, Sat 10am-6pm, Sun Noon-6pm. Purchases: BA, MC, AE. Parking: Free lot.

*Recycled Stereo* is an outgrowth of *Pacific Stereo's* trade-in policy on new equipment. It provides access to used high-fidelity equipment for those who couldn't otherwise afford it. There is a large and constantly changing selection of legitimate bargains in everything from compacts to some very exotic stuff. You can expect to save about 50% off the original retail price of this merchandise, a painless way to acquire some good-as-new stereo gear.

All parts and components are tested (and repaired, if necessary) by the service center before being offered for sale. Most equipment is covered by a 90-day warranty on parts and labor. Some gear will be sold 'as is' at even lower prices for those who like to do their own recycling. Their card file system allows them to call you when they locate your desired piece.

## E.C. WENGER ELECTRONICS CO.

1450 Harrison St., Oakland 94612. Phone: 451-1020. Hours: M-Sat 9am-5:15pm. Purchases: VISA, MC, store charge. Parking: Free lot, metered street.

**Other Stores:** 2670 Main St., Walnut Creek, 94596; 775 Arguello St., Redwood City, 94063.

I'm a little out of my depth in a store specializing in electronic needs. The merchandise—all 50,000 varieties of tubes, meters, cables, plugs, transistors, antennas, batteries, and items so foreign to me I couldn't begin to describe them—is neatly arranged on rows and rows of pegboards and display shelves. The original wholesale electronic store in the Bay Area, this is the place where all my do-it-yourselfer friends head for real savings, expert advice, good service, replacement parts for TV's, stereos and radios.

Approximately 05% of the inventory is 20-40% off retail prices. Tubes are always a great bargain at 40% off (all sales final on these). Be sure to watch the local papers for special sales.

# TOYS

**ANIMAL PUPPET OUTLET** (Furry Folk)
1219 Park Ave., Emeryville 94608. Phone: 658-7677. Hours: M-F 9am-5:30pm. Purchases: VISA, MC. Parking: Street.

These very expensive furry puppet animals have become very popular with specialty toy shops because of their unique and appealing life-like appearance. Otters, raccoons, bears, skunks, foxes, etc. look like the real animals and are a far cry from the typical puppet. In fact, they don't look like puppets at all, but more like stuffed animals. The prices on their selection of seconds with minor flaws are about 50% off retail.

**TOYS 'R' US**
1082 Blossom Hill Rd., San Jose 95123. Phone: 266-2600. Hours: M-F 10am-9pm; Sat, Sun 10am-7pm. Purchases: Cash, check. Parking: Free lot.

**Other Stores:** Daly City, Hayward, Pleasant Hill, Sunnyvale.

Just for the record, I do think that *Toys 'R' Us* is about the 'best' all around resource for toys and children's gifts when you are considering price and selection.

Their prices have stood up well in my comparison shopping. Only *Best Products* gives them serious competition in prices, but *Best* has a limited toy selection. For a big operation, I have been impressed with the no hassle, no fuss, exchange and refund policy, when you meet them half way with sales receipts as requested.

**KIDS CONSTRUCTION COMPANY**
420 Riley Street, Santa Rosa 95404. Phone: 707-526-2778. Hours: M-F 10am-5pm, Sat 10am-2pm. Purchases: Cash or Check. Parking: Street.

If stuffed animals are your special treat, you'll love Patty Cakes, a line of the softest, most hugable critters I've found. Their popular sheep and rabbits are made in soft velour fabrics that are completely washable. The outlet is easy to spot. Look for the old bright blue carriage house that accommodates both the factory and outlet. Inside you'll be charmed by the Patty Cakes animals, infant and childrens clothing with their distinctive screen prints, and kitchen aprons. Bright Ideas, a line of childrens clothing in sizes 4-14 (mostly girls) is appealing for the use of appliques and colorful fabrics. Both lines are discounted 15-50%. The minimal discounts apply to first quality in-season merchandise, while the bigger discounts apply to the overruns from previous seasons, irregulars, and production samples. These lines hold up well from year to year so it matters little that you may be buying last years clothing. This is a super place for gifts!

# Typewriters

(Also see **General Merchandise**)

**ALBANY TYPEWRITER & COMPUTER**
924 San Pablo Ave., Albany 94706. Phone: 526-1959.
Hours: M-F 9am-5pm, Sat 10am-4pm. Purchases:
VISA, MC. Parking: Street.

If you're looking for a good typewriter to use in your office or for heavy home typing you might expect to pay $300-$500 for a machine that will be reliable and durable. *Albany Typewriter* will soften the blow with their policy that states "We will not be undersold." They carry a complete selection of Smith Corona, Brother, Olympia, Facit, Olivetti, Adler and IBM re-conditioned typewriters. I noted that their regular price on a leading Smith Corona model was $60 less than a competitor's sale price. They work on a very small mark-up, and volume basis figuring that if they give you a good price on the typewriter, you'll return when the typewriter needs servicing. I was impressed that in discussing the merits of two similar models by one manufacturer that had a noticeable difference in price due to cosmetic differences, they did not push the higher priced model. Their prices on home computers, Atari, Commodore and Xerox are very good.

**CHERIN'S**
(See **Appliances**)

**HOUSE OF LOUIE**
(See **Appliances**)

# WALLPAPER

**CONTRACT DESIGN CENTER**
(See **Furniture—Catalog Discounters**)

**DOMICILE**
(See **Furniture & Accessories—Catalog Discounters**)

**HOMEWORKS**
(See **Furniture & Accessories—Catalog Discounters**)

**LAWRENCE CONTRACT FURNISHERS**
(See **Carpets**)

**THE PAPER TREE**
12175 Alcosta Blvd., San Ramon 94583. Phone: 828-4696. Hours: T-Sat 9am-5pm, Thurs till 9pm. Purchases: BA, MC. Parking: Lot.

The owner of this wallpaper store handpicks discontinued wallpapers from the distribution warehouses of major wallpaper companies in the Bay Area. This choice selection is sold for $4/single roll or $8/double roll. Savings on the discontinued rolls can range from 50-80% on papers that originally sold for $16-$60. All the patterns are displayed on rods that allow you to un-roll the pattern and get a good look and an overall impression of how each pattern will appear in a large area. For the cautious, you can take rolls home on approval before purchasing. Once you've made up your mind, be sure to estimate correctly, because if you run short, you may not be able to obtain additional paper.

Even with 500 patterns to choose from you may not find the perfect pattern to suit your needs so then you can select patterns from current wallpaper books at a 30% discount off retail. Mini-blinds, posters, and framing services are also discounted. All the sundries needed to wallpaper are sold. This store is located near Alpha Beta in the Country Faire Shopping Center.

**SEM PAINT COMPANY**
120 Sem Lane & Shoreway Rd. (Bayshore Fwy, next to Holiday Inn), Belmont 94002. Phone: 592-1414. Hours: M 8:30am-2pm, T-Fri 8am-5pm, Sat 9am-5pm. Purchases: BA, MC. Parking: Lot.

*SEM* carries wallpaper from 10 major suppliers. Each book has a tag which tells you the percent of discount. Discounts on books range from 10-25%. Additional discounts are available during wallpaper manufacturers' sponsored sales.

Occasionally they sponsor free wallpaper 'How-to-hang' classes. *SEM* also sells paints at 30% discount and paint sundries at 20% off. There is a 20% handling charge on all returns.

## WALLCOVERING & FABRIC FACTORY OUTLET

2660 Harrison St., (near 23rd) San Francisco 94110. Phone: 647-6787. Hours: T-F 10am-6pm, Sat 9am-1pm. Purchases: No Cash, Checks, VISA, MC only (No Cash). Parking: Street.

At this outlet, located on the premises of San Francisco's only manufacturer of quality designer wallcoverings, you will find seconds, overruns, mill ends, and discontinued patterns. They offer wallpaper which normally retails at $18.95 to $60 a roll at prices ranging from $3.00-$7.00 a roll. They allow you to borrow samples and even take rolls home for evaluation. Many of their remnant rolls are sold for small change and are great for gift wrapping. They can help you determine just how much you need for your job, but bring in complete room measurements along with measurements for large doors and windows that will figure in your computations. Designer fabrics, many of which match wallpaper, are priced at $2.-$7. a yard. Many fabrics are bought for the outlet from Eastern mills and the values are mind boggling. For best results, come with an open mind and be prepared to be versatile. If you can start your decorating project with the wallpaper selection *first*, it's a cinch to coordinate the other elements. Note: they do not take cash!

## WESTERN CONTRACT FURNISHERS

(See **Furniture and Accessories—Catalog Discounters**)

## WALLPAPERS FOR LESS

1036 El Camino Real (El Camino Plaza), Sunnyvale 94086. Phone: 408-730-1373. Hours: M-Th 10am-6pm, Fri 10am-9pm, Sat 10am-6pm, Sun Noon-5pm.

**Other Stores:** 1777 South Bascom Ave., Campbell; Walls 'N' Windows, 1669 Willow Pass Rd., Concord; 5353 Almaden Expressway, San Jose.

Approximately 50% of the selection of wallpapers sold here are seconds which means that the papers did not meet the manufacturers' rigid standards. The colors may vary, patterns may be off register, or small flaws may exist. You can save 50% and also have the opportunity to see each paper unrolled for inspection before you buy. Other discontinued patterns, European papers and grasscloths also sell for 50% discounts. Current patterns ordered from wallpaper books are 25% off retail. Window coverings like mini blinds vertical louvers and woven woods are 50% off. Installation is not provided. All the sundries are sold at straight retail.

# 2

**Sometimes Tearfully Abandoned, Almost All Previously Owned, Some New, Perhaps Damaged, But All in All, Useful and Useable Merchandise**

# UCTIONS

Art and nostalgia combined have made the auction big business in California. Sometimes the bargains are fantastic, sometimes they're not.

Auctions must be announced in advance, and this is generally done in the Sunday edition of the metropolitan newspapers, under "Auctions." Most of the art and real estate auction firms have descriptive brochures of items to be sold, and offer previews prior to the sale.

Bidding at almost all auctions proceeds according to the mood and pocketbook of the crowd. Size up your competition: customs, police, and railroad auctions attract average citizens, while art and antique auctions appeal to the moneyed collectors.

Many auction houses require a buyer's registration prior to the sale; others have a loose "walk in and bid" arrangement. Purchases are usually by cash, or by certified or cashier's check.

There are many different types of auctions listed on the next few pages. Take your choice and have fun.

## Art and Furniture

Follow the classified ads of the following auction houses for antiques, furnishings, estate sales and art objects. There are many good auctions in the Bay Area, but I have found the following to have auctions more frequently and with a larger selection of goods than most.

### AARCO AUCTION STUDIO
661 Golden Gate Ave., San Francisco 94102. Phone: 863-3850. Hours: Previews: Tues. 10am-4pm. Auctions occur on Wed. at 11am every 3-4 weeks. Mailing list by request. Parking: Street.

### HARVEY CLAR'S ESTATE GALLERY
4364 Piedmont Ave., Oakland 94611. Phone: 428-0100. Hours: Preview Sat & Sun Noon-5pm, Auctions every 3 weeks M, T, W, evenings at 7:30pm (subject to change). Mailing list by request. Purchases: BA, MC. Parking: Private lot.

### McCOY AUCTION CO.
35201 Newark Blvd., Newark 94560. Phone: 793-9511. Business hours: W-Fri 9am-5pm. Auction every Tuesday 7pm for American and European antiques only (subject to change). Purchases: BA, MC.

# Police

Local police departments hold auction sales to dispose of goods which were confiscated in police cases but not reclaimed by their original owners. The range of merchandise is limited only by the ingenuity of the burglar. Bicycles are the hot items at these sales, followed by radios, tape decks, televisions, small appliances, cameras, tools, and furniture. Sometimes there is no prior inspection of merchandise, so bid with care. It's all sold "as-is," strictly cash-and-carry. Bidding depends on the mood and pocketbook of the crowd, and since buyers are usually average citizens, bargain buying prevails. Auction dates must be publicized in local newspapers. Call your local department to find out when the next auction will be, mark it on your calendar. The sales usually begin about 9am and last until mid afternoon.

San Francisco is the only police department that holds frequent auctions. Starting at 9am they are held at the Hall of Justice, 850 Bryant St., (basement), San Francisco. For dates and information call 553-0123.

# U.S. Government

### U.S. BUREAU OF CUSTOMS

630 Sansome St., Room 400, San Francisco 94114. Phone: 556-4340. Purchases: Cash only. Parking: Street.

Several auctions are held each year by the *U.S. Department of Customs* to dispose of the thousands of items confiscated by San Francisco customs agents for various violations of the Tariff Act of 1930. Many unique articles from all over the world take this route to auction block. Items up for auction are liquor (which goes for about the same as regular retail, because bidding starts at the amount of federal tax on each item), clothing, cutlery, cameras, watches, lamps, pottery, gift items, jewelry, radios, tools, and some furniture. While some of the auction prices here are close to retail, many sell for 50% or less. Watch Bay Area newspapers for auction dates.

### U.S. POSTAL SERVICE AUCTIONS

Civic Center (Polk & Grove), San Francisco 94102. Phone: 556-2500. Hours: About every 3 months. Purchases: Cash only. Parking: Street.

San Francisco is the dead letter and package center for California; all lost and unclaimed mail ends up here. It is auctioned periodically depending on how much mail has accumulated; usually, however, an auction is held about every 3 to 6 months. All items are just as they were received at the post office. Both single items and lots are sold; almost anything a person could conceivably mail might be included. The dead letter center sends bulletins to all post offices designating times of auctions. It's best to call, though, and have your name put on the mailing list.

# CHARITY AND RUMMAGE SALES

## OAKLAND MUSEUM WHITE ELEPHANT SALE

Oakland (address to be announced). Phone: 893-4257 for information. Hours: To be announced. Purchases: Cash, check.

This sale, conducted by the Oakland Museum Women's Board, is one of the most successful fund-raising efforts in the Bay Area each year. In 1982 the sale earned more than $300,000! It is usually held in a different downtown Oakland location each February (last year in an empty department store scheduled for demolition).

Every possible type of merchandise is available for sale, including large quantities of new, first-quality goods donated by local merchants. One store donated 5,000 pairs of new shoes for the sale! Clothing is popular and accounts for a substantial portion of the sale; it is always arranged neatly in department-store style on racks according to size and quality. There is an elegant designer section, a better-dress section, a nice selection of furs—and budget dresses as low as $1. There are linens, toys, housewares, books, records, appliances, and great buys in furniture.

One year I purchased a sturdy though somewhat worn desk for $11. After I antiqued it and fitted it with new hardware, I could hardly recognize my ugly duckling.

The sale is announced in newspapers and on radio and television.

## LAZARUS SALES CO.

2133 Taraval, San Francisco 94116. Phone: 661-9450. Hours: M-Sat 10am-5:30pm, Sun Noon-5pm. Purchases: VISA, MC. Parking: Street.

You can't help but wonder where they get all this 'stuff' when you take a look around. Imagine anything sold in a department or variety store and you've about covered all the types of merchandise that are jammed into every nook and cranny. As a salvage dealer, the selection is rarely predictable, but you can always find at least one or two things worth buying. I stocked up on light bulbs at $1.00/pkg. of four on my last visit. The regular price is $2.28 at my local supermarket. Some outstanding buys can be made on furniture that was freight damaged but repaired then priced approximately 50% below retail. The owners delight in telling you what was wrong with each piece, then describe with pride their professional repair work. To further tempt you they've expanded into clothing areas with some wonderful bargains if you're in sync with their shipments.

## PAUL'S DEPARTMENT STORES
645 Howard, San Francisco 94103. Phone: 861-1122. Hours: M-Sat 8:30am-5pm. Purchases: BA, MC. Parking: Street, pay lots.

**Other Stores:** 716 K St., Sacramento; 1122 Howard, 556 Golden Gate, 465 Pine, 1623 Pine, 654 Pacific, San Francisco; 390 Grand, South San Francisco.

You know that this is one of "those" places when you walk in the door and see all the people scrambling through jumbled displays of merchandise. Most of the goods in this store are acquired through factory overstocks, liquidations, salvage or insurance writeoffs. New merchandise is always arriving; what's here today will be gone tomorrow. You are likely to find almost anything here; cosmetics, household needs, small appliances, goods for the handyman, and—best of all—really great buys on clothing. At first glance it's hard to believe that you could find anything good on these bulging racks—much of the merchandise is 'tired'. However, you'll find closeouts, salesmen's samples, name-brand seconds, and irregulars at a fraction of retail prices. This is strictly a self-service store. Cash refunds are available on all but special sale merchandise.

## SELECT SALVAGE
1796 Willow Pass Road, Concord 94520. Phone: 687-0480. Hours: W-Sat 10am-5pm. Purchases: Cash or Check. Parking: Lot.

Shopping at this place is like going to a surprise party. Not even the salespeople know from one week to the next what's going to be in their inventory. This store is a clearinghouse for *Pacific Intermountain Express Trucking*. Every Tuesday a *P.I.E.* truck arrives with merchandise that has been refused by *P.I.E.*'s customers. The merchandise may be slightly damaged, or part of a shipment that was damaged. Most of the items seem to be in perfect condition. The firm is able to recoup some of its losses by selling the merchandise here for prices low enough to insure quick sales to savvy customers. You should note that the store is only open Wednesday through Saturday. Come Wednesday if you want first crack at the selection and don't mind elbow-to-elbow shoppers. You won't always find furniture or appliances, but you can expect to find just about everything else: drugs, giftwares, household items, toys, books, clothing, shoes, yardage and on and on. I loved their sign over a popular poster: "This is somewhere in the store, probably in the last place you'll look."

# FLEA MARKETS

Attending flea markets is getting to be a national weekend pastime. On any leisurely Saturday or Sunday, many families leave their all-too-peaceful homes to enjoy the harried, tumultuous bargaining and selling at a nearby swap meet or flea market. Absolutely everything imaginable is for sale, from post-World War II surplus wheelbarrows for $10 (the sturdy heavy-duty kind) to eggs, bakery goods, and produce so cheap it makes you wonder why everyone doesn't shop here instead of their local supermarket. Most flea markets require a hopeful seller to pay a fee to set up a booth. Sometimes prospective customers are also charged a token amount to park or to enter. The booths are arranged sometimes haphazardly, in a large fenced-in field or yard. Cheerful chaos is the order of the day. Items for sale are those the sellers have carried from their homes (like a portable garage sale) or have acquired through liquidating stores; some items are from closeouts or from auctions of surplus goods. Some people sell things at flea markets as a regular business, spending the days between weekends collecting stuff for the next sale. Prices are often a problem though, for most sellers are amateurs in the retailing business—sometimes they price too high, sometimes too low. Get into the swing of things—if you see something you want, make an offer (remembering that the seller is as anxious to sell as you are to buy). Haggling is part and parcel of the flea-market way of life.

It may take all day just to navigate through the crowds and see everything. Most clothing must be purchased without trying on, since few vendors have dressing rooms (a few with campers as their base of operations will allow you to wiggle and squeeze into your garments inside their vans). Most merchandise is sold "as-is," and it's strictly "buyer beware." Most of the small appliance and home entertainment equipment booths give written guarantees and will make exchanges on defective merchandise if the proper receipt is presented. Most vendors operate on a cash-only basis; only a few accept credit cards.

Listed here are some of the better-known markets in the area; these are held regularly throughout the year. Other markets occur on some other basis—maybe monthly or annually. These smaller fairs can be fantastic sources of bargains by virtue of the fact that they are not as well traveled as the others. Check your local paper for notices of these events.

## ALAMEDA PENNY MARKET
Island Auto Movie, 791 Thau Way (3 blocks south of the Alameda Tube), Alameda 94501. Phone: 522-7206. Hours: Sat, Sun 7am-4pm. Purchases: Cash only. Parking: Free.

*The Penny Market* at the Island Auto Movie Drive-in Theatre is a bargain hunter's paradise. Spaces are rented by the day, weekend, or month to anyone wishing to sell merchandise. Many vendors make a handsome living selling name-brand, first-quality stereo equipment, tapes, clothing, etc., in this low-overhead type of operation. Clothing, household goods, toys, and furniture (you name it) are available new and used.

## CASTRO VALLEY FLEA MARKET

20820 Oak St. (at Castro Valley Blvd.), Castro Valley. Phone: 582-0396. Hours: Sat, Sun 7am-5pm. Purchases: Cash only. Parking: Free.

Admission is free.

## DE ANZA COLLEGE FLEA MARKET

21250 Stevens Creek Blvd., Cupertino 95014. Phone: 408-996-4756. Hours: 1st Saturday & 3rd Sunday of every month.

Admission is free. Flea market is located in parking lot A on campus.

## HILLTOP DRIVE-IN FLEA MARKET

Hilltop Dr. & Hwy. 80, Richmond 94804. Phone: 467-4849 for information. Hours: Sun 7am-4pm. Purchases: Cash only. Parking: Free.

On Sundays a modest 50¢ is charged per car. There are approximately 150 booths with new and used general merchandise. (All potential sellers must first fill out a police report describing their wares and leave proof of their identification such as driver's license, which prevents the sale of stolen merchandise.)

## LOST FLEA MARKET

1940 Monterey Hwy., San Jose 95112. Phone: 293-2323. Hours: Wed-Sun 8:30am-5pm.

Admission is free.

## MARIN CITY FLEA MARKET

Location: Marin City. (Just off Hwy. 101, Marin City exit). Phone: 332-1441. Hours: Sat & Sun 6:30am-4:30pm. Parking: Free.

Admission is free.

## MIDGLEY'S COUNTRY FLEA MARKET

2200 Gravenstein Highway South, Sebastopol. Phone: 707-823-7874. Hours: Sat & Sun 6:30am-4pm. Ample Parking.

Admission is free.

## NAPA-VALLEJO FLEA MARKET AND AUCTION

303 Kelly Road (Just off Hwy. 29, between Napa and Vallejo). Phone: 707-643-3977 or 226-8862. Hours: Sun 7am-4:30pm. Parking: 50¢.

Admission is free.

## SAN FRANCISCO FLEA MARKET
601 Tunnel Ave., San Francisco 94134. Phone: 467-4849. Hours: Sat, Sun 7am-5pm. Purchases: Cash only. Parking: Free lot.

Admission is 25¢ per person.

## SAN JOSE FLEA MARKET
12000 Berryessa Rd., San Jose 95133. Phone: 289-1550. Hours: Sat, Sun 7:30am-sundown. Purchases: Cash only. Parking: Pay lot.

Admission is free.

## SANTA CLARA FLEA MARKET
5500 Lafayette St. (Mountain View-Alviso Rd., Route 237), Santa Clara 95050. Phone: 988-0850. Hours: Sat, Sun 7am-6pm. Purchases: Cash only. Parking: Free lot.

Nonprofit organizations sell free here. Sellers pay $3 for Saturday and $4 on Sunday.

## SOLANO DRIVE-IN FLEA MARKET
Solano Way & Hwy. 4, Concord 94521. Phone: 467-4849 for information. Hours: Sat, Sun 7am-4pm. Purchases: Cash only. Parking: Free.

On Saturday admission is free; on Sunday it is 50¢ per car. There are approximately 200 booths selling new and used general merchandise.

# RESALE SHOPS

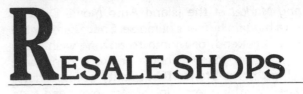

Here's your chance to have finer clothes at prices you can afford. A resale shop is the "top drawer" of the used clothing business. Usually their prices are higher than thrift shops. The affluent (who often do wear their clothes only a few times and then discard them) use these shops as a moneymaking outlet for disposing of their apparel. Most of the resale shops operate on a consignment basis. It works this way: the potential seller brings in any items she wants to dispose of, and the store agrees to try to sell the items for her for a certain percentage of the price. Other stores agree on the price the item will go for (the amount depending on item's condition and age), and this is split fifty-fifty with the shop owner. Other shops buy outright. On this kind of a deal, everyone makes some money: the socialite makes a profit, the store owner makes a profit, and you the customer, make good buys on clothing you couldn't otherwise afford. You will be saving 50-70% buying this way; when you pay $40 for a dress, it probably cost about $200 new. You'll find some very sophisticated clothes with designer labels like Givenchy, Oscar de la Renta, and Donald Brooks, as well as labels from local finer department and speciality stores. It is impossible to list all the many better resale shops which abound in the Bay Area. Your best resource is the yellow pages of the phone book. Check listings under "Clothing: Used." I have always found that the Junior Leagues' Next to New Shops in San Francisco and Oakland to be excellent for quality of merchandise and selection. The Heritage House at 3333 Mt. Diablo Blvd., Lafayette is—hands down—the best consignment shop in Contra Costa County.

# SURPLUS STORES

### AAA EQUIPMENT
745 50th Ave., Oakland 94601. Phone: 261-2443. Hours: M-F 8am-4:30pm; Sat 8am-Noon. Purchases: MC, VISA, check. Parking: Street.

A sign "Something for everyone" would seem appropriate on the outside of this business, located on three acres near the Nimitz Freeway in Oakland. A stack of magazines in the office is for the diversion of the customers waiting for service; another sign in the office boasts "We Talk Hardhat Here." It behooves you to avoid shopping on rainy days, since most of the merchandise is displayed outdoors. You can buy everything here from small hand tools (new and used) to huge pieces of construction equipment. Contractors, firms, and handymen come to *AAA* to avail themselves of the tremendous selection of government surplus and bankrupt stock. Savings of 50% are not unusual on used machinery like air compressors, generators, portable power plants, roller conveyors, and stainless steel items.

This is the place to shop for concrete trucks, crawler tractors, yard cranes, or fork lifts. The yard man will direct you through the maze of equipment to your special need and will gladly test the equipment for you. Anyone contemplating a purchase is free to bring in outside experts to appraise and evaluate the equipment. All equipment and machinery is in working order when sold. Although no guarantees are given, *AAA* tries to stand behind its merchandise.

## BONANZA SURPLUS DISTRIBUTORS
3617 E. 14th St., Oakland 94601. Phone: 534-3030. Hours: M-F 8:30am-5:30pm, Sat 8:30am-5:30pm. Purchases: BA, MC. Parking: Street.

This is a gadgeteer's paradise. A friend tells me he comes here when he can't find what he's looking for anywhere else. There are tons of tools, hardware, bolts, tape, cable, chain, compressors, motors, wheels, plumbing supplies, and on and on. You'll probably have to ask for assistance to locate your particular item amid the organized chaos that prevails. I did notice that all nails, screws, and bolts were neatly arranged in boxes according to size, and I was told that a reorganization is under way to label all those cluttered aisles.

All new electrical motors are given a 90-day guarantee; used motors carry a 30-day guarantee and are tested for you in the store. Prices are lower than those of your neighborhood hardware store, since most merchandise comes from government or industrial surplus or from stores going out of business. Special shipments are advertised in the sports section of the Oakland "Tribune" every Friday.

## J & H OUTLET
476 Industrial Way, San Carlos 94070. Phone: 591-7113. Hours: M-F 10am-6pm, Sat 10am-3pm. Purchases: Cash, check. Parking: Street.

*J & H Outlet* is tailor-made for all you tinkerers with components and audio equipment. It consists of a cavernous room filled with practically everything you could possibly need at low, low prices. There are literally millions of surplus items—thousands of components, lots of wires, all kinds of parts, and very good buys on copper and brass remnants for jewelrymakers and sculptors. Mr. Ingethron, owner of *J & H*, is helpful and nice. He and his staff are willing to help you find what you need or get it for you if they possibly can.

## UNITED SURPLUS SALES
(See **Part I: Arts, Crafts, Hobby Supplies**)

# THRIFT SHOPS

Moving, remodeling, marriage, divorce, and death all contribute to the unearthing of items no longer needed but too good to throw away. At least half of the "too good to throw away" items end up being donated to charitable organizations which redistribute them through thrift shops. The donations come from many sources; sometimes a will leaves an entire estate to an organization, or a large corporation redoing its offices will simply hand its old stuff to a thrift shop for a tax deduction rather than incur the headache and expense of moving. Of course, there are also those who are simply cleaning out their attic, closet, or basement and call their favorite thrift shop to remove the discards. Whatever the reason, many valuable antiques and collectables with obscure histories often end up here; for the "pro" bargain hunter thrift shops are a must. These places are also becoming more and more "in" for the decorators and collectors (which ought to tell you something). Most larger thrift stores operate on a similar basis, with the same store policies on exchanges, returns, etc. Most of them have everything priced clearly and arranged neatly for your perusal. We suggest checking out your smaller thrift shop from time to time, too; smaller stores are often less picked over than the larger ones. I've not listed three good old standbys—*Goodwill Industries, Salvation Army,* and *St. Vincent de Paul Society.* All offer great bargains and there are many located throughout the Bay Area. Check the white pages of your phone book.

# WRECKING AND SALVAGE YARDS

## CHAS. S. CAMPANELLA WRECKING
5401 San Leandro Blvd., Oakland 94601. Phone: 536-7002. Hours: M-F 8am-5pm, Sat 9am-4pm. Purchases: BA, MC. Parking: Street.

If you're trying to achieve that "funky" look in your decorating or if you're just leery of putting new wood on top of old wood, try browsing through the assortment of old doors, windows, and artifacts often available at this wrecking yard. *Campanella* frequently demolishes old Victorian houses, amassing an assortment of newel posts, footed bathtubs, wooden columns, or windows (curved or straight, made of leaded, stained, or beveled glass), and the like. You'll be saving 50-70% off the cost of new doors or windows, and all you have to do is measure the doors and windows for yourself when making your choice.

There is also a big selection of used plywood, large beams (good for sub-flooring), used brick, concrete foundation blocks, aluminum windows, plumbing fittings, molding and many other types of used building materials—great dollar savings for a thrifty remodeling job or even new construction. Occasionally they run ads in the Oakland "Tribune" when an interesting inventory is acquired through a wrecking job.

## CLEVELAND WRECKING COMPANY
Cargoway at Amador (1 block off 3rd St.), San Francisco. Phone: 824-1804. Hours: M-F 8am-4:30pm, Sat 8am-12:30pm. Purchases: BA, MC. Parking: Street, free lot.

Much of what the San Francisco branch of this large wrecking company demolished is for sale in their yard. Any kind of building material you may need—used plywood, paneling, lumber, doors, windows and glass, electrical or plumbing equipment—is for sale here for a fraction of its original price. The stock changes constantly, depending on the building currently being demolished.

You can save even more when you buy the materials directly at the demolition site. You can learn about site sales by calling the office or by checking the San Francisco "Chronicle" under 'Announcements.' Know your measurements before you buy; there are no returns without the original sales slip and they charge for all merchandise returned (on new material, 10% of the cost; on used material, 20%). All new items for sale (lumber, heaters, roofing materials) go for discount prices.

You can find some really arty stuff here if you take your time and don't mind venturing into their big yard.

# BARGAIN HUNTER'S MAPS

It's clearly impossible to include maps for all the businesses listed in Bargain Hunting in the Bay Area. Because of the close proximity of many San Francisco businesses, several maps are provided to help you locate outlets of neighborhood shopping areas within San Francisco.

## Mission and Potrero

1. Canned Foods, 87
2. S. Beressi, 81
3. Gallery West, 110 (in same building as S. Beressi, #2)
4. Arvey Paper, 139
5. Royal Supply Co., 74
6. Designer's Exchange, 35
7. **M.C.O. of S.F., 39**
8. **Lilli Ann, 23**
9. **S & R Fashion Center, 32**
10. P.J.'s Appliance, 47
11. Cherin's, 45
12. **Clothes Encounter II, 28**
13. **Better Dress Outlet, 18,** & Decorative Ceramics Outlet, (same building)
14. Wallcovering & Fabric Outlet, 157
15. Esprit Factory Outlet, 20

*Bold numbers indicate apparel stores/outlets.

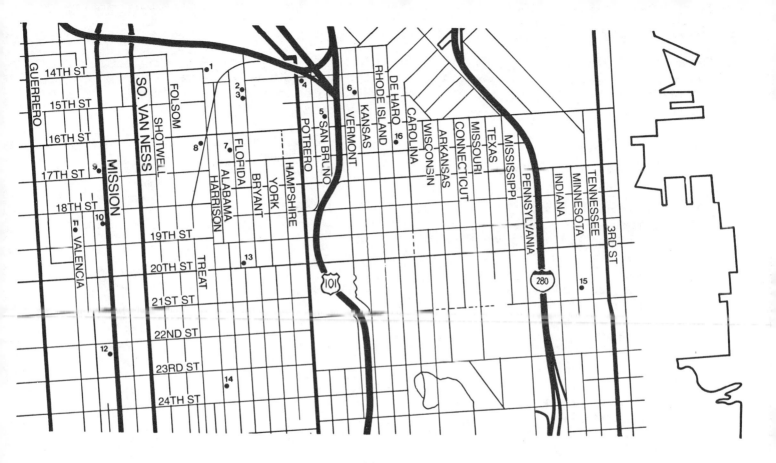

GUERRERO

14TH ST

15TH ST

16TH ST

17TH ST

18TH ST

19TH ST

20TH ST

21ST ST

22ND ST

23RD ST

24TH ST

SO. VAN NESS

MISSION

VALENCIA

SHOTWELL

FOLSOM

TREAT

HARRISON

ALABAMA

FLORIDA

BRYANT

YORK

HAMPSHIRE

POTRERO

SAN BRUNO

VERMONT

KANSAS

RHODE ISLAND

DE HARO

CAROLINA

WISCONSIN

ARKANSAS

CONNECTICUT

MISSOURI

TEXAS

MISSISSIPPI

PENNSYLVANIA

INDIANA

MINNESOTA

TENNESSEE

3RD ST

101

280

1
2
3
4
5
6
7
8
9
10
12
13
14
15
16
F

# South of Market

1. Great Blouse Separates ,22
2. Gunne Sax, 22
3. End of the Line, 20
4. Raincoat Outlet, 25
5. Fashion Express, 36
6. Designers' Loft, 35
7. Kutler Bros., 13
8. Patti Quinn's, 31
9. Clothes Rack, 28
10. Pioneer Home Supply, 113
11. AAA Luggage Repair Depot, 134
12. Harband's Luggage, 135 (next to Patti Quinn's, see #8)
13. Cottage Tables, 97
14. Terry McHugh Outlet, 24
15. Paul's Dept. Stores, 163
16. Bluxome Factory Outlet, 19
17. Factory Outlet (Kids Clothing), (in same building as Bluxome, #16),197
18. Fantastico, 50
19. Flower Mart, 83
20. Clothing Clearance Center, 12
21. Rucker Fuller South, 116
22. Jeffrey Kriger Framing, 51
23. Silky Way, 26
24. Display Dimensions, 71
25. House of Karlson, 111
26. Western Fur Traders Outlet, 26
27. Sausalito Designs Clearance Center, 103

28. SF Ski/Sports Outlet, 4
29. Factory Store—Outerware, 36
30. Flax's Warehouse, 50
31. House of Louie, 36

*Bold numbers indicate apparel stores/outlets.

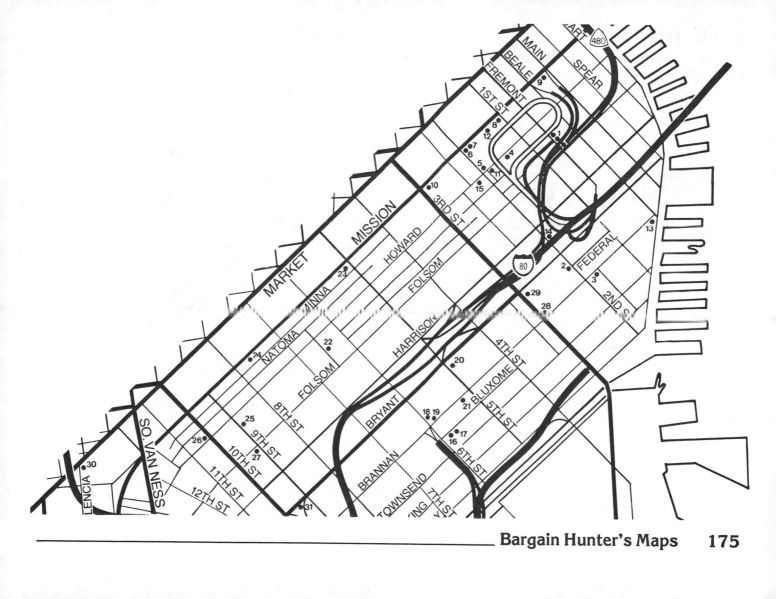

## Pacific Heights

1. San Francisco Mercantile Co., 26
2. The Company Store, 19

## Columbus & Bay

1. Dunnegan Furniture, 109
2. Cheap 'n' Cheerful, 78
3. Jeanne Marc Outlet, 23

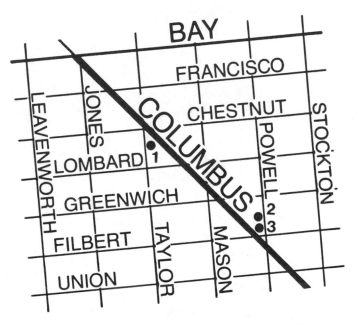

*Bold numbers indicate apparel stores/outlets.

# Union Square

1. Deovlet Furniture, 108
2. Nigel's Furniture, 102
3. Cresalia Jewelers, 127
4. Azevedo Jewelers, 127
5. S. Christian of Copenhagen, 72
6. Niederholzer, 128
7. Merchandisers, Inc., 16, (also on South of Market Map)
8. A Small Things Co., 128 & Zwillinger Jewelry, 129 (same building)
9. My Favorite Clothing Store, 31
10. Executive Clothes, 12
11. Merchandisers, Inc., 16
12. Clothes Rack, 28
13. Clothes Encounter, 28
14. For Eyes, 77
15. Guitar Center, 136

# ALPHABETICAL INDEX

# GEOGRAPHICAL INDEX

# SUBJECT INDEX

# Late Additions

## Apparel

### CLOTHES VAULT

MacArthur/Broadway Shopping Center, Oakland 94611. Phone: 428-2288. Hours: M-Th 10am-7pm, Fri 10am-7pm, Sat 10am-6pm, Sun, 11am-5pm. Purchases: MC, VISA. Parking: Lot.

Oakland teenagers and younger working women can stretch their limited shopping dollars at this fashion discount store, in the MacArthur/Broadway shopping Center across from Kaiser Hospital. Most merchandise is purchased in L.A. although I spotted some popular lines from Bay Area manufacturers. Discounts range from 25-60% off original retail, and all are first quality. My first few visits to the *Clothes Vault* did not impress me, but it appears that the owners have more closely defined their market and they're now providing a good selection of manufacturers overruns that are very current most of the time. A larger store that will cater to the downtown Oakland working women is planned for the near future. Sizes range from 4-16.

### DESIGNERS CLOSET

68 Coombs St., Napa 94559. Phone: 707-252-0923. Hours: Thurs-Monday 10am-4:30pm. Closed Tues & Wed. Purchases: VISA, MC. Parking: Lot.

The owner of *Designers Closet*, a former buyer for Bloomingdales, is putting her years of experience and valuable contacts to good use by keeping an intriguing selection of merchandise well displayed in this outlet. She has leased a section of the Sheepskin Outlet where she sells her fashions to those who desire an updated image. These are usually women from the baby boom era who have outgrown or become too sophisticated for most Junior lines. Sizes range from 4-14 on the dresses and separates from well known manufacturers like Carol Little, Stanley Blacker, John Henry, Jag, Condor, and many others. The average discount is about 25% off retail but often is as much as 40%. These are very current fashions, all first quality, and selected to *"Put you together. . .to set you apart"*. To find the outlet in Napa, remember that Coombs is off Imola (Hwy 121).

### FACTORY OUTLET (KIDS CLOTHING)

173 Bluxome St., San Francisco 94107. Phone: 957-9355. Hours: Thurs, Fri, Sat only 10am-4pm. Purchases: Cash preferred. Parking: Very limited.

A visit to this outlet may be hazardous to your piece of mind when you consider the parking limitations. Bluxome is a small street crowded with delivery trucks during the week and has few legal parking spaces. It's best to park on streets which border Bluxome; Brannan, Townsend and 5th St. At this manufacturers outlet most clothing is geared for girls in infant sizes through pre-teen. The line is sold at better stores around the country including Bloomingdales. Wholesale prices on fashions that are overruns, irregulars, and samples are the only way many people could afford this quality line. Prices generally range from $5-$25 on the playclothes, coordinated separates, school clothing and special occasion apparel. Their sweat shirt and terry lines are very popular. In addition to their own line they anticipate bringing in other lines to provide a wider range of fashion for both girls and boys. These lines will also be discounted substantially. All sales final!

## SYMBRAETTE FACTORY OUTLET
21 Janis Way, Scotts Valley 95066. Phone: 408-438-1711. Hours: M-F 9am-4pm. Closed 12:30-1pm for lunch. Purchases: Cash or Check. Parking: Lot.

Scotts Valley is a long way to drive to buy a bra, bathing suit or girdle, yet, there are several reasons why many will go to the trouble. First, if you have a fitting problem, you're too big, too small, uneven, or something, Symbraette can custom fit and design a bra that will give you support and comfort. Their largest custom made bra to date was a 64-Q. Their regular size range is 28-46 AA-O. Bras are fancy, basic, pretty, padded, sheer, in other words, something for everyone including mastectomy, surgical, and nursing bras. Bras sold at the factory outlet are discontinued, overruns, or have been in stock too long. Prices range from 75 cents to about $6.50 on their standard sizes, go up to $12.50 on special sizes, and even higher for custom designed and fitted bras. Their girdles are popular with weight lifters and bodybuilders as well as those who need support for health reasons. Panty girdles and waist cinchers are also sold. Bathing suits are taking a larger share of their production and the styles are typical of what you would find in most major department store selections. At the factory just about everything is sold at wholesale or less. If the name Symbraette is unknown to you it's probably because they have functioned for over 20 years as a direct merchandising company selling through home parties and only recently have expanded their business to conventional retail establishments. To find the outlet, from Hwy 17, take Scotts Valley Drive to El Pueblo, and turn left on Janis. The factory is at the end of the street, the outlet at the back of the parking lot. Don't hesitate to call for directions or to inquire about special sizes or fitting.

# Arts and Crafts

## BLUEGATE CANDLE FACTORY OUTLET
Airport Street, Moss Beach 94037. Phone: 728-3301. Hours: M-F 10am-4pm. Weekends before Xmas. Purchases: Cash or Check. Parking: Lot.

The *Bluegate Candle Company* makes a beautiful line of candles and acessories that are sold in specialty shops and major department stores. Their reputation is based upon their own special candle techniques, painstakingly combined dyes, waxes and perfumes in great variety to achieve the highest quality, handcrafted product possible. Their colors are selected each year to coordinate with the home furnishings industries latest color trends. Their candles are expensive at retail!

Savvy shoppers wait for their big sales which occur twice a year, before Mothers Day and before Xmas to make a big haul. In this instance, it's wise to bring boxes so your candles can be packed properly for the trip home. At the outlet you can save 30-70% on seconds which are usually just slightly off color, discontinued colors, and overstock candles. When necessary they even pull additional merchandise from their warehouse to complete your order. Along with candles they also sell a complete line of accessories, i.e. brass and wrought iron candle holders, candle wreaths, votives etc.

The factory is difficult to find. They are located immediately west of the Half Moon Bay Airport in Moss Beach. Highway One passes along the East side of the airport. A driver, looking west across the airport, can see their building on the other side (Airport St.). One can turn West off of Highway One at the Pillar Point Harbor intersection in El Granada, or on Cypress St. at the North end of the airport. Either way one will end up crossing Airport St. which runs along the West side of the Airport.

## JERRY KRIGER FRAMING
156 Russ Street, San Francisco 94103. Phone: 621-4226. Hours: M-F 10:30am-5:15pm, Sat 11am-2pm. Purchases: VISA, MC. Parking: Very limited.

If you don't like the do-it-yourself frame shops because you don't like to do the work yourself and their prices don't seem to be that much of a bargain, you'll be pleased to do business with Jeffrey Kriger. First, he does the work himself, and second his prices are almost always less than the do-it-yourself shops. You can elect to save more just by buying all the framing materials, i.e. glass, mats, backings, frame, fasteners etc. and then doing the work at home. Your one limitation is that he only sells aluminum framing yet when you see the many frame styles, finishes, and colors you won't think this is so limiting. His labor charge on most jobs ranges from $1.50-$7.50. Savings do add up if you do-it-yourself when you have many pictures to frame or if you're an artist with a show to get ready for. Additionally, he has rasonable rates for vacuum dry mounting. He offers several qualities of materials for framing that allow you to frame a magazine picture with inexpensive materials or to frame a fine work of art with museum quality mats and backings. The studio is located in an offbeat alley-type street south of Market. Russ St. is between 6th and 7th Streets and between Howard and Folsom. Parking is always at a premium!

## BABY SUPER DISCOUNT

522 So. Bascom Ave., San Jose, 95126. Phone: 408-293-0358. Hours: M-Sat 9:30am-5:30pm, Thurs eve till 9pm. Purchases: VISA, MC, Lay-a-Way. Parking: Lot.

It's not easy to keep prices low when competing with catalog discount firms like Best Products and Consumers Distributing. *Super Baby Discount* often beats their prices and offers more by way of selection both in quality and merchandise. Prospective parents can completely prepare for the coming 'event' in purchasing anything that a baby would require for the first 18 months. This includes infant clothing, diapers, blankets, plus cribs, high chairs, car seats etc. The owners of *Baby Super Discount* are pros. If you're overwhelmed with choices, they can help you determine your needs and also keep you within your budget. It helps that they offer a six month no interest lay-a-way period. Occasionally they take advantage of manufacturers overruns or overproduction, and irregulars, because then they can discount even more. Their selection of car seat covers is particularly extensive. Be sure to check their newest venture just a few doors away, *Children's Super Discount*, where clothing for older kids and juvenile furniture i.e. bunk beds, trundle beds, chests, etc., are sold at solid discounts. Both stores will order special lines form catalogs if they don't have this merchandise on the floor.

## WALLPAPERS N-STOCK

1639 No. Main Street, Walnut Creek 94596. Phone: 932-8957. Hours: M-F 10:30am-5:30pm, Sat 11am-5pm. Purchases: Cash or Check. Parking: Street.

If monthly payments have wiped out your decorating budget you can still manage a little decorating with wallpaper at *Wallpapers N-Stock*. It's possible to wallpaper an entire room for $40 because all their papers are $4.00/roll. These are manufacturers discontinued papers from local distributors. The selection is ho-hum to wonderful. Don't bring baby in a stroller or you'll never be able to navigate around the boxes of wallpapers that cover the entire floor area. The owner brings in new papers every week, so often it's just a matter of what-and-see. Buy what you need when you see it, may not be there if you want more!